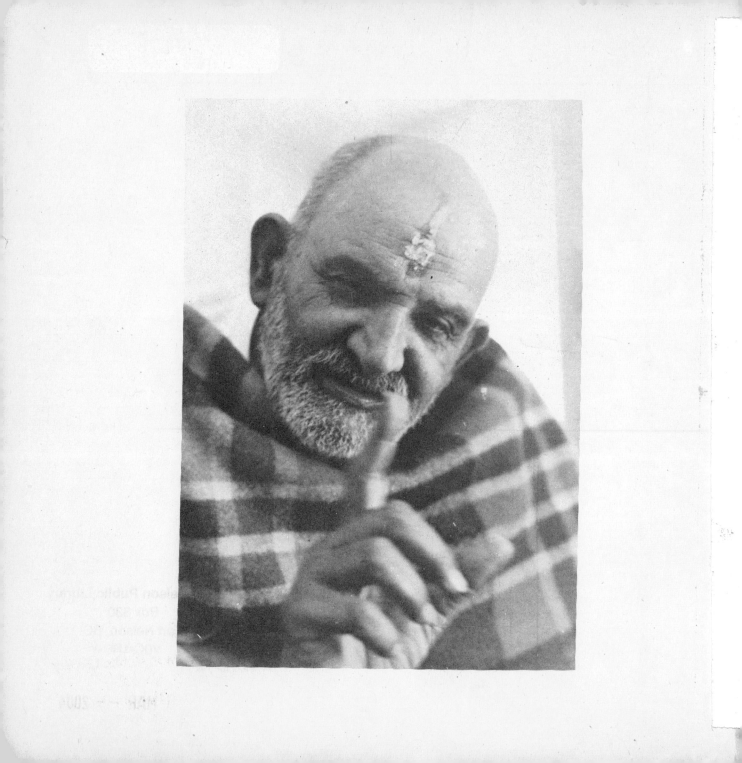

REMEMBER
BE HERE NOW

**• LAMA FOUNDATION • 1971 • YEAR OF THE EARTH MONKEY
BOX 240 • SAN CRISTOBAL, NEW MEXICO 87564**

First printing through forty-third printing, 962,824 copies

• HANUMAN FOUNDATION 1978

Printed at: Kingsport Press
Kingsport, Tennessee

46 47 48 49 50

0-517-54305-2

**Distributed by:
The Crown Publishing Group, New York, New York**

CONTENTS:

1

JOURNEY

THE TRANSFORMATION:
DR. RICHARD ALPERT, Ph.D
INTO
BABA RAM DASS

2

FROM BINDU TO OJAS

THE CORE BOOK

3

COOKBOOK FOR A SACRED LIFE

A MANUAL FOR CONSCIOUS BEING

4

PAINTED CAKES

BOOKS

COST DISTRIBUTION

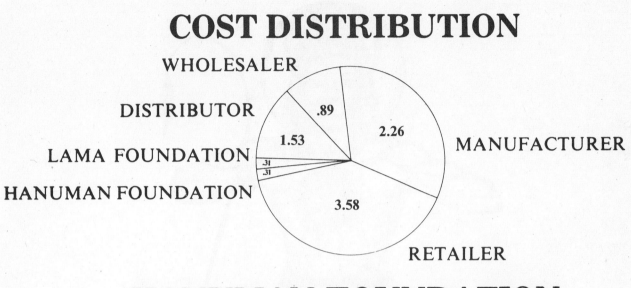

WHOLESALER

DISTRIBUTOR

LAMA FOUNDATION

HANUMAN FOUNDATION

.89

1.53

.31

.31

2.26

MANUFACTURER

3.58

RETAILER

HANUMAN FOUNDATION

A CURRENT NOTE

BE HERE NOW was originally distributed in pamphlet form by Lama Foundation and was subsequently published by Lama Foundation as this book, more than 928,300 copies of which have been distributed by Crown Publishers to date. In the summer of 1977 Lama Foundation decided to give the copyright and half the proceeds from BE HERE NOW to Hanuman Foundation to further distribute the energy generated by this book through the projects of Hanuman Foundation. For this generous sacrifice and gesture of faith, Hanuman Foundation would like to thank Lama Foundation.

Hanuman Foundation, instigated by Ram Dass, was incorporated in California in 1974 as a tax-exempt non-profit corporation to "promulgate spiritual well-being among members of the society as a whole through education and service, by spiritual training and by publications and recordings, and to promote the study, practice, and teaching of spiritual knowledge." A newsletter and catalog are sent semi-annually describing the activities of Hanuman Foundation, which include the Prison-Ashram Project, Dying Project, Hanuman Tape Library, Ram Dass' lecture tours and retreats, and other tentative projects. If you would like to receive this newsletter please include a first-class stamp with your name and address to Hanuman Foundation, Box 203, 524 San Anselmo Avenue, San Anselmo, CA 94960.

JAI HANUMAN!

JOURNEY

THE TRANSFORMATION

DR. RICHARD ALPERT, Ph.D INTO BABA RAM DASS

NAMASTÉ

OUR-STORY

There are three stages in this journey that I have been on! The first, the social science stage; the second, the psychedelic stage; and the third, the yogi stage. They are summating—that is, each is contributing to the next. It's like the unfolding of a lotus flower. Now, as I look back, I realize that many of the experiences that made little sense to me at the time they occurred were prerequisites for what was to come later. I want to share with you the parts of the internal journey that never get written up in the mass media: I'm not interested in the political parts of the story; I'm not interested in what you read in the Saturday Evening Post about LSD. This is the story of what goes on inside a human being who is undergoing all these experiences.

SUCCESS

In 1961, the beginning of March, I was at perhaps the highest point of my academic career. I had just returned from being a visiting professor at the University of California at Berkeley: I had been assured of a permanent post that was being held for me at Harvard, if I got my publications in order. I held appointments in four departments at Harvard—the Social Relations Department, the Psychology Department, the Graduate School of Education, and the Health Service (where I was a therapist); I had research contracts with Yale and Stanford. In a worldly sense, I was making a great income and I was a collector of possessions.

I had an apartment in Cambridge that was filled with antiques and I gave very charming dinner parties. I had a Mercedes-Benz sedan and a Triumph 500 CC motorcycle and a Cessna 172 airplane and an MG sports car and a sailboat and a bicycle. I vacationed in the Caribbean where I did scuba-diving. I was living the way a successful bachelor professor is supposed to live in the American world of "he who makes it." I wasn't a genuine scholar, but I had gone through the whole academic trip. I had gotten my Ph.D.; I was writing books. I had research contracts. I taught courses in Human Motivation, Freudian Theory, Child Development. But what all this boils down to is that I was really a very good game player.

My lecture notes were the ideas of other men, subtly presented, and my research was all within the Zeitgeist—all that which one was supposed to research about.

In 1955 I had started doing therapy and my first therapy patient had turned me on to pot. I had not smoked regularly after that, but only sporadically, and I was still quite a heavy drinker. But this first patient had friends and they had friends and all of them became my patients. I became a "hip" therapist, for the hip community at Stanford. When I'd go to the parties, they'd all say "Here comes the shrink" and I would sit in the corner looking superior. In addition, I had spent five years in psychoanalysis at a cool investment of something like $26,000.

Before March 6th, which was the day I took Psylocybin, one of the psychedelics, I felt something was wrong in my world, but I couldn't label it in any way so as to get hold of it. I felt that the theories I was teaching in psychology didn't make it, that the psychologists didn't really have a grasp of the human condition, and that the theories I was teaching, which were theories of achievement and anxiety and defense mechanisms and so on, weren't getting to the crux of the matter.

My colleagues and I were 9 to 5 psychologists: we came to work every day and we did our psychology, just like you would do insurance or auto mechanics, and then at 5 we went home and were just as neurotic as we were before we went to work. Somehow, it seemed to me, if all of this theory were right, it should play more intimately into my own life. I understood the requirement of being "objective" for a scientist, but this is a most naive concept in social sciences as we are finding out. And whatever the psychoanalysis did (and it did many things, I'm sure) I still was a neurotic at the end of those five years of psychoanalysis. Even my therapist thought so, because when I stopped analysis to go to Harvard, he said, "You are too sick to leave analysis." Those were his final words. But because I had been trained in Freudian theory, I knew his game well enough to enjoy this terribly sophisticated, competitive relationship with my analyst, and I would say to him, "Well in Freud's 1906 paper, don't you recall he said this, and when I'm saying this you should be interpreting . . ." For this I was paying $20 an hour!

Something was wrong. And the something wrong was that I just didn't know, though I kept feeling all along the way that somebody else must know even though I didn't. The nature of life was a mystery to me. All the stuff I was teaching was just like little molecular bits of stuff but they didn't add up to a feeling anything like wisdom. I was just getting more and more knowledgeable. And I was getting very good at bouncing three knowledge balls at once. I could sit in a doctoral exam, ask very sophisticated questions and look terribly wise. It was a hustle.

DISSATISFACTION

Now my predicament as a social scientist was that I was not basically a scholar. I came out of a Jewish anxiety-ridden high-achieving tradition. Though I had been through five years of psychoanalysis, still, every time I lectured, I would get extraordinary diarrhea and tension. Lecturing five days a week made it quite a complex problem to keep my stomach operating. But whatever my motivations, they drove me so hard that despite the fact that I was a very mediocre student (in fact, I could never get into Harvard no matter how hard I tried, even using all my father's political influence) I finally found myself on the faculty of the "good" universities.

I could study 10 hours and prepare a really good lecture on Freud or Human Motivation, but it was all as if it were behind a wall. It was theoretical. I theorized this or that. I espoused these ideas, these intellectual concepts, quite apart from my own experiential base. Although I could bring all kinds of emotional zeal to bear on my presentation, there was a lack of validity in my guts about what I was doing. And, to my suppressed dismay, I found that this stance was considered acceptable by most of my colleagues who seemed, in their attempt to become "scientific", to think of personality in terms of variables. Children were nothing but ambulatory variables, and no matter how hard we tried, by the time we got to the legitimacy of a highly operationally-defined variable, it had lost its gut feeling. So the concepts we were working with were intellectual fun and games, but they weren't affecting my life.

Here I was, sitting with the boys of the first team in cognitive psychology, personality psychology, developmental psychology, and in the midst of this I felt here were men and women who, themselves, were not highly evolved beings. Their own lives were not fulfilled. There was not enough human beauty, human fulfillment, human contentment. I worked hard and the keys to the kingdom were handed to me. I was being promised all of it. I had felt I had got into whatever the inner circle meant: I could be Program Chairman for Division 7 of the A.P.A. and I could be on government committees, and have grants, and travel about and sit on doctorate committees. But there was still that horrible awareness that I didn't know something or other which made it all fall together. And there was a slight panic in me that I was going to spend the next forty years not knowing, and that apparently that was par for the course. And in off hours, we played "Go", or poker, and cracked old jokes. The whole thing was too empty. It was not honest enough.

And there was some point as a professor at Stanford and Harvard when I experienced being caught in some kind of a meaningless game in which the students were exquisite at playing the role of students and the faculty were exquisite at playing the role of faculty. I would get up and say what I had read in books and they'd all write it down and give it back as answers on exams but nothing was happening. I felt as if I were in a sound-proof room. Not enough was happening that mattered—that was real.

And as a therapist I felt caught in the drama of my own theories. The research data showed that Rogerian patients ended up saying positive statements, and Freudian patients ended up talking about their mother because of subtle reinforcement clues—it was so obvious. I would sit with my little notebook and when the person would start talking about his mother, I'd make a note and it didn't take long for the patient to realize that he got his "note" taken, he got his pellet, every time he said certain things. And pretty soon he would be "Freudianized".

In the face of this feeling of malaise, I ate more, collected more possessions, collected more appointments and positions and status, more sexual and alcoholic orgies, and more wildness in my life.

Everytime I went to a family gathering, I was the boy who made it. I was a Professor at Harvard and everybody stood around in awe and listened to my every word, and all I felt was that horror that I knew inside that I didn't know. Of course, it was all such beautiful, gentle horror, because there was so much reward involved.

I had an empire in a place called Center for Research in Personality: a corner office in a building I'd helped design; with two secretaries and many graduate and undergraduate research assistants. I had done all this in about three years. I was really driven. Until you know a good, Jewish middleclass, upwardly mobile, anxiety-ridden neurotic, you haven't met a real achiever!

My Judaism was a political Judaism. I came out of a tradition of folk religion—the spirit escaped me somehow, although we did all the Yom Kippur and Passover Services. But Dad was on the Board of Trustees that hired and fired Rabbis, so how could I get into a feeling with a spiritual leader if my father was hiring and firing these guys.

Down the hall from my big empire, there was a little office. It had been a closet and they needed an extra office, so they cleared out the closet and put a desk in there and in that closet was Timothy Leary. He had been bicycling around Italy, bouncing checks, and David McClelland found him and brought him back as a creative gift to western science. Tim and I became drinking buddies together. Then we started to teach courses together, such as the first year clinical course—practicum—on "Existential Transactional Behavior Change."

The more time I spent with Tim, the more I realized he had an absolutely extraordinary intellect. He really knew a lot. I found him extremely stimulating and the students found him exciting to be around, because of his openness to new ideas and his willingness to take wild risks in thinking.

One night when we were drinking together, we plotted a trip across North and South America, and when I said I flew a plane, he said, "Great, we'll fly in your plane."

And I said, "Wonderful", and neglected to tell him that I had only a student license.

So I secretly set about getting a license in order to meet him on August 1st in Cuernavaca, Mexico, where he was summering. There we would start our journey.

At that time I was a consultant for a School Mathematics Study Group, a mathematics program in Education at Stanford. I got my license and an airplane on the same day and flew to Mexico the next day in a death-defying leap. When I got there, I found that Timothy had done some other type of flying, just about the week before. Frank Baron, who was a psychologist at Cal, an old friend of Tim's, had introduced him to an anthropologist in Mexico and they had come to know about the Tionanactyl, the flesh of the Gods, the Magic Mushrooms of Mexico, which one obtained from Crazy Juanna, a woman up in the mountains who ate the mushrooms all the time. Contact was made with her and the mushrooms were obtained.

Tim had eaten nine of these mushrooms—so many male and so many female mushrooms—with a group of others around a swimming pool and had had a profound experience. He said, "I learned more in the six or seven hours of this experience than I had learned in all my years as a psychologist."

That is a strong statement!

When I arrived in Cuernavaca, the mushrooms were all gone, and so was the zeal to go on a trip across South America, because what was the sense in doing external journeying when obviously what Timothy had been looking for was inside his own head.

So I hung out in Tepetzlan with David McClelland and his family and in Cuernavaca with Tim and his entourage, and then flew back to the United States with Tim and Jackie his son, and an Iguana.

And I went to be a visiting professor at Cal and Tim went back to Harvard. And by the time I got back, Timothy had a large psychedelic project going.

He had consulted with Aldous Huxley, who was then visiting at M.I.T., and Aldous and Tim and a number of graduate students had contacted Sandoz, who produced a synthetic of the magic mushrooms called Psylocybin, and they had gotten a test batch of this and were busy taking it and administering it. When I got back to Cambridge in the spring, I was invited to share in this bounty.

TURNING ON

The night that was chosen turned out to be the night of the biggest snowstorm of the year and it was to be at Tim's home in Newton, a few blocks from the home of my parents where I had been visiting for dinner. I plowed through the snow, came in and we sat around the kitchen table and there were about three or four of us and we passed the bottle of pills and I took my 10 milligrams. That was my preparation and my set and setting, but beyond that I trusted Timothy. I had seen that Timothy had had a profound experience and he was somebody with an intellect that I understood. I knew that he was not interpersonally destructive—he might be destructive of institutions, but not of individuals. He was a very loving person.

We took a very small dosage, (later we were using 5 or 10 times as much) and the first part of the experience was comparable to a strong pot-high, I'd say. A little more dramatic, a little more intense. Clearly though something happened.

During the first part of this experience with Psylocybin, we got into a very low-level tragi-comedy type thing. Tim's son's dog had been running in the snow and upon entering the warm kitchen lay gasping and panting. To our timeless minds, his struggle for breath continued too long and we thought he was about to expire. What could we do? We could hardly carry the dog through a blizzard in the early Sunday morning to the vet's, some four miles away, especially since we were all very high, and thus not sure about the dog's state. It seemed our concern mounted and the dog passed into a nearby room where it appeared to collapse. We finally decided the only path was to summon 11-year old Jackie from the Late TV show upstairs. Since he wasn't under a chemical influence, we would watch his interaction with the dog, rather than frighten him with our own suspicions.

Jackie was not pleased at being disturbed by us, (merely to find out what he was watching on TV), but the problem was quickly solved by the dog, who, upon hearing Jackie's voice, leapt back to life, ready to play.

Now a few hours later I had gone off by myself to reflect upon these new feelings and senses. A deep calm pervaded my being. The rug crawled and the pictures smiled, all of which delighted me. Then I saw a figure standing about 8 feet away, where a moment before there had been none. I peered into the semi-darkness and recognized none other than myself, in cap and gown and hood, as a professor. It was as if that part of me, which was Harvard professor, had separated or disassociated itself from me.

"How interesting . . . an external hallucination," I thought. "Well, I worked hard to get that status but I don't really need it." Again I settled back into the cushions, separate now from my professorness, but at that moment the figure changed. Again I leaned forward straining to see. "Ah, me again." But now it was that aspect of me who was a social cosmopolite. "Okay, so that goes too," I thought. Again and again the figure changed and I recognized over there all the different aspects I knew to be me . . . cellist, pilot, lover, and so on. With each new presentation, I again and again reassured myself that I didn't need that anyway.

Then I saw the figure become that in me which was Richard Alpert-ness, that is, my basic identity that had always been Richard. I associated the name with myself and my parents called me Richard: "Richard, you're a bad boy." So Richard has badness. Then "Richard, aren't you beautiful!" Then Richard has beauty. Thus develop all these aspects of self.

Sweat broke out on my forehead. I wasn't at all sure I could do without being Richard Alpert. Did that mean I'd have amnesia? Was that what this drug was going to do to me? Would it be permanent? Should I call Tim? Oh, what the hell—so I'll give up being Richard Alpert. I can always get a new social identity. At least I have my body . . . But I spoke too soon.

As I looked down at my legs for reassurance, I could see nothing below the kneecaps, and slowly, now to my horror, I saw the progressive disappearance of limbs and then torso, until all I could see with my eyes open was the couch on which I had sat. A scream formed in my throat. I felt that I must be dying since there was nothing in my universe that led me to believe in life after leaving the body.

Doing without professorness or loverness, or even Richard Alpertness, okay, but I did NEED the body.

The panic mounted, adrenalin shot through my system—my mouth became dry, but along with this, a voice sounded inside—inside what, I don't know—an intimate voice asked very quietly, and rather jocularly, it seemed to me, considering how distraught I was, ". . . but who's minding the store?"

When I could finally focus on the question, I realized that although everything by which I knew myself, even my body and this life itself, was gone, still I was fully aware! Not only that, but this aware "I" was watching the entire drama, including the panic, with calm compassion.

Instantly, with this recognition, I felt a new kind of calmness—one of a profundity never experienced before. I had just found that "I", that scanning device—that point—that essence—that place beyond. A place where "I" existed independent of social and physical identity. That which was I was beyond Life and Death. And something else—that "I" Knew—it really Knew. It was wise, rather than just knowledgeable. It was a voice inside that spoke truth. I recognized it, was one with it, and felt as if my entire life of looking to the outside world for reassurance—David Reisman's other-directed being, was over. Now I need only look within to that place where I Knew.

Fear had turned to exaltation. I ran out into the snow laughing as the hugh flakes swirled about me. In a moment the house was lost from view, but it was all right because inside I Knew.

Around 5 in the morning I walked back, plowing through the snow to my parents' home, and I thought, "Wouldn't it be nice; I'll shovel the walk—young tribal buck shovels the walk." So I started to shovel the walk and my parents' faces appeared at the upstairs window.

"Come to bed, you idiot. Nobody shovels snow at 5 in the morning."

And I looked up at them and I heard the external voice I had been listening to for 30 years, and inside me, something said, "It's all right to shovel snow and it's all right to be happy."

And I looked up at them and I laughed and did a jig and went back to shoveling snow. And they closed the windows and then I looked up and inside they were smiling too. That was my first experience of giving a contact high!

But also, you can see in that moment in the early morning the seeds of the breakaway. The seeds of the ability to be able to confront, and even disagree with, an existing institution and know and trust that inside place that says it's all right. It's something I could never have done without anxiety until that moment—until that day.

Now I thought at that moment, "Wow, I've got it made. I'm just a new beautiful being—I'm just an inner self—all I'll ever need to do is look inside and I'll know what to do and I can always trust it, and here I'll be forever."

But two or three days later I was talking about the whole thing in the past tense. I was talking about how I "experienced" this thing, because I was back being that anxiety-neurotic, in a slightly milder form, but still, my old personality was sneaking back up on me.

Well, the next day I had to give my lecture in Social Relations 143, Human Motivation, and it presented me with a bit of a problem because I couldn't find anywhere in the psychology teachings anything about what had happened to me the night before.

Now, what we did at first at Harvard was to tell all of our colleagues about this extraordinary thing that was happening to us, and they all shared our delight, as any scientists do when a fellow scientist finds a new avenue into the unknown. And so the first week they listened with delight. And then at the end of the first week we all went back into our experimental cell—the living room by the fire and opened the bottle again and took some more psylocybin to chart this course further. And the next week we had shared a deeper experience and we came back and we spoke to our colleagues. Now they couldn't hear us quite as well. It wasn't that they were changing, it was that we were. We were developing a language among ourselves. If Admiral Byrd and an exploratory party are going deeper and deeper into the polar region, the things they think about and are concerned about and are interested in become less and less relevant to somebody living in New York City. This was our situation.

We had the choice along the way of stopping to bring everybody else along, or going on. But these experiences quickly became indescribable. I'd get to a point with my colleagues when I couldn't explain any further, because it came down to "To him who has had the experience no explanation is necessary, to him who has not, none is possible." And we would feel this frustration when they'd say "It sounds very interesting." And we'd say, "In order to know, you've got to try it." And they'd say, "No, that isn't scientific. It isn't appropriate to test your own product. You do it first on animals and then on graduate students . . ."

So then the next week, we'd sit around on Saturday night and say, "What should we do?" and we all knew what we were going to do, and we would "turn on." We were exploring this inner realm of consciousness that we had been theorizing about all these years and suddenly we were traveling in and through and around it. At the same time, of course, by the second week, it was as though we had just been traveling in Tibet, and now, back in the school lunchroom, who do we hang out with? We hang out with the guy with whom we went to Tibet, because we shared this very powerful experience.

Pretty soon there were five or six of us and we were hanging out together and our colleagues said, "Ah ha, a cult is forming," which was true for us. A cult is a shared system of belief.

As to how to work with this stuff, Tim said, "We don't know what this is about yet and there are many models, but it would be best not to impose a model too soon, because a model that exists in the west for these states is pathological, and the model that exists in the primitive cultures is mystical and religious and it's better we keep wide open . . ."

So we did what would be called a naturalistic study: we gave the Psylocybin to maybe 200 people who were physically healthy enough and we said, "You take it under any conditions you want and all you've got to do is answer this questionnaire at the end, so we'll know what happened. You do it however you want to."

So we gave it to jazz musicians and physicists and philosophers and ministers and junkies and graduate students and social scientists. And at the end we had these 200 protocols and the first analysis we did showed up very clearly that the reactions were a function of set and setting—a function of their expectations of what was going to happen, and the environment in which they took the drug. If they had it in a very paranoid environment, and they were expecting to have excitement, they tended to have paranoid excitement. All it did was intensify one's expectations.

However, the data also showed something else. Out of these first few hundred, you could see that there was some kind of a step ladder of experience. There was a kind of probablistic hierarchy of experience, so that the most likely experience everybody had was a heightened sensitivity to all of their five senses and speeding up of the thought process.

Then the next type of experience that people would frequently report was an interpersonal shift of figure and ground, where they would look at another person and see the way in which the other person was similar, rather than different from themselves. And it was as if the whole western mind-training of individual differences had been made background instead of figure, so that you'd look at another human being and say, "Here we are." You'd see differences more as clothing, rather than as core stuff. This was a profound perceptual experience for many people.

For example, we had a Negro psychiatrist, Madison Presnell, working with us, and I had been trained to be a very liberal person about Negroes, which meant that you didn't have feelings. It was a phony kind of liberal thing. I went out of my way to be liberal. You know, that very self-conscious kind of equality. And Madison and I turned on together and I looked at Madison, and there we were, the same human beings. It was just that he was wearing that skin and I was wearing this skin. And it was no more or less than that. It was that shirt and this shirt and it had no more relevance than that.

And I looked at that and suddenly there we were, whereas before I had been so busy with my super-liberal reaction to color of skin, that I couldn't relax enough to share this unitive place.

Then there was a still less frequent type of experience reported: a oneness, in which subjects would say,

". . . I remember being in a dark room with another person and one of us spoke and one of us said, "Who spoke, you or me?" It wasn't clear from who's mouth the words came.

And then there was a still less frequent experience where one looked at somebody and he started to see the other person as cellular structure or patterns of energy rather than as a person.

And finally, a few subjects (maybe 3% or something like that) transcended all form and saw just pure energy—a homogeneous field. It has been called the White Light.

There was research being done by the group with prisoners, to try to change their rate of recidivism. And there were attempts with ministers: a study was run by Walter Pankhe and a group of the research community on Good Friday in Boston University chapel, with twenty ministers—advanced minister-training students—ten received psylocybin and ten a placebo. It was a double-blind study on Good Friday in a chapel. It was absurd, because a double-blind study was absurd. Everybody knew something was happening. It was as if you were proving the obvious. Somebody who had taken the placebo which made their skin crawl reacted by saying, "Well, maybe something's happening", and then another minister would stagger into the room and say, "I see God! I see God!" and it was all too obvious in a short time who had had the psylocybin.

Now my own experiences were horrible and beautiful and I kept working in different environments and settings and whenever anybody that I trusted brought along some new chemical, I would open my mouth and off I'd go. I was interested in doing this exploring.

For example, at one point I had been in the meditation room in the community house we had in Newton, and I was for four hours in a state of total homogeneous light, bliss, and then I recall starting to "come down" and this huge red wave rolled in across the room. It looked like a cross between a William Blake (that picture of the wave) sketch and a Hieronymous Bosch painting, and it was all my identities, all rolling in over me. I remember holding up my hand and saying, "NO, NO, I don't want to go back." It was like this heavy burden I was going to take on myself. And I realized I didn't have the key—I didn't know the magic words, like "Abracadabra" or "Hocus Pocus" or whatever it was going to be that would stop that wave, and it rolled in over me and then . . . "Oh, here I am again—Richard Alpert—what a drag!"

COMING DOWN

In these few years we had gotten over the feeling that one experience was going to make you enlightened forever. We saw that it wasn't going to be that simple.

And for five years I dealt with the matter of "coming down." The coming down matter is what led me to the next chapter of this drama. Because after six year, I realized that no matter how ingenious my experimental designs were, and how high I got, I came down.

At one point I took five people and we locked ourselves in a building for three weeks and we took 400 micrograms of LSD every four hours. That is 2400 micrograms of LSD a day, which sounds fancy, but after your first dose, you build a tolerance; there's a refractory period. We finally were just drinking out of the bottle, because it didn't seem to matter anymore. We'd just stay at a plateau. We were very high. What happened in those three weeks in that house, no one would ever believe, including us. And at the end of the three weeks, we walked out of the house and within a few days, we came down!

And it was a terribly frustrating experience, as if you came into the kingdom of heaven and you saw how it all was and you felt these new states of awareness, and then you got cast out again, and after 2 or 300 times of this, began to feel an extraordinary kind of depression set in—a very gentle depression that whatever I knew still wasn't enough!

ENVIRONMENTAL CHANGES

Now at the same moment, there were obvious changes going on, because that checking back, over and over again, to the inner place inside myself, made me less and less attached to reassurance from the environment that I was all right. So I remember the moment when I was thrown out of Harvard . . .

There was a press conference and all of the reporters looked at me as if I was a prizefighter who had just lost a major fight, and was headed for oblivion, that kind of look you have for losers—real losers! And they stood there looking at me that way. Everybody was looking at me that way, and inside I felt, "What I'm doing is all right."

Everybody, parents, colleagues, public, saw it as a horrible thing; I thought inside "I must really be crazy, now—because craziness is where everybody agrees about something,—except you!" And yet I felt saner than I had ever felt, so I knew this was a new kind of craziness or perhaps a new kind of saneness. But the thing was, I always seemed to be able to skirt the line: to keep it together. I didn't ever DO anything quite crazy enough.

I was the guy that people would come to and say, "Look, would you calm Tim Leary—he's too far out. If you'll calm him and protect him and so on." And I'd say, "I'll help him with pleasure 'cause he's that great a being." And I'd help raise money and run the kitchen and clean the house and raise the children . . .

Well, we realized then that what we needed to do was to create certain kinds of environments which would allow a person, after being into another state of consciousness, to retain a certain kind of environmental support for new ways of looking at himself. After all, if you see yourself as God and then you come back from this state and somebody says, "Hey, Sam, empty the garbage!" it catches you back into the model of "I'm Sam who empties the garbage." You can't maintain these new kinds of structures. It takes a while to realize that God can empty garbage.

Now in 1962 or 3, Tim and Ralph Metzner with him (I was just given author's credit because I took care of the kitchen) had come across the Tibetan Book of the Dead, which was a very close description of a number of these experiences. This book was 2500 years old, at least, and it had been used all those years for preparing Tibetan Lamas to die and be reincarnated. And when we opened it, we would find descriptions of the 49 days after death before rebirth, that were perfect descriptions of sessions we were having with psychedelics.

How could this be? The parallel was so close. Tim rewrote the book as a manual called "The Psychedelic Experience", a manual for psychological death and rebirth, arguing that this was really a metaphor about psychological death and rebirth and not necessarily physical death and reincarnation.

Tim had gone to India, Ralph had gone to India, Allen Ginsberg had gone to India. I checked with everybody when they came back. There was Tim, being Tim and there was Ralph, being Ralph, and there was Allen, being Allen—and I realized that they had all had lovely experiences and seen a beautiful country and so on, but they were not finished looking for something.

And by 1966-7, I was in the same predicament. I was aware that I didn't know enough to maintain these states of consciousness. And I was aware that nobody else around me seemed to know enough either. I checked with everybody I thought might know, and nobody seemed to know.

So I wasn't very optimistic about India or psychedelics. By 1967 I had shot my load! I had no more job as a psychologist in a respectable establishment and I realized that we didn't know enough about psychedelics to use them profitably.

But at that time I was still lecturing around the country on psychedelics to such diverse groups as the Food and Drug Administration, and the Hell's Angels.

Then, along came a very lovely guy whom I had guided through some psychedelic sessions, an interesting guy, who had gone to the University of Chicago in his early teens and had taught seminars in Chinese Economics, had started a company called Basic Systems, which had been sold to Xerox, and now he had retired. He was about 35 and he had retired and taken his five million dollars or whatever he made, and was now becoming a Buddhist. He wanted to make a journey to the east to look for holy men and he invited me to go along. He had a Land Rover imported into Teheran and this was my way out. What else was I going to do at this point.

So I left to go to India, and I took a bottle of LSD with me, with the idea that I'd meet holy men along the way, and I'd give them LSD and they'd tell me what LSD is. Maybe I'd learn the missing clue.

We started out from Teheran, and for the next three months we had lovely guides and a most beautiful time and we scored great hashish in Afghanistan, and at the end of three months, I had seen the inside of the Land Rover, I had 1300 slides, many tape recordings of Indian music; I had drunk much bottled water, eaten many canned goods: I was a westerner traveling in India. That's what was happening to me when I got to Nepal.

We had done it all. We had gone to see the Dalai Lama, and we had gone on horseback up to Amanath Cave up in Kashmir; we had visited Benares, and finally we ended up in Katmandu, Nepal. I started to get extremely, extremely depressed. I'm sure part of it was due to the hashish. But also, part of it was because I didn't see what to do next.

I had done everything I thought I could do, and nothing new had happened. It was turning out to be just another trip. The despair got very heavy. We didn't know enough and I couldn't figure out how to socialize this thing about the new states of consciousness. And I didn't know what to do next. It wasn't like I didn't have LSD. I had plenty of LSD, but why take it. I knew what it was going to do, what it was going to tell me. It was going to show me that garden again and then I was going to be cast out and that was it. And I never could quite stay. I was addicted to the experience at first, and then I even got tired of that. And the despair was extremely intense at that point.

We were sitting in a hippie restaurant, called the Blue Tibetan, and I was talking to some French hippies . . .

I had given LSD to a number of pundits around India and some reasonably pure men:

An old Buddhist Lama said, "It gave me a headache."

Somebody else said, "It's good, but not as good as meditation."

Somebody else said, "Where can I get some more?"

And I got the same range of responses I'd get in America. I didn't get any great pearl of wisdom which would make me exclaim, "Oh, that's what it is—I was waiting for something that was going to do that thing!"

So I finally figured, "Well, it's not going to happen." We were about to go on to Japan and I was pretty depressed because we were starting the return now, and what was I returning to? What should I do now?

I decided I was going to come back and become a chauffeur. I wanted to be a servant, and let somebody else program my consciousness. I could read holy books while I'd wait for whoever it was I was waiting for while they were at Bergdorf Goodman's and I'd just change my whole style of life around. I could just get out of the whole drama of having to engineer my own ship for a while. This is a funny foreshadowing, as you'll see.

The despair was extremely intense at that point. I was really quite sad.

BHAGWAN DASS

I was in the Blue Tibetan with my friend and these other people, and in walked this very extraordinary guy, at least extraordinary with regard to his height. He was 6'7" and he had long blonde hair and a long blonde beard. He was a Westerner, an American, and was wearing holy clothes—a dhoti (a cloth Indian men wear instead of pants) and so on, and when he entered, he came directly over to our table and sat down.

Now, up until then, I had found this interesting thing that I don't think I could have labeled until that moment. Once, when I had met Gesha Wangyal at Freehold, N.J., I knew I was meeting a being who "knew", but I couldn't get to it because I wasn't ready, somehow. We were very close—we loved each other extraordinarily, but I hadn't been able to really absorb whatever I needed to absorb. Now here was this young fellow and again, I had the feeling I had met somebody who "Knew".

I don't know how to describe this to you, except that I was deep in my despair; I had gone through game, after game, after game, first being a professor at Harvard, then being a psychedelic spokesman, and still people were constantly looking into my eyes, like "Do you know?" Just that subtle little look, and I was constantly looking into their eyes—"Do you know?" And there we were, "Do you?" "Do you?" "Maybe he . . ." "Do you . . .?" And there was always that feeling that everybody was very close and we all knew we knew, but nobody quite knew. I don't know how to describe it, other than that.

And I met this guy and there was no doubt in my mind. It was just like meeting a rock. It was just solid, all the way through. Everywhere I pressed, there he was!

We were staying in a hotel owned by the King or the Prince, or something, because we were going first class, so we spirited this fellow up to our suite in the Sewalti Hotel and for five days we had a continuing seminar. We had this extraordinarily beautiful Indian sculptor, Harish Johari, who was our guide and friend. Harish, this fellow, Bhagwan Dass and David and I sat there and for five days high on Peach Melbas and Hashish and Mescaline, we had a seminar with Alexandra David Neehl's books and Sir John Woodroffe's Serpent Power, and so on. At the end of five days, I was still absolutely staggered by this guy. He had started to teach me some mantras and working with beads. When it came time to leave, to go to Japan, I had the choice of going on to Japan on my first class route, or going off with this guy, back into India on a temple pilgrimage. He had no money and I had no money and it was going to change my style of life considerably. I thought. "Well, look, I came to India to find something and I still think this guy knows—I'm going to follow him."

But there was also the counter thought, "How absurd—who's writing this bizarre script. Here I am—I've come half-way around the world and I'm going to follow, through India, a 23 year old guy from Laguna Beach, California."

I said to Harish and to David, "Do you think I'm making a mistake?" And Harish said, "No, he is a very high guy." And so I started to follow him—literally follow him.

Now, I'm suddenly barefoot. He has said, "You're not going to wear shoes, are you?" That sort of thing. And I've got a shoulder bag and my dhoti and blisters on my feet and dysentery, the likes of which you can't imagine, and all he says is, "Well, fast for a few days."

He's very compassionate, but no pity.

And we're sleeping on the ground, or on these wooden tables that you get when you stop at monasteries, and my hip bones ache. I go through an extraordinary physical breakdown, become very childlike and he takes care of me. And we start to travel through temples—to Baneshwar and Konarak and so on.

I see that he's very powerful, so extraordinarily powerful—he's got an ectara, a one-stringed instrument, and I've got a little Tibetan drum, and we go around to the villages and people rush out and they touch our feet because we're holy men, which is embarrassing to me because I'm not a holy man—I'm obviously who I am—a sort of overage hippie, western explorer, and I feel very embarrassed when they do that and they give us food. And he plays and sings and the Hindu people love him and revere him. And he's giving away all my money . . .

But I'm clinging tight to my passport and my return ticket to America, and a traveler's check that I'll need to get me to Delhi. Those things I'm going to hold on to. And my bottle of LSD, in case I should find something interesting.

And during these travels he's starting to train me in a most interesting way. We'd be sitting somewhere and I'd say,

"Did I ever tell you about the time that Tim and I . . ."

And he'd say, "Don't think about the past. Just be here now."

Silence.

And I'd say, "How long do you think we're going to be on this trip?"

And he'd say, "Don't think about the future. Just be here now."

I'd say, "You know, I really feel crumby, my hips are hurting . . ."

"Emotions are like waves. Watch them disappear in the distance on the vast calm ocean."

He had just sort of wiped out my whole game. That was it—that was my whole trip—emotions, and past experiences, and future plans. I was, after all, a great story teller.

So we were silent. There was nothing to say.

He'd say, "You eat this." or, "Now you sleep here." And all the rest of the time we sang holy songs. That was all there was to do.

Or he would teach me Asanas—Hatha Yoga postures.

But there was no conversation. I didn't know anything about his life. He didn't know anything about my life. He wasn't the least bit interested in all of the extraordinary dramas that I had collected . . . He was the first person I couldn't seduce into being interested in all this. He just didn't care.

And yet, I never felt so profound an intimacy with another being. It was as if he were inside of my heart. And what started to blow my mind was that everywhere we went, he was at home.

If we went to a Thereavaden Buddhist monastery, he would be welcomed and suddenly he would be called Dharma Sara, a Southern Buddhist name, and some piece of clothing he wore, I suddenly saw was also worn by all the other monks and I realized that he was an initiate in that scene and they'd welcome him and he'd be in the inner temple and he knew all the chants and he was doing them.

We'd come across some Shavites, followers of Shiva, or some of the Swamis, and I suddenly realized that he was one of them. On his forehead would be the appropriate tilik, or mark, and he would be doing their chanting.

We'd meet Kargyupa lamas from Tibet and they would all welcome him as a brother, and he knew all their stuff. He had been in India for five years, and he was so high that everybody just welcomed him, feeling 'he's obviously one of us'.

I couldn't figure out what his scene was. All I personally felt was this tremendous pull toward Buddhism because Hinduism always seemed a little gauche—the paintings were a little too gross—the colors were bizarre and the whole thing was too melodramatic and too much emotion. I was pulling toward that clean, crystal-clear simplicity of the Southern Buddhists or the Zen Buddhists.

After about three months, I had a visa problem and we went to Delhi, and I was still quite unsure of my new role as a holy man and so when I got to Delhi, I took $4.00 out of my little traveler's check and bought a pair of pants and a shirt and a tie and took my horn-rimmed glasses out of my shoulder bag and stuck them back on and I became again Dr. Alpert, to go to the visa office. Dr. Alpert, who had a grant from the Folk Art Museum of New Mexico for collecting musical instruments and I did my whole thing.

I kept my beads in my pocket. Because I didn't feel valid in this other role. And then the minute I got my visa fixed, he had to have his annual visa worked over, and he had to go to a town near-by, which we went to, and we were welcomed at this big estate and given a holy man's house, and food brought to us, and he said, "You sit here. I'm going to see about my visa."

He told me just what to do. I was just like a baby. "Eat this." "Sit here." "Do this." And I just gave up. He knew. Do you know? I'll follow you.

He spoke Hindi fluently. My Hindi was very faltering. So he could handle it all.

We had spent a few weeks in a Chinese Buddhist monastery in Sarnath, which was extraordinarily powerful and beautiful, and something was happening to me but I couldn't grasp the total nature of it at all.

There was a strange thing about him. At night he didn't seem to sleep like I did. That is, any time I'd wake up at night, I'd look over and he would be sitting in the lotus position. And sometimes I'd make believe I was asleep and then open sort of a half-eye to see if he wasn't cheating—maybe he was sleeping Now—but he was always in the lotus posture.

Sometimes I'd see him lie down, but I would say that 80% of the time when I would be sleeping heavily, he would be sitting in some state or other, which he'd never describe to me. But he was not in personal contact—I mean, there was no wave or moving around, or nothing seemed to happen to him.

The night at that estate, I went out—I had to go to the bathroom and I went out under the stars and the following event happened . . .

The previous January 20th, at Boston in the Peter Bent Brigham Hospital, my mother had died of a spleen illness—the bone marrow stopped producing blood and the spleen took over and grew very large and they removed it and then she died. It had been a long illness and I had been with her through the week prior to her death and through it we had become extremely close. We had transcended mother-child and personalities and we had come into true contact. I spent days in the hospital just meditating. And I felt no loss when she died. Instead there was a tremendous continuing contact with her. And in fact, when I had been in Nepal, I had had a vision of her one night when I was going to bed. I saw her up on the ceiling and I was wondering whether to go to India or go on to Japan and she had a look that was the look of "You damn fool—you're always getting into hot water, but go ahead, and I think that's great." She looked peeved-pleased. It was like there were two beings in my mother. She was a middle class women from Boston, who wanted me to be absolutely responsible in the most culturally acceptable fashion, and then there was this swinger underneath—this spiritual being underneath who said, "—go, baby." And I felt these two beings in that look which supported my going back into India.

This night I'm under the stars, and I hadn't thought about her at all since that time. I'm under the stars, urinating, and I look up and the stars are very close because it's very dark and I suddenly experience a presence of mother, and I'm thinking about her—not about how she died or anything about that. I just feel her presence. It's very very powerful. And I feel great love for her and then I go back to bed.

Of course, Bhagwan Dass is not the least interested in any of my life, so he'd be the last person I'd talk to about my thoughts or visions.

The next morning he says, "We've got to go to the mountains. I've got a visa problem. We've got to go see my Guru."

Now the term "Guru" had meant for me, in the West, a sort of high grade teacher. There was a Life article about Allen Ginsberg—"Guru goes to Kansas" and Allen was embarrassed and said, "I'm not really a Guru." And I didn't know what a Guru really was. . .

Bhagwan Dass also said we were going to borrow the Land Rover, which had been left with this sculptor, to go to the mountains. And I said, I didn't want to borrow the Land Rover. I'd just gotten out of that horrible blue box and I didn't want to get back into it, and I didn't want the responsibility. David had left it with this Indian sculptor and he wouldn't want to loan it to us anyway. I got very sulky. I didn't want to go see a guru—and suddenly I wanted to go back to America in the worst way.

I thought, "What am I doing? I'm following this kid and all he is . . ." But he says, "We've got to do this," and so we go to the town where the sculptor lives and within half an hour the sculptor says, "You have to go see your Guru? Take the Land Rover!"

Well, that's interesting.

We're in the Land Rover and he won't let me drive. So I'm sitting there sulking. He won't let me drive and we are in the Land Rover which I don't want to have and I'm now really in a bad mood. I've stopped smoking hashish a few days before because I'm having all kinds of reactions to it, and so I'm just in a very, very uptight, negative paranoid state and all I want to do is go back to America and suddenly I'm following this young kid who wants to drive and all he wanted me for was to get the Land Rover and now the whole paranoid con world fills my head. I'm full of it.

We go about 80 or 100 miles and we come to a tiny temple by the side of the road in the foothills of the Himalayas. We're stopping and I think we're stopping because a truck's coming by, but when we stop, people surround the car, which they generally do, but they welcome him and he jumps out. And I can tell something's going to happen because as we go up into the hills, he's starting to cry.

We're singing songs and tears are streaming down his face, and I know something's going on, but I don't know what.

We stop at this temple and he asks where the guru is and they point up on a hill, and he goes running up this hill and they're all following him, so delighted to see him. They all love him so much.

I get out of the car. Now I'm additionally bugged because everybody's ignoring me. And I'm following him and he's way ahead of me and I'm running after him barefoot up this rocky path and I'm stumbling—by now my feet are very tough—but still his legs are very long and I'm running and people are ignoring me and I'm very bugged and I don't want to see the guru anyway and what the hell—

We go around this hill so that we come to a field which does not face on the road. It's facing into a valley and there's a little man in his 60's or 70's sitting with a blanket around him. And around him are 8 or 9 Hindu people and it's a beautiful tableau—clouds, beautiful green valley, lovely, lovely place—the foothills of the Himalayas.

And this fellow, Bhagwan Dass, comes up, runs to this man and throws himself on the ground, full-face doing 'dunda pranam,' and he's stretched out so his face is down on the ground, full-length and his hands are touching the feet of this man, who is sitting cross-legged. And he's crying and the man is patting him on the head and I don't know what's happening.

I'm standing on the side and thinking "I'm not going to touch his feet. I don't have to. I'm not required to do that." And every now and then this man looks up at me and he twinkles a little. But I'm so uptight that I couldn't care less. Twinkle away, man!

Then he looks up at me—he speaks in Hindi, of which I understand maybe half, but there is a fellow who's translating all the time, who hangs out with him, and the Guru says to Bhagwan Dass, "You have a picture of me?"

Bhagwan Dass nods, "Yes".

"Give it to him," says the man, pointing at me.

"That's very nice, I think, giving me a picture of himself, and I smile and nod appreciatively. But I'm still not going to touch his feet!

Then he says, "You came in a big car?" Of course that's the one thing I'm really uptight about. "Yeah."

So he looks at me and he smiles and says, "You give it to me?"

I started to say, "Wha . . ." and Bhagwan Dass looks up—he's lying there—and he says, "Maharaji, (meaning 'great king'), if you want it you can have it—it's yours."

And I said, "No—now wait a minute—you can't give away David's car like that. That isn't our car . . ." and this old man is laughing. In fact, everyone is laughing . . . except me.

Then he says, "You made much money in America?"

"Ah, at last he's feeding my ego." I think.

So I flick through all of my years as a professor and years as a smuggler and all my different dramas in my mind and I said, "Yeah."

"How much you make?"

Well, I said, at one time—and I sort of upped the figure a bit, you know, my ego—$25,000.

So they all converted that into rupees which was practically half the economic base of India, and everybody was terribly awed by this figure, which was complete bragging on my part. It was phony—I never made $25,000. And he laughed again. And he said,

"You'll buy a car like that for me?"

And I remember what went through my mind. I had come out of a family of fund-raisers for the United Jewish Appeal, Brandeis, and Einstein Medical School, and I had never seen hustling like this. He doesn't even know my name and already he wants a $7,000 vehicle.

And I said, "Well, maybe . . ." The whole thing was freaking me so much.

And he said, "Take them away and give them food." So we were taken and given food—magnificent food—we were together still, and saddhus brought us beautiful food and then we were told to rest. Some time later we were back with the Maharaji and he said to me, "Come here. Sit." So I sat down and he looked at me and he said,

"You were out under the stars last night."
"Um-hum."
"You were thinking about your mother."
"Yes." ('Wow', I thought, 'that's pretty good. I never mentioned that to anybody').
"She died last year."
"Um-hum."
"She got very big in the stomach before she died."
. . . Pause . . . "Yes."
He leaned back and closed his eyes and said, "Spleen. She died of spleen".

    Well, what happened to me at that moment, I can't really put into words. He looked at me in a certain way at that moment, and two things happened—it seemed simultaneous. They do not seem like cause and effect.

The first thing that happened was that my mind raced faster and faster to try to get leverage—to get a hold on what he had just done. I went through every super CIA paranoia I've ever had:

"Who is he?" "Who does he represent?"

"Where's the button he pushes where the file appears?" and "Why have they brought me here?" None of it would jell.

It was just too impossible that this could have happened this way. The guy I was with didn't know all that stuff, and I was a tourist in a car, and the whole thing was just too far out. My mind went faster and faster and faster.

Up until then I had two categories for "psychic experience." One was 'they happened to somebody else and they haven't happened to me, and they were terribly interesting and we certainly had to keep an open mind about it'. That was my social science approach. The other one was, 'well, man, I'm high on LSD. Who knows how it really is? After all, under the influence of a chemical, how do I know I'm not creating the whole thing?' Because, in fact, I had taken certain chemicals where I experienced the creation of total realities. The greatest example I have of this came about through a drug called JB 318, which I took in a room at Millbrook. I was sitting on the 3rd floor and it seemed like nothing was happening at all. And into the room walked a girl from the community with a pitcher of lemonade and she said, would I like some lemonade, and I said that would be great, and she poured the lemonade, and she poured it and she kept pouring and the lemonade went over the side of the glass and fell to the floor and it went across the floor and up the wall and over the ceiling and down the wall and under my pants which got wet and it came back up into the glass—and when it touched the glass the glass disappeared and the lemonade disappeared and the wetness in my pants disappeared and the girl disappeared and I turned around to Ralph Metzner and I said,

"Ralph, the most extraordinary thing happened to me," and Ralph disappeared!

I was afraid to do anything but just sit. Whatever this is, it's not nothing. Just sit. Don't move, just sit!

So I had had experiences where I had seen myself completely create whole environments under psychedelics, and therefore I wasn't eager to interpret these things very quickly, because I, the observer, was, at those times, under the influence of the psychedelics.

But neither of these categories applied in this situation, and my mind went faster and faster and then I felt like what happens when a computer is fed an insoluble problem; the bell rings and the red light goes on and the machine stops. And my mind just gave up. It burned out its circuitry . . . its zeal to have an explanation. I needed something to get closure at the rational level and there wasn't anything. There just wasn't a place I could hide in my head about this.

And at the same moment, I felt this extremely violent pain in my chest and a tremendous wrenching feeling and I started to cry. And I cried and I cried and I cried. And I wasn't happy and I wasn't sad. It was not that kind of crying. The only thing I could say was it felt like I was home. Like the journey was over. Like I had finished.

Well, I cried and they finally sort of spooned me up and took me to the home of devotee, K.K. Sah, to stay overnight. That night I was very confused. A great feeling of lightness and confusion.

At one point in the evening I was looking in my shoulder bag and came across the bottle of LSD.

"Wow! I've finally met a guy who is going to Know! He will definitely know what LSD is. I'll have to ask him. That's what I'll do. I'll ask him." Then I forgot about it.

The next morning, at 8 o'clock a messenger comes. Maharaji wants to see you immediately. We went in the Land Rover. The 3 miles to the temple. When I'm approaching him, he yells out at me, "Have you got a question?"

And he's very impatient with all of this nonsense, and he says, "Where's the medicine?"

I got a translation of this. He said medicine. I said, "Medicine?" I never thought of LSD as medicine! And somebody said, he must mean the LSD. "LSD?" He said, "Ah-cha—bring the LSD."

So I went to the car and got the little bottle of LSD and I came back.

"Let me see?"

So I poured it out in my hand—"What's that?"

"That's STP . . . That's librium and that's . . ." A little of everything. Sort of a little traveling kit.

He says, "Gives you siddhis?"

I had never heard the word "siddhi" before. So I asked for a translation and siddhi was translated as "power". From where I was at in relation to these concepts, I thought he was like a little old man, asking for power. Perhaps he was losing his vitality and wanted Vitamin B 12. That was one thing I didn't have and I felt terribly apologetic because I would have given him anything. If he wanted the Land Rover, he could have it. And I said, "Oh, no, I'm sorry." I really felt bad I didn't have any and put it back in the bottle.

He looked at me and extended his hand. So I put into his hand what's called a "White Lightning". This is an LSD pill and this one was from a special batch that had been made specially for me for traveling. And each pill was 305 micrograms, and very pure. Very good acid. Usually you start a man over 60, maybe with 50 to 75 micrograms, very gently, so you won't upset him. 300 of pure acid is a very solid dose.

He looks at the pill and extends his hand further. So I put a second pill—that's 610 micrograms—then a third pill—that's 915 micrograms—into his palm.

That is sizeable for a first dose for anyone!

"Ah-cha."

And he swallows them! I see them go down. There's no doubt. And that little scientist in me says, "This is going to be very interesting!"

All day long I'm there, and every now and then he twinkles at me and nothing—nothing happens! That was his answer to my question. Now you have the data I have.

ASHTANGA YOGA

I was taken back to the temple. It was interesting. At no time was I asked, do you want to stay? Do you want to study? Everything was understood. There were no contracts. There were no promises. There were no vows. There was nothing.

The next day Maharaji instructed them to take me out and buy me clothes. They gave me a room. Nobody ever asked me for a nickel. Nobody ever asked me to spread the word. Nobody ever did anything. There was no commitment whatsoever required. It was all done internally.

This guru — Maharaji — has only his blanket. You see, he's in a place called SAHAJ SAMADHI and he's not identified with this world as most of us identify with it. If you didn't watch him, he'd just disappear altogether into the jungle or leave his body, but his devotees are always protecting him and watching him so they can keep him around. They've got an entourage around him and people come and bring gifts to the holy man because that's part of the way in which you gain holy merit in India. And money piles up, and so they build temples, or they build schools. He will walk to a place and there will be a saint who has lived in that place or cave and he'll say, "There will be a temple here," and then they build a temple. And they do all this around Maharaji. He appears to do nothing.

As an example of Maharaji's style, I was once going through my address book and I came to Lama Govinda's name (he wrote *Foundations of Tibetan Mysticism* and *Way of the White Cloud*) and I thought, "Gee, I ought to go visit him. I'm here in the Himalayas and it wouldn't be a long trip and I could go and pay my respects. I must do that some time before I leave."

And the next day there is a message from Maharaji saying, "You are to go immediately to see Lama Govinda."

Another time, I had to go to Delhi to work on my visa and I took a bus. This was the first time after four months that they let me out alone. They were so protective of me. I don't know what they were afraid would happen to me, but they were always sending somebody with me . . . They weren't giving me elopement privileges, as they say in mental hospitals.

But they allowed me to go alone to Delhi and I took a 12 hour bus trip. I went to Delhi and I was so high. I went through Connaught Place. And I went through that barefoot, silent with my chalkboard — I was silent all the time. At American Express, writing my words it was so high that not at one moment was there even a qualm or a doubt.

So after all day long of doing my dramas with the Health Department and so on, it came time for lunch. I had been on this very fierce austere diet and I had lost 60 lbs. I was feeling great—very light and very beautiful—but there was enough orality still left in me to want to have a feast. I'll have a vegetarian feast, I thought. So I went to a fancy vegetarian restaurant and I got a table over in a corner and ordered their special deluxe vegetarian dinner, from nuts to nuts, and I had the whole thing and the last thing they served was vegetarian ice cream with 2 english biscuits stuck into it. And those biscuits . . . the sweet thing has always been a big part of my life, but I knew somehow, maybe I shouldn't be eating those. They're so far out from my diet. It's not vegetables—it's not rice. And so I was almost secretly eating the cookies in this dark corner. I was feeling very guilty about eating these cookies. But nobody was watching me. And then I went to a Buddhist monastary for the night and the next day took the bus back up to the mountain.

Two days later, we heard Maharaji was back—he had been up in the mountains in another little village. He travels around a lot, moves from place to place. I hadn't seen him in about a month and a half—I didn't see much of him at all. We all went rushing to see Maharaji and I got a bag of oranges to bring to him and I came and took one look at him, and the oranges went flying and I started to cry and I fell down and they were patting me. Maharaji was eating oranges as fast as he could, manifesting through eating food the process of taking on the karma of someone else.

Women bring him food all day long. He just opens his mouth and they feed him and he's taking on karma that way. And he ate eight oranges right before my eyes. I had never seen anything like that. And the principal of the school was feeding me oranges and I was crying and the whole thing was very maudlin, and he pulls me by the hair, and I look up and he says to me, "How did you like the biscuits?"

I'd be at my temple. And I'd think about arranging for a beautiful lama in America to get some money, or something like that. Then I'd go to bed and pull the covers over my head and perhaps have a very worldly thought; I would think about what I'd do with all my powers when I got them; perhaps a sexual thought. Then when next I saw Maharaji he would tell me something like, "You want to give money to a lama in America." And I'd feel like I was such a beautiful guy. Then suddenly I'd be horrified with the realization that if he knew that thought, then he must know that one, too . . . ohhhhh . . . and that one, too! Then I'd look at the ground. And when I'd finally steal a glance at him, he'd be looking at me with such total love.

Now the impact of these experiences was very profound. As they say in the Sikh religion—One you realize God knows everything, you're free. I had been through many years of psychoanalysis and still I had managed to keep private places in my head—I wouldn't say they were big, labeled categories, but they were certain attitudes or feelings that were still very private. And suddenly I realized that he knew everything that was going on in my head, all the time, and that he still loved me. Because who we are is behind all that.

I said to Hari Dass Baba, my teacher at the time, "Why is it that Maharaji never tells me the bad things I think?", and he says, "It does not help your sadhana - your spiritual work. He knows it all, but he just does the things that help you."

The sculptor had said he loved Maharaji so much, we should keep the Land Rover up there. The Land Rover was just sitting around and so Maharaji got the Land Rover after all, for that time. And then one day, I was told we were going on an outing up in the Himalayas for the day. This was very exciting, because I never left my room in the temple. Now in the temple, or around Maharaji, there were eight or nine people. Bhagwan Dass and I were the only westerners. In fact, at no time that I was there did I see any other westerners. This is clearly not a western scene, and in fact, I was specifically told when returning to the United States that I was not to mention Maharaji's name or where he was, or anything.

The few people that have slipped by this net and figured out from clues in my speech and their knowledge of India where he was and have gone to see him, were thrown out immediately . . . very summarily dismissed, which is very strange. All I can do is pass that information on to you. I think the message is that you don't need to go to anywhere else to find what you are seeking.

So there were eight or nine people and whenever there was a scene, I walked last. I was the lowest man on the totem pole. They all loved me and honored me and I was the novice, like in a karate or judo class, where you stand at the back until you learn more. I was always in the back and they were always teaching me.

So we went in the Land Rover. Maharaji was up in the front—Bhagwan Dass was driving. Bhagwan Dass turned out to be very high in this scene. He was very very highly thought of and honored. He had started playing the sitar; he was a fantastic musician and the Hindu people loved him. He would do bhajan—holy music—so high they would go out on it. So Bhagwan Dass was driving and I was way in the back of the Land Rover camper with the women and some luggage.

And we went up into the hills and came to a place where we stopped and were given apples, in an orchard and we looked at a beautiful view. We stayed about 10 minutes, and then Maharaji says, "We've got to go on."

We got in the car, went further up the hill and came to a Forestry camp. Some of his devotees are people in the Forestry department so they make this available to him.

So we got to this place and there was a building waiting and a caretaker—"Oh, Maharaji, you've graced us with your presence." He went inside with the man that is there to take care of him or be with him all the time—and we all sat on the lawn."

After a little while, a message came out, "Maharaji wants to see you." And I got up and went in, and sat down in front of him. He looked at me and said,

"You make many people laugh in America?"

I said, "Yes, I like to do that."

"Good . . . You like to feed children?"

"Yes. Sure."

"Good."

He asked a few more questions like that, which seemed to be nice questions, but . . .? Then he smiled and he reached forward and he tapped me right on the forehead, just three times. That's all.

Then the other fellow came along and lifted me and walked me out the door. I was completely confused. I didn't know what had happened to me—why he had done it—what it was about.

When I walked out, the people out in the yard said that I looked as if I were in a very high state. They said tears were streaming down my face. But all I felt inside was confusion. I have never felt any further understanding of it since then. I don't know what it was all about. It was not an idle movement, because the minute that was over, we all got back in the car and went home.

I pass that on to you. You know now, what I know about that. Just an interesting thing. I don't know what it means, yet.

Hari Dass Baba was my teacher. I was taught by this man with a chalkboard in the most terse way possible. I would get up early, take my bath in the river or out of a pail with a lota (a bowl). I would go in and do my breathing exercises, my pranayam and my hatha yoga, meditate, study, and around 11:30 in the morning, this man would arrive and with chalkboard he would write something down:

"If a pickpocket meets a saint, he sees only his pockets."

Then he'd get up and leave. Or he'd write,

"If you wear shoeleather, the whole earth is covered with leather."

These were his ways of teaching me about how motivation affects perception. His teaching seemed to be no teaching because he always taught from within . . . that is, his lessons aroused in me just affirmation . . . as if I knew it all already.

When starting to teach me about what it meant to be 'ahimsa' or non-violent, and the effect on the environment around you of the vibrations—when he started to teach me about energy and vibrations, his opening statement was "Snakes Know Heart." "Yogis in jungle need not fear." Because if you're pure enough, cool it, don't worry. But you've got to be very pure.

So his teaching was of this nature. And it was not until a number of months later that I got hold of Vivekananda's book "Raja Yoga" and I realized that he had been teaching me Raja Yoga, very systematically—an exquisite scientific system that had been originally enunciated somewhere between 500 BC and 500 AD by Patanjali, in a set of sutras, or phrases, and it's called Ashtanga Yoga, or 8-limbed yoga—and also known as Raja or Kingly yoga. And this beautiful yogi was teaching me this wisdom with simple metaphor and brief phrase.

Now, though I am a beginner on the path, I have returned to the West for a time to work out karma or unfulfilled commitment. Part of this commitment is to share what I have learned with those of you who are on a similar journey. One can share a message through telling 'our-story' as I have just done, or through teaching methods of yoga, or singing, or making love. Each of us finds his unique vehicle for sharing with others his bit of wisdom.

For me, this story is but a vehicle for sharing with you the true message . . . the living faith in what is possible.

—OM—

JAGAT GURUDEV BABA
NEEM KAROLIE MAHARAJ

MAHASAMADHI
SEPTEMBER 11 - 1973

Baba Ram Dass is a friend of the Lama Foundation, but we are not affiliated in any official way. Since his most recent return to the West from India he has been floating about on an ocean of love . . . carried by the winds of desire of beings he can serve.

TO
MAHARAJ-JI

OF WHOSE
ASHIRBAD
(BLESSING)
THIS
IS
A   MANIFESTATION

ॐ

THE HEART CAVE

"EXCEPT YE BE CONVERTED
&
BECOME AS LITTLE CHILDREN
YE SHALL NOT ENTER
THE KINGDOM OF HEAVEN"

✠ ✠

UNLESS ★ YOU

START AGAIN

BECOME   THAT   TRUSTING

OPEN   SURRENDERED   BEING

THE ENERGY CAN'T COME IN

THAT IS THE KINGDOM OF HEAVEN

❖ THE ENERGY ❖

IT IS THE SAME THING

COSMIC CONSCIOUSNESS

ॐ 1

CONSCIOUSNESS EQUALS

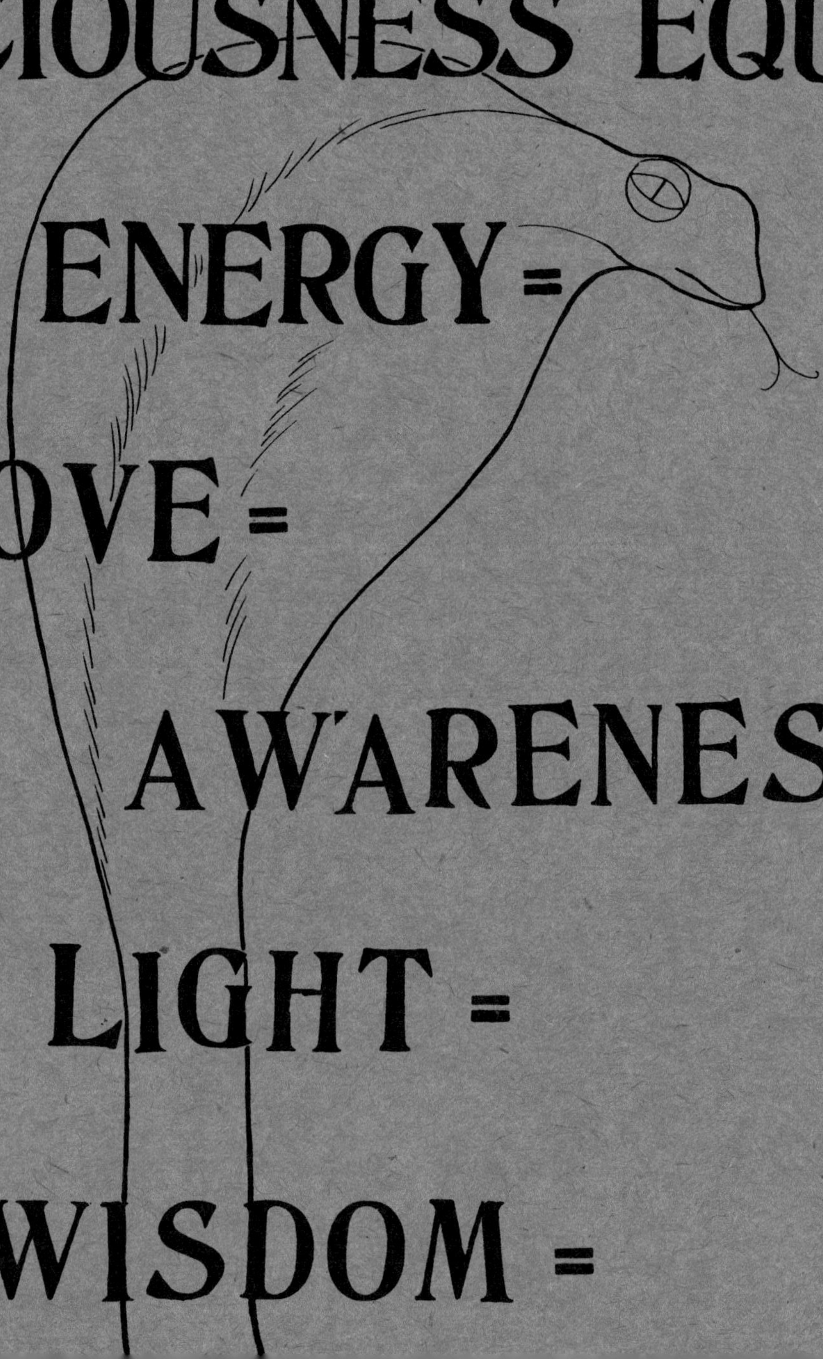

ENERGY =

LOVE =

AWARENESS =

LIGHT =

WISDOM =

BEAUTY =

TRUTH =

PURITY.

IT'S ALL THE SAME TRIP

IT'S ALL THE SAME

ANY TRIP YOU WANT TO TAKE

LEADS TO THE SAME PLACE ॐ

ॐ2

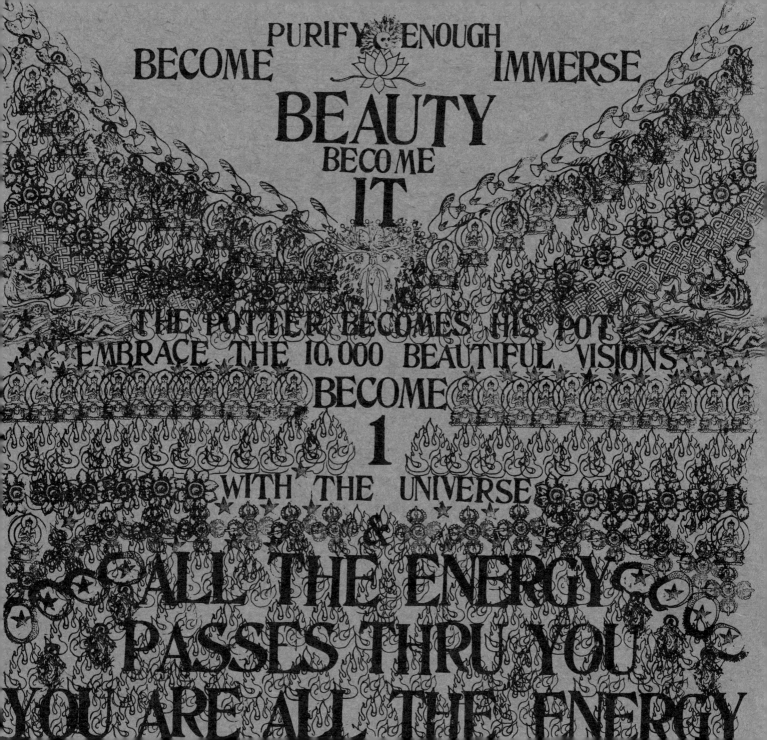

PURIFY ENOUGH

BECOME IMMERSE

BEAUTY

BECOME

IT

THE POTTER BECOMES HIS POT

EMBRACE THE 10,000 BEAUTIFUL VISIONS

BECOME

1

WITH THE UNIVERSE

&

ALL THE ENERGY

PASSES THRU YOU

YOU ARE ALL THE ENERGY

& IT ALL RESIDES IN YOU . HEAR

F YOU CAN GO WITHIN TO YOUR SPIRITUAL HEART

YOUR HRIDAYAM

YOU WILL THEN KNOW THAT:

YOU ARE HE

& IT IS FROM THIS PLACE IN OUR HEART CAVE
WHERE WE ARE NOW
WE WATCH THE ENTIRE DRAMA
THAT IS OUR LIVES
WE WATCH THE ILLUSION
WITH

UNBEARABLE COMPASSION

ॐ3

THERE IS WRITING   HAPPENING
MAYBE THATS HARD FOR YOU TO UNDERSTAND
I AM HERE BUT "I" AM NOT HERE.
I AM WRITING   BUT "I" AM NOT WRITING
INSIDE OF ME IN THE HEART CAVE IS A
MANTRA GOING ON THAT REMINDS ME
WHO I REALLY AM

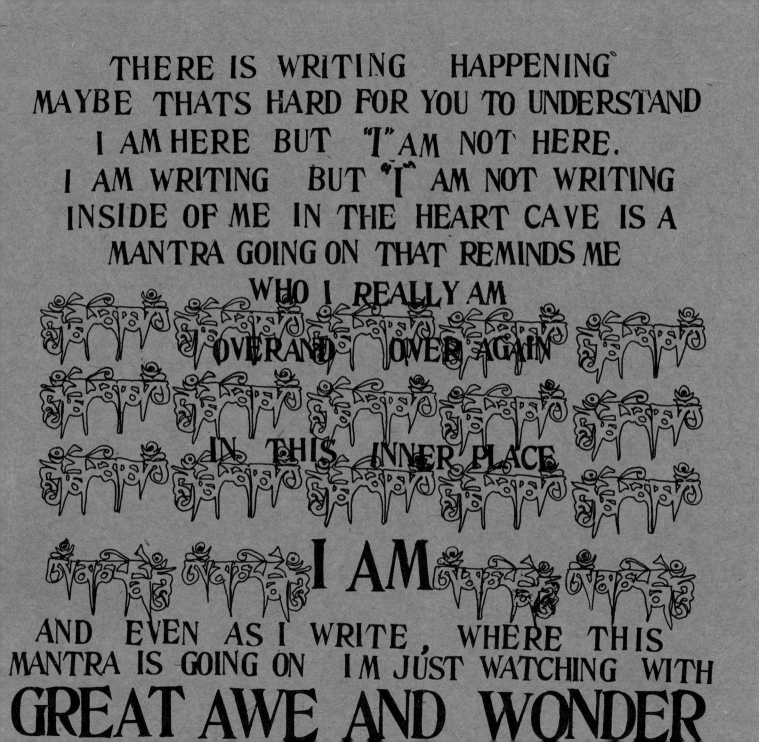

OVER AND   OVER AGAIN

IN THIS INNER PLACE

I AM

AND EVEN AS I WRITE WHERE THIS
MANTRA IS GOING ON   I'M JUST WATCHING WITH
GREAT AWE AND WONDER

THE AWESOME DRAMA OF NATURE

UNFOLD BEFORE MY VERY EYE

BEFORE THAT EYE I I WHICH

SEES ALL AND KNOWS ALL.

AND ON ॐ मणि पद्मे हूँ   ॐ मणि पद्मे हूँ   ॐ मणि पद्मे हूँ

AND ON

INSIDE GOES: ॐ मणि पद्मे हूँ   ॐ मणि पद्मे हूँ

AUM MANI PADME HUM

ALWAYS BRINGING ME RIGHT TO MY HEART

WHERE I DWELL ETERNALLY.

WHEN YOU HAVE QUIETED YOUR MIND
ENOUGH
AND TRANSCENDED YOUR EGO
ENOUGH
YOU CAN HEAR HOW IT REALLY IS. SO:
WHEN YOU ARE WITH A CANDLEFLAME
YOU ARE THE CANDLEFLAME
AND WHEN
YOU ARE WITH ANOTHER BEING'S MIND
YOU ARE THE OTHER BEING'S MIND
WHEN
THERE IS A TASK TO DO
YOU ARE THE TASK

THE MINDLESS QUALITY OF TOTAL INVOLVEMENT
THAT COMES ONLY WHEN THE EGO IS QUIET
AND THERE IS NO ATTACHMENT

IT IS ONLY WHEN YOU RESIDE QUIETLY

IN YOUR OWN HRIDAYAM

THAT YOU BECOME

HE OF TOTAL LIGHT

UNBEARABLE COMPASSION

AND INFINITE POWER

ॐ 5

SEE:
IF YOU GET FAR ENOUGH   IN
YOU CAN SEE... .....KARMA
YOU CAN SEE PATTERNS UNFOLDING

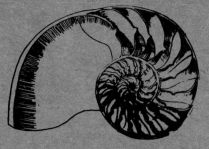

(OF WHICH THIS LIFE
IS ONLY A PART
PART OF A MOSAIC)

BUT:

IN ORDER TO DO THAT
YOU HAVE TO HAVE   LEFT

THE GRAVITATIONAL FIELD
OF
TIME AND SPACE
(AS A MATRIX)

YOU CAN'T THINK IN.......TIME & SPACE

YOU CAN'T BE IN........YOUR THOUGHTS

☞ ANY MORE! ☜

BECAUSE: YOUR THOUGHTS ARE STILL IN TIME & SPACE & YOU CAN'T GET OUT OF TIME THROUGH THEM. YOU'VE GOT TO BE OUTSIDE THAT. YOU'VE GOT TO BE IN THE PLACE WHERE

YOU SEE YOUR OWN

CONCEPTION★BIRTH★CHILDHOOD★ADOLESCENCE★MATURITY★AGE★DEATH★

AND: NOT ONLY THAT ONE BUT 3☽6 THAT ONE & THAT TOO... THAT ONE &.......

THE BUTTERFLY

I AM WITHOUT FORM,
WITHOUT LIMIT
BEYOND SPACE   BEYOND TIME
I AM IN EVERYTHING
EVERYTHING IS ME
I AM THE BLISS OF THE UNIVERSE,
EVERYTHING
AM I

RAM TIRTHA

BUT YOU'RE STILL ONLY SEEING HINTS
YOU'VE GOT A WAY TO GO YET

GÄTĒ/GÄTĒ/PÄRÄGÄTĒ
PÄRÄSÄMGÄTĒ
BODHĬ SVÄHÄ!

GONE/GONE/GONE BEYOND/GONE BEYOND BEYOND
HAIL THE GOER

BEYOND EVEN CONCEIVING OF A PLACE
BEYOND WHICH YOU CAN GO BEYOND

WHO'S ADVENTUROUS ENOUGH TO WANT TO GO
ON THAT JOURNEY?
DO YOU REALIZE WHEN YOU GO ON THAT JOURNEY
IN ORDER TO GET TO THE DESTINATION
YOU
CAN NEVER GET TO THE DESTINATION?
IN THE PROCESS
YOU
MUST DIE

MUST 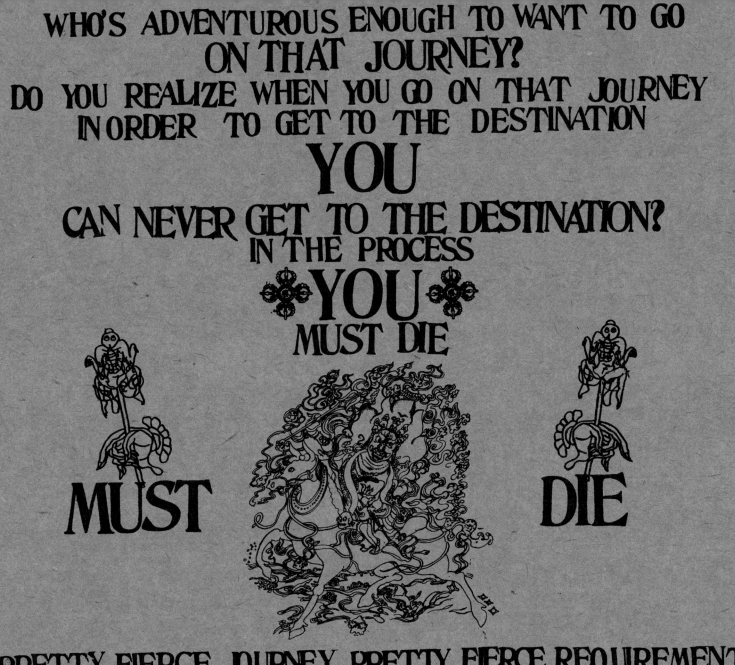 DIE

PRETTY FIERCE JOURNEY PRETTY FIERCE REQUIREMENT
WE WANT VOLUNTEERS

NOW: WE'LL MAKE THE JOURNEY
AS COMFORTABLE AS POSSIBLE
BUT: YOU HAVE TO REALIZE THAT
(AFTER YOU PASS THROUGH THE VAN ALLEN BELT)
YOU'RE GOING TO GET OUT
TO ANOTHER BELT OF RADIATION
WHICH IS GOING TO CRISP YOU COMPLETELY
AND
YOU WILL DIE
BUT THERE WILL BE AN
ESSENCE
LEFT THAT WILL GET THROUGH.
NOW: WHO WOULD LIKE TO VOLUNTEER?
READY?

WELL: COULDN'T WE MAKE
A SPECIALLY INSULATED SUIT?
NO. SORRY. CAN'T DO IT.
BUT: IF YOU PROPEL HARD ENOUGH
THERE WILL BE GOING THROUGH—
THERE WILL BE SOMETHING THAT WILL
GET THROUGH TO THE OTHER SIDE
WE CAN'T REALLY DEFINE WHAT YOU'LL BE...
BUT YOU'LL BE BEYOND THAT
WHY WOULD ANYONE GO ON A TRIP LIKE THAT?
ADVENTURE?
WELL: THE ONE THING ABOUT AN ADVENTURE IS:
THE ADVENTURER WANTS TO STAY AROUND
AND ADVENTURE. AND:
IF HE'S GOING TO BE CRISPED IN THE PROCESS
THERE'S GOING TO BE NO ADVENTURER LEFT
TO HAVE HAD THE ADVENTURE.

BUT YOU SEE: THERE'S SOMETHING THAT
PULLS A PERSON TOWARD THIS JOURNEY 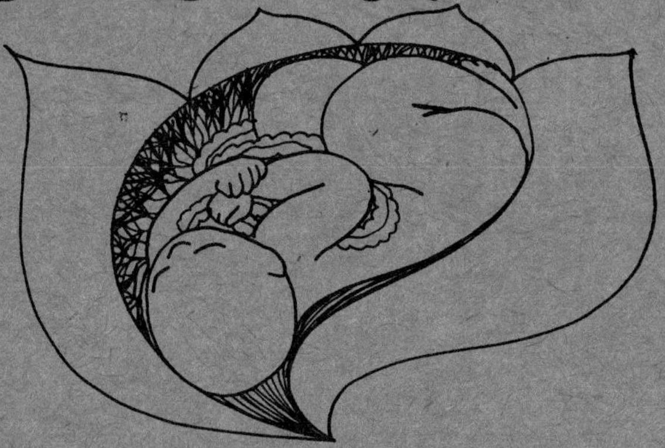
WAY AWAY BACK
DEEP INSIDE
IS A MEMORY
THERE IS SOMETHING

INSIDE EACH OF US
THAT COMES FROM BEHIND THAT VEIL
BEHIND THE PLACE OF OUR OWN BIRTH
IT'S AS IF YOU HAVE TASTED OF SOMETHING
SOMEWHERE IN YOUR PAST
THAT'S BEEN SO HIGH
SO MUCH LIGHT
SO MUCH ENERGY

THAT NOTHING
YOU CAN EXPERIENCE
THROUGH ANY OF YOUR
SENSES
OR YOUR THOUGHTS

CAN BE
ENOUGH !

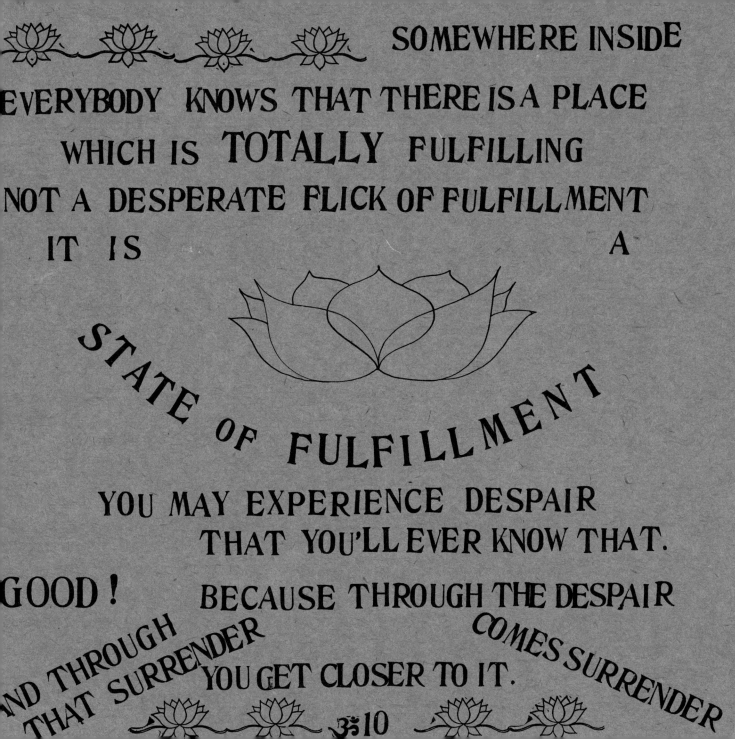

SOMEWHERE INSIDE
EVERYBODY KNOWS THAT THERE IS A PLACE
WHICH IS TOTALLY FULFILLING
NOT A DESPERATE FLICK OF FULFILLMENT
IT IS   A
STATE OF FULFILLMENT
YOU MAY EXPERIENCE DESPAIR
THAT YOU'LL EVER KNOW THAT.
GOOD! BECAUSE THROUGH THE DESPAIR
AND THROUGH THAT SURRENDER COMES SURRENDER
YOU GET CLOSER TO IT.

3ॐ10

AND WHAT KEEPS YOU FROM

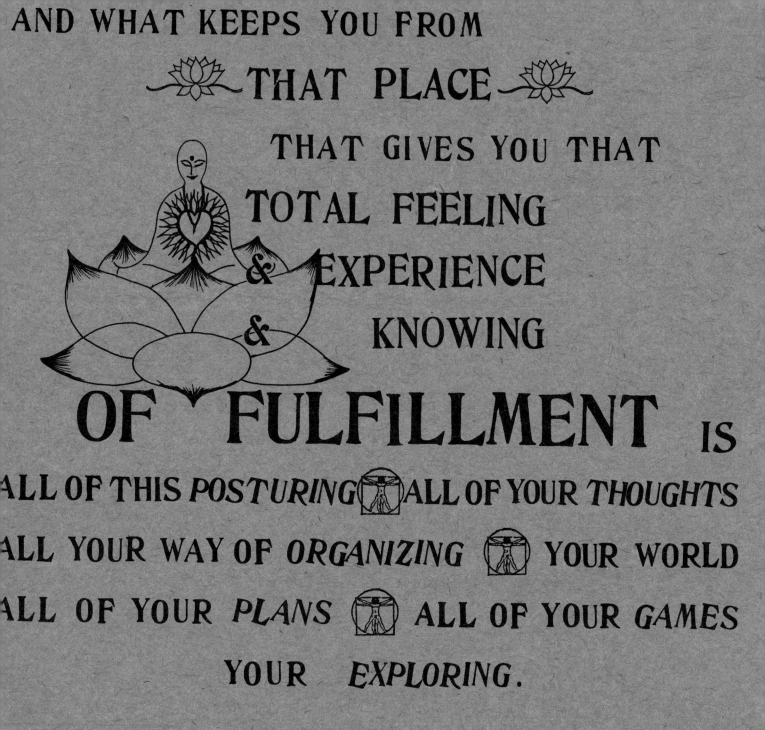

THAT PLACE

THAT GIVES YOU THAT

TOTAL FEELING

& EXPERIENCE

& KNOWING

OF FULFILLMENT IS

ALL OF THIS POSTURING ALL OF YOUR THOUGHTS

ALL YOUR WAY OF ORGANIZING YOUR WORLD

ALL OF YOUR PLANS ALL OF YOUR GAMES

YOUR EXPLORING.

SOME OF US DO GO ON THIS JOURNEY
WE DIDN'T STAND UP AND SAY WE VOLUNTEER
(IT DIDN'T WORK THAT WAY AT ALL
IT'S NOT LIKE YOU HAD A CHOICE
        OF VOLUNTEERING OR NOT VOLUNTEERING)
    THAT ISN'T THE WAY IT WORKS.
IT'S AS IF YOU'RE PROPELLED INTO IT

    LIKE THE MOTH INTO THE FLAME.

    BUT YET NOBODY'S
    PUSHING YOU. NOBODY'S
    STANDING AROUND SAYING: GET IN !
    TAKE EVERY THIRD MAN !   HE   GOES !

    IT DOESN'T WORK THAT WAY EITHER.

ॐ॥

IT'S A LITTLE MORE LIKE THE IMAGE OF A
CATERPILLAR—ENCLOSING ITSELF
IN A COCOON IN ORDER TO GO THROUGH THE
METAMORPHOSIS
TO EMERGE AS A BUTTERFLY
THE CATERPILLER DOESN'T SAY:
" WELL NOW. I'M GOING TO CLIMB
INTO THIS COCOON AND COME OUT
A BUTTERFLY.

IT'S JUST AN INEVITABLE PROCESS

IT'S INEVITABLE

IT'S JUST HAPPENING

IT'S GOT TO HAPPEN THAT WAY . ✤

3·12

WE'RE TALKING ABOUT A METAMORPHOSIS
WE'RE TALKING ABOUT
GOING FROM A CATERPILLAR TO BUTTERFLY
WE'RE TALKING ABOUT
HOW TO BECOME A BUTTERFLY.
I MEAN: THE CATERPILLAR ISN'T WALKING AROUND
SAYING: MAN I'LL SOON BE A BUTTERFLY
BECAUSE: AS LONG AS HE'S BUSY
BEING A CATERPILLAR
HE CAN'T BE A BUTTERFLY.
IT'S ONLY WHEN CATERPILLARNESS IS DONE
THAT ONE STARTS TO BE A BUTTERFLY
AND THAT AGAIN IS PART OF THIS PARADOX
YOU CANNOT RIP AWAY
CATERPILLARNESS

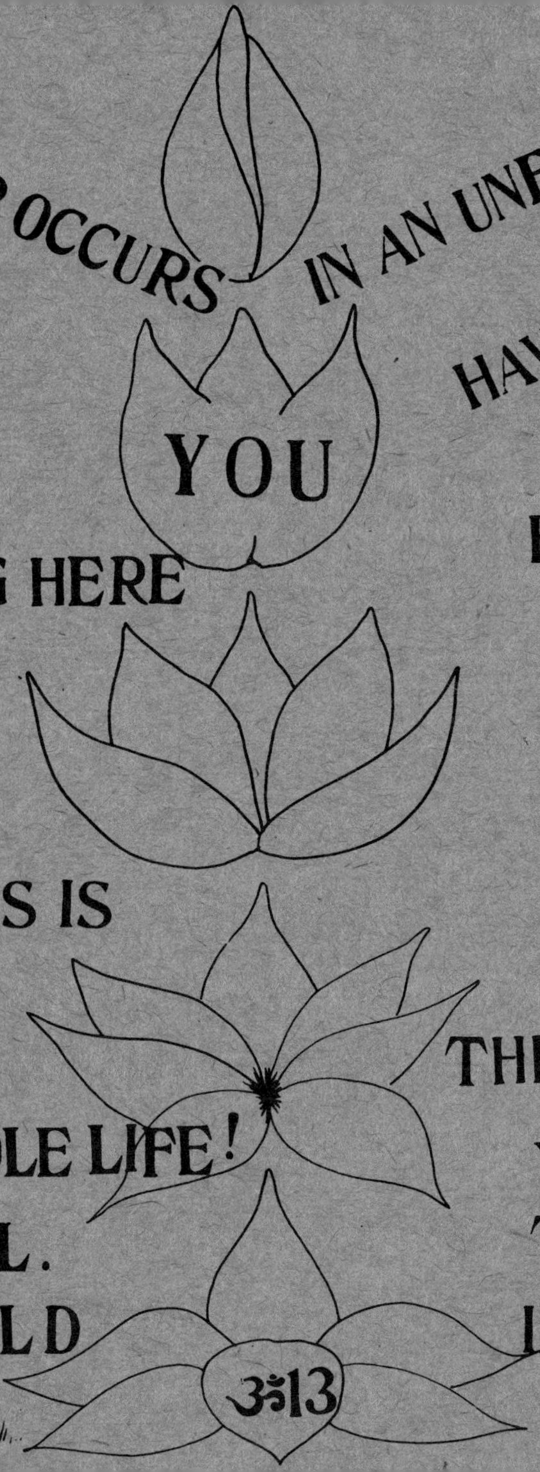

THE WHOLE TRIP OCCURS IN AN UNFOLDING PROCESS

UNDER WHICH

HAVE NO CONTROL

YOU

THAT'S A

HARD ONE !

WELL:
WHAT AM I DOING HERE
IF I HAVE
NO CONTROL?

YOU MEAN
I DON'T HAVE
ANY CHOICE?

CAN'T I SAY THIS IS
NONSENSE ?

CAN'T I SAY
THIS IS IMPORTANT?

YOUR LECTURE
CHANGED MY WHOLE LIFE !

YOU THINK
THAT'S CHOICE?

NO. NOT AT ALL.
IT'S AN UNFOLD

ING PROCESS.

ॐ13

NO ACCIDENTS

IF YOU COULD STAND BACK FAR ENOUGH AND
WATCH THE WHOLE PROCESS YOU WOULD SEE

YOU ARE A TOTALLY
DETERMINED BEING

THE VERY MOMENT YOU WILL WAKE UP
IS TOTALLY DETERMINED
HOW LONG YOU WILL SLEEP
IS TOTALLY DETERMINED
WHAT YOU WILL HEAR OF WHAT I SAY
IS TOTALLY DETERMINED
THERE ARE NO ACCIDENTS IN THIS BUSINESS
AT ALL. ACCIDENTS ARE JUST FROM WHERE
YOU'RE LOOKING. TO THE EGO, IT LOOKS LIKE
IT'S MIRACLES AND ACCIDENTS.

NO MIRACLES. NO ACCIDENTS.

IT'S JUST YOUR VANTAGE POINT THAT
YOU'RE SORT OF.....STUCK IN.

3:14

THIS WHOLE TRIP I'M TALKING ABOUT IS FRAUGHT WITH

PARADOX PARADOX PARADOX PARADOX

THE MOST EXQUISITE PARADOX
AS SOON AS YOU GIVE IT ALL UP
YOU CAN HAVE IT ALL

HOW ABOUT THAT ONE ?

AS LONG AS YOU WANT POWER
YOU CAN'T HAVE IT.
THE MINUTE YOU DON'T WANT POWER
YOU'LL HAVE MORE THAN YOU EVER DREAMED
POSSIBLE

WHAT A WEIRD THING!

AS LONG AS YOU HAVE AN EGO
YOU'RE ON A LIMITED TRIP

YOU'RE ON A TRIVIAL TRIP THAT'S GOING TO LAST
?MAYBE WHAT? 60 — SAY 70 — MAYBE 80 YEARS
AND FULL WITH FEAR OF ITS END
TRYING TO MAKE ITS OWN ETERNITY.

WELL: IF 'I' AM NOT SPEAKING
IF 'I' AM NOT WHAT 'I' THOUGHT 'I' WAS
HOW DID 'I' GET INTO THIS
WHO   AM 'I'

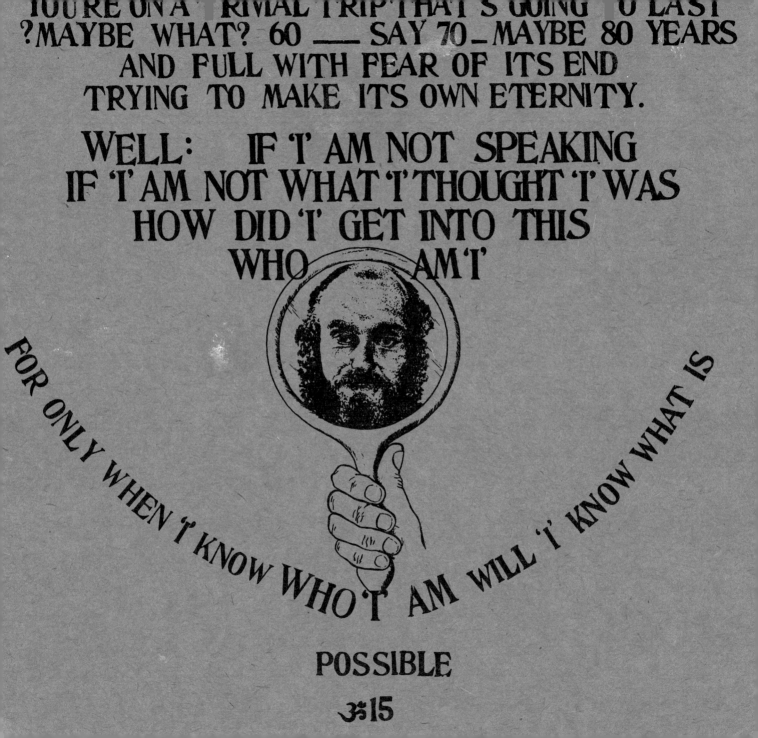

FOR ONLY WHEN 'I' KNOW WHO 'I' AM WILL 'I' KNOW WHAT IS

POSSIBLE

ॐ 15

UNDERSTANDING   THE
POSSIBILITY

THERE ARE 3 WAYS IN WHICH ONE KNOWS
WHAT WE ARE TALKING ABOUT TONIGHT
ONE WAY IN WHICH YOU KNOW ABOUT IT IS
THRU   DIRECT EXPERIENCE
THRU SOME WAY OR ANOTHER
THRU BEING ALONE IN THE DESERT
THRU FALLING IN LOVE
THRU BEARING A CHILD
THRU NEARLY DYING
THRU TURNING ON
THRU YOGA
THRU TAKING ANY ONE OF YOUR SENSES
& PUSHING IT BEYOND ITSELF

GOING THRU IT YOU HAVE TOUCHED A PLACE INSIDE
YOURSELF THAT HAS AN INTUITIVE VALIDITY

I'VE B EN W TH (L TE RALLY NOW) WEL OVER
100 PEOPLE WHO HAVE HAD SUCH AN EXPERIENCE
WHICH WAS POWERFUL AND VALID BUT IT WAS SO
DISCONTINUOUS WITH THEIR NORMAL CONSCIOUSNESS
THAT THEY SCREAMED FOR HELP

THE HELP
THAT WAS
AVAILABLE
TO THEM

WAS A
GROUP
OF MINDS
WHICH SAID

'THAT'S ALL RIGHT
YOU'VE JUST GONE CRAZY'
THAT IS
'THE EXPERIENCE YOU'VE JUST HAD
IS THE EXPERIENCE OF PSYCHOSIS'

ॐ 16

WILLIAM JAMES SAID

OUR NORMAL WAKING CONSCIOUSNESS
IS BUT ONE SPECIAL TYPE OF CONSCIOUSNESS
WHILST ALL ABOUT IT
PARTED FROM IT BY THE FILMIEST OF SCREENS
THERE LIE POTENTIAL FORMS OF CONSCIOUSNESS ENTIRELY DIFFERENT
WE MAY GO THROUGH LIFE
WITHOUT SUSPECTING THEIR EXISTENCE
BUT APPLY THE REQUISITE STIMULUS AND AT A TOUCH
THEY ARE THERE IN ALL THEIR COMPLETENESS
DEFINITE TYPES OF MENTALITY WHICH PROBABLY SOMEWHERE
HAVE THEIR FIELD OF APPLICATION AND ADAPTATION

NO ACCOUNT OF THE UNIVERSE IN ITS TOTALITY
CAN BE FINAL WHICH LEAVES THESE OTHER FORMS
OF CONSCIOUSNESS QUITE DISREGARDED.
HOW TO REGARD THEM IS THE QUESTION
FOR THEY ARE SO DISCONTINUOUS WITH ORDINARY
CONSCIOUSNESS. THEY MAY DETERMINE
ATTITUDES, THOUGH THEY CANNOT FURNISH FORMULAS,
AND OPEN A REGION THOUGH THEY FAIL TO GIVE A MAP.

AT ANY RATE, CONCLUDES JAMES,

THEY FORBID OUR PREMATURE CLOSING OF ACCOUNTS
WITH REALITY.

IN SPITE OF WHAT HE SAID
WE'VE CLOSED OUR ACCOUNTS WITH REALITY.

(MOST OF US)

3-17

'THAT EXPERIENCE YOU HAD IS PSYCHOTIC'
'I'LL GIVE YOU THORAZINE'
'IT'S NOT VALID'
'YOU'RE HALLUCINATING'
'WHAT DO YOU MEAN YOU'RE GOD?'

THE UNDERSTANDING OF THE POSSIBILITY MAY
HAVE COME TO YOU DIRECTLY THROUGH THE
EXPERIENCE ITSELF OR:
IT MAY HAVE COME TO YOU THROUGH INFERENCE,
THROUGH YOUR INTELLECT:
YOU MAY HAVE REASONED & REASONED UNTIL YOU
SAW THE PECULIAR POSITION THAT RATIONAL MAN
IS IN & YOU REALIZED THAT THERE MUST BE
SOMETHING ELSE ALTHOUGH YOU HAVE NOT
EXPERIENCED IT. YOU JUST INFER THE PRESENCE
OF
"SOMETHING ELSE"

IT DOESN'T QUITE MAKE SENSE
NOTHING "TURNS YOU ON"
YOU HAVEN'T EXPERIENCED IT DIRECTLY BUT
YOU FIGURED THERE MUST BE
SOMETHING ELSE SOMETHING THERE

& THEN YOU READ ALL THE WRITINGS OF
ST. JOHN OF THE CROSS & ST. THERESA AVILA
& ON & ON ALL THE MYSTICS
& VISIONARIES IN RECORDED HISTORY

& YOU SAY: 'WELL, THEY CAN'T ALL BE NUTS
THEY MUST BE TALKING ABOUT SOMETHING'
SO YOU SORT OF INFER THE PRESENCE OF THIS
OTHER THING, BUT YOU DON'T KNOW IT IN YOUR GUTS

NOW THAT'S A TOUGH ONE,
TO BE IN THAT POSITION

ॐ 18

THEN THE THIRD WAY IS
YOU TRUST THE FACT THAT
THERE ARE
REALIZED BEINGS
AND THEY SAID IT 
& THEREFORE YOU KNOW IT TO BE TRUE
IT'S NOT INFERENCE ANY MORE
IT'S NOT AN INTELLECTUAL PROCESS
YOU JUST ACCEPT WHAT THEY HAVE SAID

THAT'S FAITH

SE : WE'VE GOTTEN SO SUPER-SOPHISTICATED
IN OUR EVALUATIVE MECHANISMS
THAT YOU QUESTION EVERYTHING YOU HEAR
HOW DO YOU KNOW YOU'RE NOT BEING HUSTLED ?
I MEAN: WHAT WAS JESUS UP TO ?
WHAT'S THE GAME, MAN ?
WHAT'S HE INTO ?
& YOU ESPECIALLY FEEL PARANOID
F YOU ARE ONE OF THE KEEPERS OF THE TABLES
IN THE TEMPLE
IF YOU ARE COMMITTED TO AN EXISTING SYSTEM
WITH GREAT ATTACHMENT
WITH GREAT ATTACHMENT

SOME WAY OR OTHER
MOST OF YOU IN THIS ROOM
(MOST OF YOU, NOT ALL OF YOU) MOST OF YOU
HAVE SENSED THE POSSIBILITY
BUT YOU CAN'T QUITE........!

ॐ19

SURRENDER

WHAT ARE YOU GIVING UP? — A HOLLOW LITTLE TRIP
THAT'S GOOD FOR ANOTHER 40 YEARS AT BEST.
YOU'RE GIVING IT UP FOR:

ETERNAL UNION
WITH
PURE ENERGY & PURE LIGHT

BECAUSE: SURRENDER MEANS

YOU

NO LONGER DIE

IT'S AS SIMPLE
AS THAT
THAT'S WHAT IT MEANS.

BECAUSE: YOU THAT LIVES AND DIES IS
YOU......EGO
AND FEAR OF DEATH ONLY COMES THROUGH
THE BRITTLENESS OF THE EGO

TOTAL TOTAL

SURRENDER SURRENDER

THERE'S NO MORE YOU, NO MORE
LIFE AND DEATH

YEAH I'M GOING TO DIE WOW! DIG THAT! I'M GOING
TO LIVE WOW! DIG THAT! GARBAGE WOW!
NEW BLOSSOMS ON THE TREE WOW!

PATTERNS OF ENERGY
ALL PATTERNS OF ENERGY

YOU'RE PART OF IT ALL

THAT'S THE PLACE!

3520

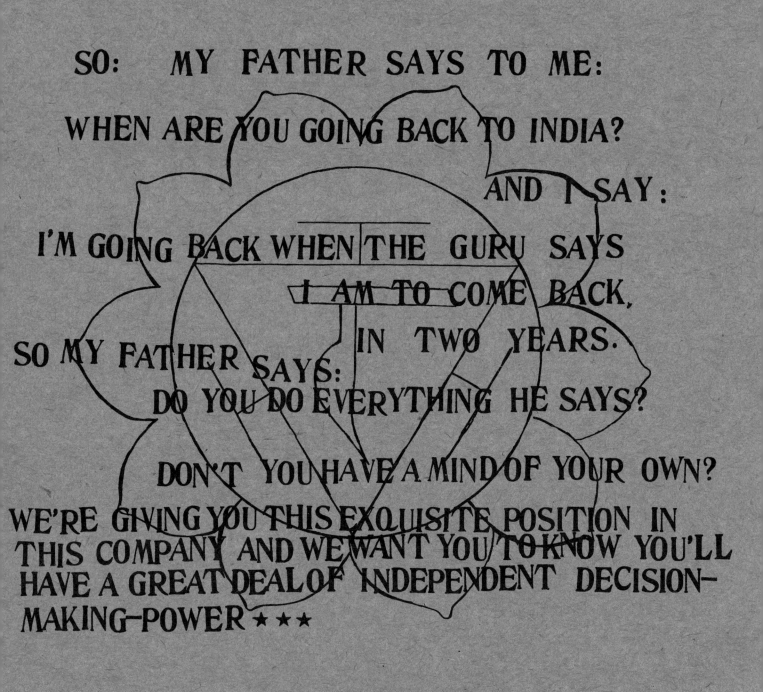

SO: MY FATHER SAYS TO ME:

WHEN ARE YOU GOING BACK TO INDIA?

                              AND I SAY:

I'M GOING BACK WHEN THE GURU SAYS
            I AM TO COME BACK,
                  IN TWO YEARS.
SO MY FATHER SAYS:
      DO YOU DO EVERYTHING HE SAYS?

      DON'T YOU HAVE A MIND OF YOUR OWN?

WE'RE GIVING YOU THIS EXQUISITE POSITION IN
THIS COMPANY AND WE WANT YOU TO KNOW YOU'LL
HAVE A GREAT DEAL OF INDEPENDENT DECISION-
MAKING-POWER ★ ★ ★

WHAT DO YOU WANT TO DO TODAY, MARTY?

I DON'T CARE

WHAT DO YOU WANT TO DO?

HERE

I REMEMBER A FEW DAYS STAYING IN LONDON. WE HAD FLED FROM COPENHAGEN WHERE WE HAD A VERY UNFORTUNATE SCENE AT A PSYCHOLOGICAL CONVENTION. WE WERE IN LONDON AND TIM AND BILL BURROUGHS AND I WERE WALKING DOWN THE STREET HIGH ON SOMETHING OR OTHER AND WE WERE SPENDING DAYS GOING FROM PARK TO TEA ROOM TO PARK TO TEA ROOM; AND EVERY NOW AND THEN WE'D HIT A CORNER AND SOMEBODY WOULD SAY: WELL SHOULD WE CROSS THE STREET AND WE'D STAND THERE AND NOBODY WOULD SEEM TO CARE. BECAUSE WE WERE ALL FULFILLED AT THAT MOMENT. RIGHT THERE ON THE STREETCORNER IN LONDON. WE WERE ALL JUST

VERY

VERY

HIGH

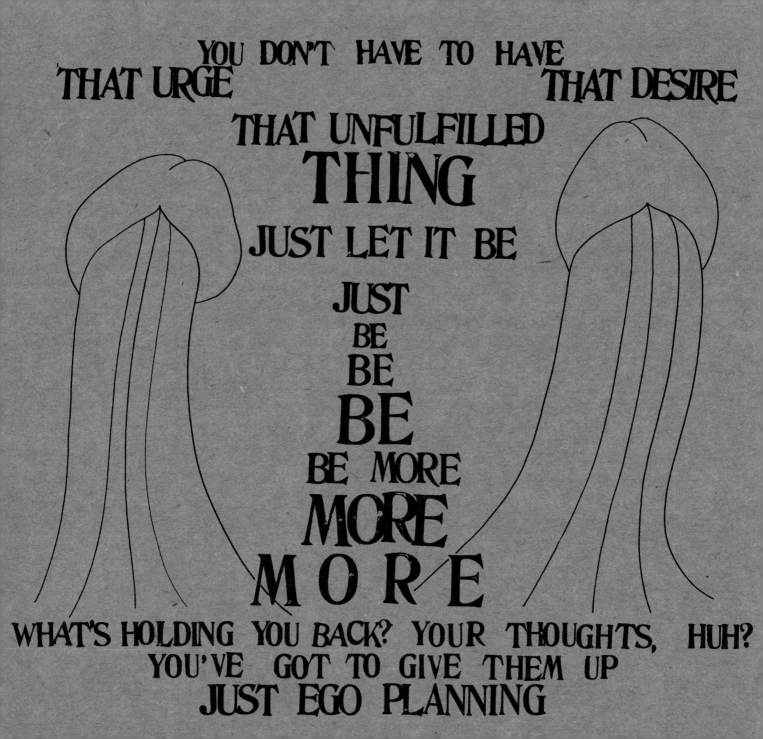

WHAT ARE YOU DOING?
PLANNING FOR THE FUTURE?

WELL

IT'S ALL RIGHT NOW

BUT LATER?....................... FORGET IT BABY

THAT'S LATER
NOW IS

NOW

ARE YOU GOING TO

BE HERE

OR NOT?

IT'S AS SIMPLE AS THAT!

ॐ 22

BUT I'M SO YOUNG!
I HAVE SO MANY THINGS TO DO YET!

WELL! THAT'LL SURE KEEP YOU FROM
BEING HERE & NOW
LIFE IS PASSING ME BY!

HMMMMM
BUT, IF I LIVE JUST IN THE HERE & NOW
WON'T THERE BE CHAOS? WHAT HAPPENS
IF THE TELEPHONE RINGS?

WELL: THE HERE & NOW IS THE FACT
THAT THE TELEPHONE IS RINGING!
PICK IT UP!

WELL: WHAT IF SOMEBODY WANTS TO
MAKE AN APPOINTMENT TO SEE ME
3 WEEKS FROM NOW?

RIGHT!
WRITE IT DOWN. THAT'S HERE & NOW

WELL, WHAT HAPPENS 3 WEEKS FROM NOW
?

3 WEEKS FROM NOW THERE'S THAT
APPOINTMENT. THEN: THAT IS HERE & NOW

WHEN YOUR CHILD COMES DOWN THE STAIRS

THIS IS THE **FIRST MOMENT** ALL OVER AGAIN

THIS IS

BUDDHA MEETING BUDDHA

OVER TOAST   & COFFEE

OVER MILK   & PORRIDGE

OVER MU TEA   & BROWN RICE

WE NEVER HAD BREAKFAST BEFORE!

THIS IS IT !!

THIS IS ALL THERE IS

RIGHT NOW!

IF IT'S NOT GOOD ENUF, MAN, IT'S NOT GOOD ENUF

ॐ23

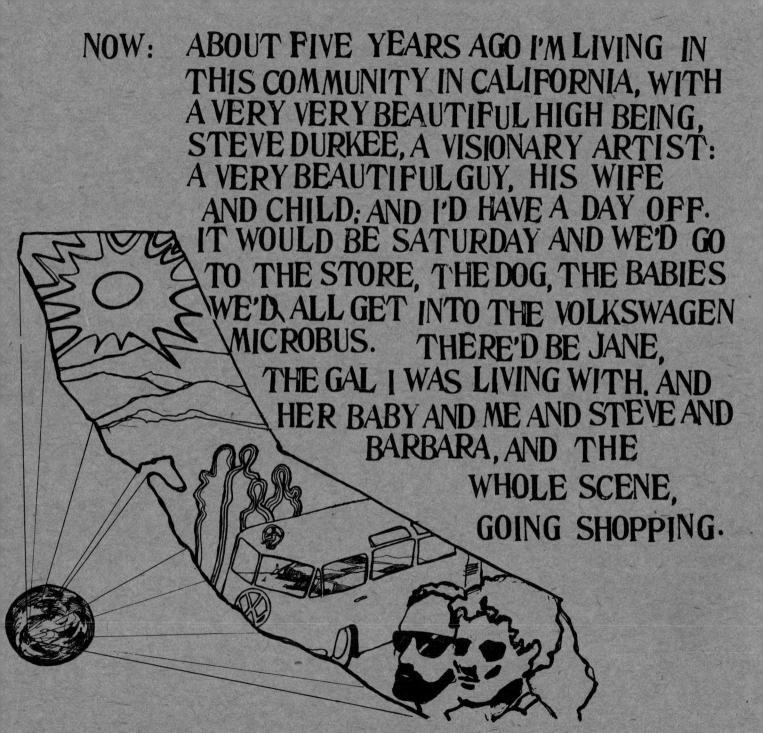

NOW: ABOUT FIVE YEARS AGO I'M LIVING IN THIS COMMUNITY IN CALIFORNIA, WITH A VERY VERY BEAUTIFUL HIGH BEING, STEVE DURKEE, A VISIONARY ARTIST: A VERY BEAUTIFUL GUY, HIS WIFE AND CHILD; AND I'D HAVE A DAY OFF. IT WOULD BE SATURDAY AND WE'D GO TO THE STORE, THE DOG, THE BABIES WE'D ALL GET INTO THE VOLKSWAGEN MICROBUS. THERE'D BE JANE, THE GAL I WAS LIVING WITH. AND HER BABY AND ME AND STEVE AND BARBARA, AND THE WHOLE SCENE, GOING SHOPPING.

AND STEVE TAUGHT ME THAT :

IF YOU GET SO EFFICIENT......
IF YOU'VE GOT TO TURN OFF ALL THE
VIBRATIONS OF THE SCENE...
BECAUSE YOU'RE SO BUSY
ABOUT THE FUTURE
OR THE PAST
OR TIME HAS CAUGHT YOU..

IT COSTS TOO MUCH !!

ॐ 25

1-2- ME

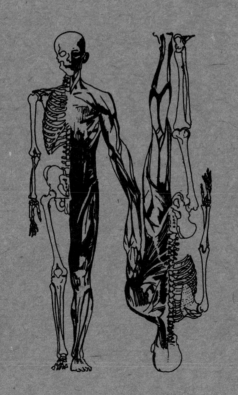

&

YOU FINALLY UNDERSTAND

THE MESSAGE YOU COMMUNICATE
WITH AN OTHER HUMAN BEING
HAS NOTHING TO DO WITH WHAT YOU SAY
IT HAS NOTHING TO DO WITH THE LOOK
ON THE MUSCULATURE OF YOUR FACE

IT'S MUCH DEEPER THAN THAT

MUCH DEEPER!

IT'S THE VIBRATIONS
THAT EMANATE FROM YOU!

ॐ 26

IF YOUR VIBRATIONS ARE PARANOID
THAT'S-WHAT'S BEING RECEIVED
AND WHEN YOU'RE AROUND PETS
(BIRDS OR CATS PARTICULARLY)
OR VERY YOUNG CHILDREN
OR VERY FLIPPED OUT PSYCHOTICS
THEY WILL KNOW YOU   IMMEDIATELY.

YOU CAN COME AND SAY
" HELLO, DEAR, HOW ARE YOU?"
AND THE DOG WILL GROWL...

YOU CAN'T COME ON BECAUSE THEY'RE LISTENING
TO THE VIBRATIONS THAT HAND IS REACHING
OUT AND SENDING.

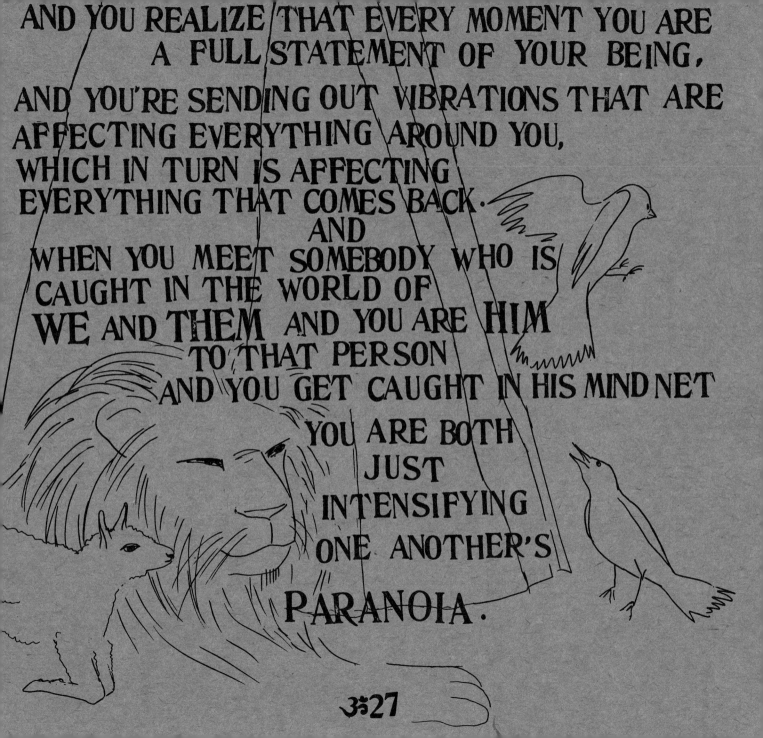

AND YOU REALIZE THAT EVERY MOMENT YOU ARE
A FULL STATEMENT OF YOUR BEING,
AND YOU'RE SENDING OUT VIBRATIONS THAT ARE
AFFECTING EVERYTHING AROUND YOU,
WHICH IN TURN IS AFFECTING
EVERYTHING THAT COMES BACK.
AND
WHEN YOU MEET SOMEBODY WHO IS
CAUGHT IN THE WORLD OF
WE AND THEM AND YOU ARE HIM
TO THAT PERSON
AND YOU GET CAUGHT IN HIS MIND NET
YOU ARE BOTH
JUST
INTENSIFYING
ONE ANOTHER'S
PARANOIA.

HIPPIES CREATE POLICE

POLICE CREATE HIPPIES

IF YOU'RE

IN POLARITY POLAR

YOU'RE CREATING OPPOSITES

YOU CAN ONLY PROTEST EFFECTIVELY

YOU LOVE THE PERSON

AS MUCH AS YOU LOVE YOURSELF

WHEN

WHOSE IDEAS YOU ARE PROTESTING AGAINST

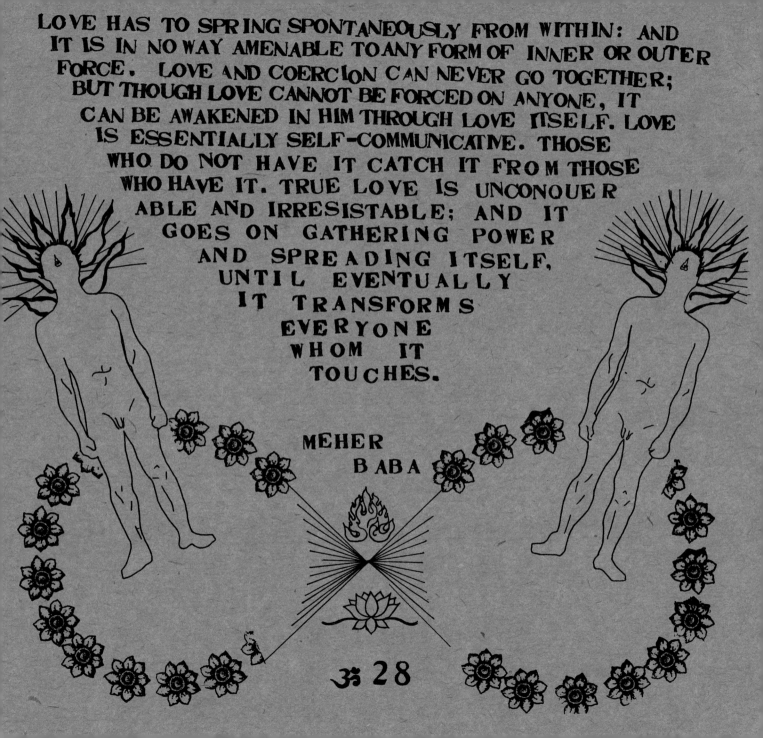

LOVE HAS TO SPRING SPONTANEOUSLY FROM WITHIN: AND
IT IS IN NO WAY AMENABLE TO ANY FORM OF INNER OR OUTER
FORCE. LOVE AND COERCION CAN NEVER GO TOGETHER;
BUT THOUGH LOVE CANNOT BE FORCED ON ANYONE, IT
CAN BE AWAKENED IN HIM THROUGH LOVE ITSELF. LOVE
IS ESSENTIALLY SELF-COMMUNICATIVE. THOSE
WHO DO NOT HAVE IT CATCH IT FROM THOSE
WHO HAVE IT. TRUE LOVE IS UNCONQUER
ABLE AND IRRESISTABLE; AND IT
GOES ON GATHERING POWER
AND SPREADING ITSELF,
UNTIL EVENTUALLY
IT TRANSFORMS
EVERYONE
WHOM IT
TOUCHES.

MEHER
BABA

ॐ 28

AND THE FACT OF THE MATTER IS:
AS YOU GO OUT ON THE ASTRAL PLANE
YOU SEE MORE & MORE
& THE FINAL THING YOU SEE
IN THE WORLD OF FORM
BEFORE YOU GO INTO THE FORMLESS
& INTO TOTAL UNITY
YOU SEE THE WORLD OF

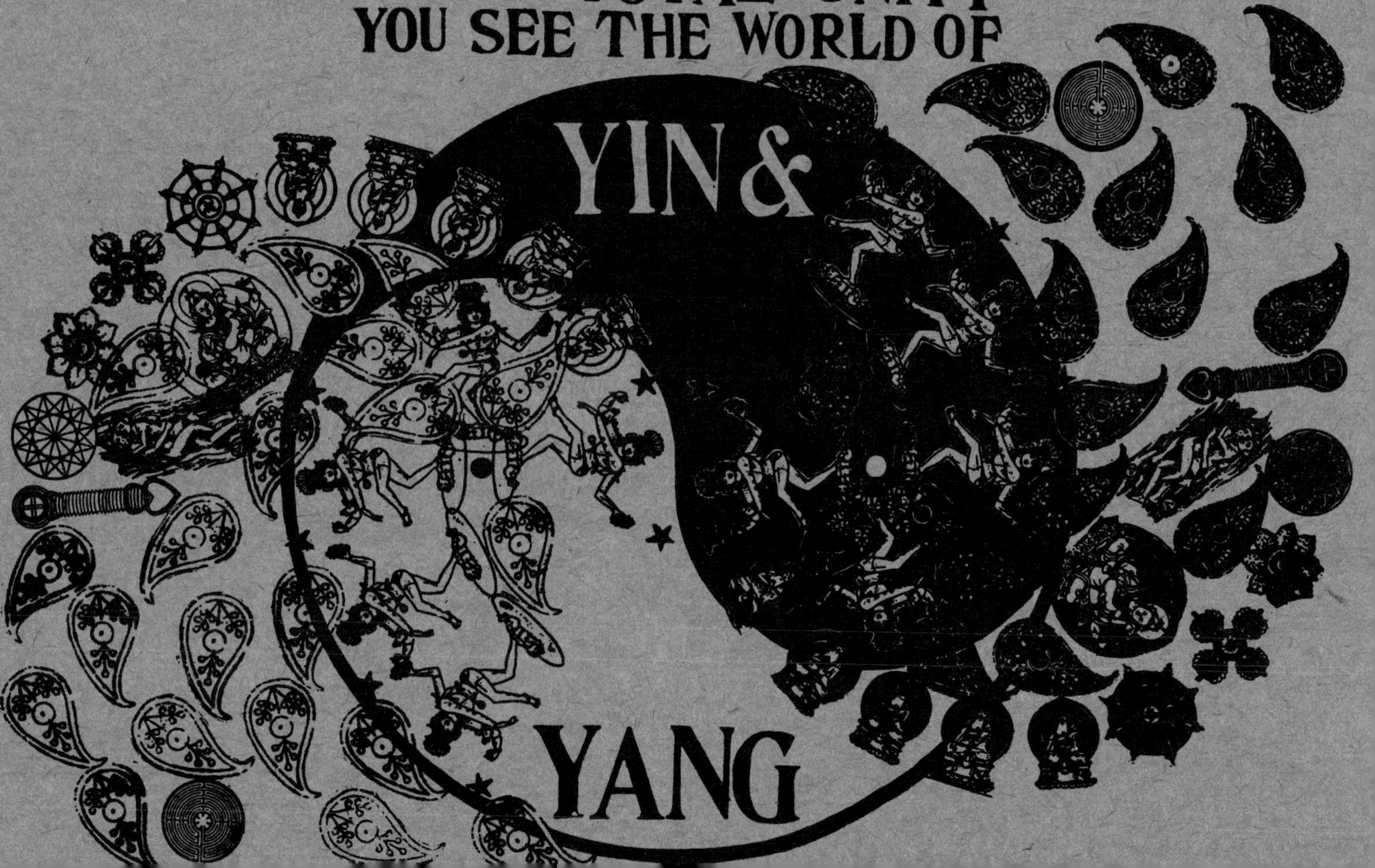

YIN&

YANG

AND THE WORLD OF YIN & YANG
IS ANOTHER ASTRAL PLANE
& IT'S ONE OF THE HIGHEST PLANES
IN THE WORLD OF FORM
BUT IT'S STILL DUALITY
IT IS STILL ☯ POLARIZATION

THERE IS GOD   THERE IS MAN

THERE IS GOOD   THERE IS EVIL

YES   NO

PLEASURE PAIN

LOSS   GAIN

THE WORLD MOST EVERYBODY IS LIVING IN
MOST OF THE TIME
ॐ 29

THE ONLY WAY OUT OF THAT IS TO TAKE
THE POLES OF EVERY SET OF OPPOSITES
AND SEE THE WAY IN WHICH

THEY ARE ONE

AND : IF YOU CAN GET INTO THAT PLACE
WHERE YOU SEE THE INTERRELATEDNESS OF
EVERYTHING
AND : YOU SEE THE ONENESS IN IT ALL

THEN : NO LONGER ARE YOU ATTACHED
TO YOUR POLARIZED POSITION

THE WHOLE THING ABOUT GENERATION GAPS
IS A HYPE

THE SPIRIT
IS
THE SPIRIT

WHEN YOU CAN CENTER AND SEE YOUR WHOLE LIFE
AS A STORY IN WHICH CHAPTERS ARE

UNFOLDING

THEN: THE MOMENT-TO-MOMENT EGO INVOLVEMENT
"AM I GETTING ENOUGH AT THIS MOMENT?"
CEASES TO BE A DOMINANT THEME
AND: YOU START TO LIVE IN THE
TAO
(THE WAY)

JESUS SAID: I AM THE WAY

IT'S THE SAME WAY!

THE WAY
IS THE WAY IS
THE WAY

THE WAY IS THE HARMONY OF THE UNIVERSE

WHEN ONE COMES INTO THE SPIRIT
WHEN ONE SEES HOW IT IS
ONE UNDERSTANDS THAT BEHIND ALL THE INDIVIDUAL DIFFERENCES

MAN-WOMBMAN

BIG-LITTLE

OLD-YOUNG

GOOD-BAD

EVERY LABEL YOU CAN THINK OF
BECOMES BACKGROUND INSTEAD OF FIGURE
WHAT STANDS OUT IS:

HERE WE ARE
HERE & NOW
THAT'S ALL THERE IS
AND IF IT ISN'T BEAUTIFUL, MAN
THERE'S NOTHING

SO YOU SAY:

WELL, I CAN'T HAVE IT BEAUTIFUL NOW. BUT. LATER! WHEN WE GET THE FOOD HOME
IT WILL BE BEAUTIFUL

LATER NEVER EXISTS

WHAT'S HAPPENED TO LIFE INSURANCE, TO TENURE, TO PLANNING, SAVING, RESPONSIBILITIES?

NOTHING'S HAPPENED TO ANY OF IT!

ॐ31

SURFING

EITHER YOU DO
IT LIKE IT'S
A BIG
WEIGHT
ON YOU

OR YOU DO IT

AS

PART OF THE DANCE

WHEN YOU UNDERSTAND
"THE THOUGHT IS THE THOUGHT
OF THE THOUGHTLESS
YOUR SINGING AND DANCING
IS NO OTHER THAN THE VOICE
OF THE DHARMA"
HAKUIN

ॐ 32

IF ONLY
YOU COULD
THROW IT OFF!

IF ONLY
I DIDN'T
HAVE THESE
KIDS AROUND
MY NECK...

YOU CAN'T GET
AWAY FOR THE DAY   BECAUSE:

IT'S IN
YOUR HEAD!

THAT YOU'RE
TRYING TO GET
AWAY FROM...AND
IS TO

THE ONLY WAY TO
GET AWAY

CHANGE YOUR HEAD!

SIMPLE AS THAT!   YOU WANT TO
CHANGE YOUR
ENVIRONMENT?

CHANGE YOUR HEAD!!
ECSTATIC MOMENT!   IT'S ALL THE

IF YOU KNOW HOW TO DIG IT... IF NOT... IT'S A
TRAVESTY...   THAT'S   ॐ33   ALL.   PROFANE....

DESIRE

THE FIRST THING IN MY TEACHER'S BOOK,
THE FIRST THING HE EVER WROTE ON HIS
SLATE (BECAUSE HE WAS SILENT) WAS:

DESIRE IS A TRAP
DESIRE-LESSNESS IS MOKSHA
(LIBERATION)

DESIRE IS THE CREATOR
DESIRE IS THE DESTROYER
DESIRE IS THE UNIVERSE

AND: THAT APPLIES TO THE PHYSICAL PLANE
THE ASTRAL PLANE
THE CAUSAL PLANE

HEAVEN

HELL

DEMONS

(THE DEMONS ON 43RD ST.
AS WELL AS THE DEMONS
ON THE ASTRAL PLANE!)

ARE ALL THE CREATIONS OF DESIRE!

ALL THE MANIFESTATIONS
OF THE DIVINE MOTHER
ARE CREATIONS OF DESIRE!

THAT'S WHY NAGA, (THE NAKED ASCETIC),
WORKED ON GETTING RAMAKRISHNA TO
GO BEYOND HIS LOVE FOR KALI.

GIVE UP EVEN THE
DESIRE TO BE EXPERIENCING THE BLISS
OF BEING IT ALL
OF BEING WITH THE DIVINE MOTHER

ॐ 34

THE BUDDHISTS SAY: (I'M TALKING ABOUT THE NON-DUALISTIC BUDDHISTS)
CUT OUT ALL THIS MIDDLE STUFF!
THEY SAY:
DON'T GET HUNG UP ON ALL THESE DIFFERENT DESIRE TRIPS. JUST GO BEYOND IT ALL.

BUDDHA'S 4 NOBLE TRUTHS
ARE VERY STRAIGHTFORWARD AND VERY SIMPLE.

THE FIRST ONE
CONCERNS THE FACT THAT LIFE ALWAYS HAS IN IT THE ELEMENT OF UNFULFILLMENT: CALL IT SUFFERING

BIRTH OLD AGE SICKNESS NOT GETTING WHAT YOU WANT GETTING WHAT YOU DON'T WANT EVEN GETTING WHAT YOU WANT IN THIS PHYSICAL WORLD IS GOING TO BE SUFFERING BECAUSE:

YOU'RE GOING TO LOSE IT!
IT'S ALWAYS IN TIME O!
ANYTHING THAT IS IN TIME O IS GOING TO PASS AWAY.

LAY NOT UP 12 YOUR TREASURES
11
1
10
2
9
3
8
4
7
5
6
WHERE MOTH AND RUST DOTH CORRUPT
THAT'S THE TRAP OF TIME O AS LONG AS YOU WANT
ANYTHING IN TIME O IT'S GOING TO PASS BECAUSE
TIME O 35 PASSES

THE SECOND NOBLE TRUTH

IS:

THE CAUSE OF SUFFERING

IS DESIRE

(OR CRAVING)

IF YOU DON'T TRY TO HOLD   YOU DON'T SUFFER

OVER THE LOSS

IF YOU DON'T   YOU DON'T

WORSHIP LIFE   FEAR DEATH

BUT IF YOU TRY TO   HOLD ON TO LIFE IT'S

VERY SAD   YOU CAN HONOR LIFE   BUT IF YOU

TRY TO HOLD ON TO LIFE ....IT'S VERY SAD

DID YOU EVER SEE A REALLY BEAUTIFUL WOMAN LIKE A TOP MODEL WHO IS JUST GETTING TO THAT POINT WHERE HER LOOKS ARE CHANGING INTO WHAT COULD BE AN INTERNAL BEAUTY IF SHE HADN'T BEEN SO BUSY WITH HER EXTERNAL BEAUTY ? SHE IS CAUGHT IN THE BEAUTY OF TIME WHICH WITHERS

HOW POIGNANT !

& YET WELL WE'VE ALL TOUCHED PEOPLE IF YOU ATTACH WHO WERE SO BEAUTIFUL YOURSELF AS BEINGS THAT WE IF YOU CRAVE NEVER NOTICE WHETHER TEMPORAL THINGS THEY ARE PHYSICALLY BEAUTY POSSESSIONS BEAUTIFUL IT'S LIKE ACHIEVEMENT AN ETERNAL BEAUTY ANYTHING LIVES WITHIN THEM HOW POIGNANT !

ॐ 36

EXAMPLE: SOME BODY LOOKS AT YOU SEDUCTIVELY...
AN ICE CREAM CONE GOES BY............WILL IT EVER BE

THE BIG ICE CREAM CONE

IN THE SKY?

WILL IT EVER BE AN ETERNAL ICE CREAM CONE?
OR....IS IT ALWAYS GOING TO MELT?
YOU GOTTA KEEP EATING IT YET IT MELTS & MELTS
THAT'S ITS PROBLEM
YOU GOTTA KEEP EATING IT CUZ IT WILL MELT......

....& THEN IT'S GONE
& YOU KNOW THAT TASTE IN YOUR MOUTH WHEN YOU
FINISH &....YOU WANT A GLASS OF WATER? RIGHT?...
THEN YOU HAVE A GLASS OF WATER & THERE'S THAT
BLOATY FEELING?..
THEN, YOU'RE READY FOR THE NEXT ONE.....
TO GET RID OF THAT ONE.........
LET'S TAKE A WALK....& YOU TAKE A WALK.....
IT'S COLD OUT. LET'S HAVE SOME HOT CHOCOLATE,
YES, LET'S HAVE SOME,& ON &ON &ON& ITS CALLED

LIFE

❀ YOU SEE: THE OPPOSITE OF CRAVING IS SAYING
BABY, THIS IS THE WAY IT IS ❀ YEAH ❀
❀ OK ❀ HERE & NOW ❀ THIS IS IT

I ACCEPT THE HERE & NOW

FULLY

· AS · IT · IS ·
RIGHT AT THIS MOMENT !!!
3ॐ37

LAME, HALT, BLIND, DYING
WE'RE ALL DYING

AT THIS MOMENT
YOUR BODY IS   DISINTEGRATING
BEFORE YOUR   VERY EYES
IF YOU'VE TAKEN   LSD YOU MAY BE
SEEING IT DO THIS   BUT YOU KNOW
IT'S HAPPENING   ANYWAY
        IT'S ALL A DOWNHILL TRIP
                                      ALL THE WAY

BOY, WHAT A FUNNY PLACE TO GET ATTACHED!
TO SOMETHING THAT'S GOT TO GO LIKE THAT
SO BUDDHA SAYS: THE CAUSE OF SUFFERING
              IS ATTACHMENT
              OR DESIRE

THEY ALL SAY THE SAME THING!

THIRD NOBLE TRUTH

GIVE UP ATTACHMENT
GIVE UP DESIRE

YOU END THE BIRTHS
YOU END THE DEATHS
YOU END THE SUFFERING
YOU END THE WHOLE THING THAT
KEEPS YOU STUCK!

IF I'M NOT ATTACHED TO THIS PARTICULAR
TIME-SPACE LOCUS THEN I CAN FREE MY
AWARENESS FROM MY BODY AND I CAN BECOME
ONE WITH IT ALL
I CAN MERGE WITH
THE DIVINE MOTHER

38

FOURTH NOBLE TRUTH IS:
THE EIGHTFOLD PATH
(FOR GETTING RID OF DESIRE)

WHICH SAYS:
GET YOUR

LIFE
STRAIGHT

THOUGHT SPEECH ACTION LIVELIHOOD EXERTION REMEM-BRANCE MEDITA-TION BELIEF

DO YOUR WORK. DO EVERYTHING YOU'VE GOT TO DO. WATCH YOUR SPEECH. WATCH YOUR THOUGHT. WATCH YOUR CALMNESS. GET YOUR CALM CENTER GOING. LIVE YOUR LIFE IN SUCH A WAY AS TO GET YOURSELF STRAIGHT, TO GET FREE OF ATTACHMENT THAT JUST KEEPS SUCKING YOU IN ALL THE TIME.

GET FREE OF DESIRE

—GET FREE OF DESIRE. IT'S A LITTLE LIKE A ROLLER COASTER. JUST THE WAY IT WORKS: THIS IS IF YOU READ ST. JOHN OF THE CROSS' "DARK NIGHT OF YOU THE SOUL" KNOW HOW IT IS YOU'VE REALLY BEEN WORKING ON YOURSELF AND YOU'RE VERY PURE AND SOMETHING VERY HIGH HAPPENS TO YOU: YOU FEEL LIBERATED. AND THEN: YOUR EGO WALKS AROUND AND PATS YOU ON THE SHOULDER: "PRETTY GOOD! LOOK HOW HOLY YOU'RE BECOMING." AND YOU FALL AGAIN.

ॐ 39

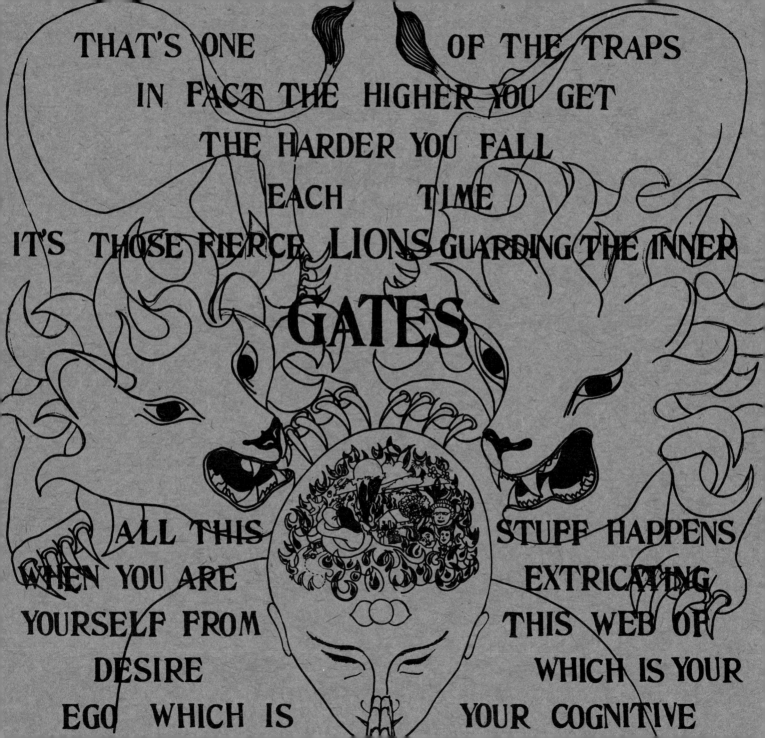

THAT'S ONE OF THE TRAPS
IN FACT THE HIGHER YOU GET
THE HARDER YOU FALL
EACH TIME
IT'S THOSE FIERCE LIONS GUARDING THE INNER
GATES
ALL THIS STUFF HAPPENS
WHEN YOU ARE EXTRICATING
YOURSELF FROM THIS WEB OF
DESIRE WHICH IS YOUR
EGO WHICH IS YOUR COGNITIVE

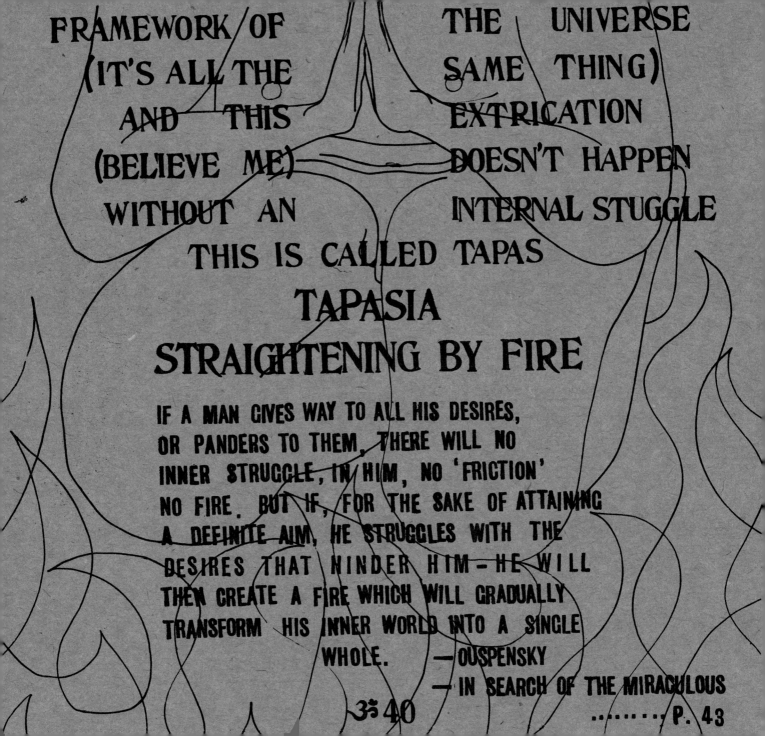

FRAMEWORK OF THE UNIVERSE (IT'S ALL THE SAME THING) AND THIS EXTRICATION (BELIEVE ME) — DOESN'T HAPPEN WITHOUT AN INTERNAL STUGGLE

THIS IS CALLED TAPAS

TAPASIA

STRAIGHTENING BY FIRE

IF A MAN GIVES WAY TO ALL HIS DESIRES, OR PANDERS TO THEM, THERE WILL NO INNER STRUGGLE, IN HIM, NO 'FRICTION' NO FIRE. BUT IF, FOR THE SAKE OF ATTAINING A DEFINITE AIM, HE STRUGGLES WITH THE DESIRES THAT HINDER HIM — HE WILL THEN CREATE A FIRE WHICH WILL GRADUALLY TRANSFORM HIS INNER WORLD INTO A SINGLE WHOLE. —OUSPENSKY

— IN SEARCH OF THE MIRACULOUS
.... P. 43

3ॐ40

FAITH

HAD YE BUT FAITH, YOU COULD
MOVE MOUNTAINS, SAID JESUS

AND THAT IS LITERALLY TRUE
THE BIBLE IS NOT A METAPHOR
IT'S NOT A STORY MADE UP TO TEACH US
HOW TO BE MORAL BEINGS

IT'S A STRAIGHT MESSAGE OF HOW IT IS
WHEN MAN LIVES IN THE SPIRIT, AND
THE SPIRIT IS RIGHT INSIDE.
THE WAY TO GET INTO THE SPIRIT
IS NOT A LOT OF HOCUS-POCUS.
IT'S A VERY SIMPLE METHODICAL,
MECHANICAL SET OF STEPS
BUT THEY'RE ONLY AVAILABLE
TO HIM WHO CAN HEAR
LET THOSE WHO HAVE EARS HEAR
TEACH NOT HIM WHO DOES NOT WANT TO KNOW.
THE WHOLE GAME   IS BASED
ON   FAITH
3:41

WHAT YOU MAY NOT UNDERSTAND IS: THE WHOLE
GAME YOU HAVE BEEN PLAYING IS ALSO BASED ON FAITH
YOU HAVE HAD FAITH IN THE RATIONAL MIND
WE ARE LIVING IN A SOCIETY WHICH IS A TEMPLE
DEDICATED TO THE RATIONAL MAN. EVEN THOUGH
THE FIRST COMMANDMENT SAYS:

I AM THE LORD THY GOD
THOU SHALT HAVE
NO OTHER GODS
BEFORE ME

EVEN THOUGH THAT HAS BEEN SAID
& EVEN THOUGH WE REPEAT IT
WE STILL WORSHIP THE RATIONAL MIND & ITS PRODUCTS
WE WORSHIP OUR OWN SENSE DATA.
IT'S ONLY WHEN WE SEE THE ASSUMPTION THAT

WE'VE ALREADY BEEN FUNCTIONING ON THAT

WE CAN START TO EXTRICATE OURSELVES.
WE HAVE GOT TO HAVE HEARD THE FIRST MESSAGE
BEFORE ANY OF THE KEYS OPEN ANYTHING.
YOU DON'T EVEN KNOW THERE ARE DOORS
UNTIL YOU HAVE HEARD THE FIRST MESSAGE.

GEORGES I. GURDJIEFF,
A WESTERNER WHO WENT ON THIS HIGHER TRIP
OR AT LEAST ON A LARGE PART OF THE TRIP, SAID:

YOU DON'T SEEM TO UNDERSTAND

YOU ARE IN PRISON

IF YOU ARE TO GET OUT OF PRISON
THE FIRST THING YOU MUST REALIZE IS:

YOU ARE IN PRISON

IF YOU THINK
YOU'RE FREE   YOU CAN'T ESCAPE.

ॐ 42

WHAT CALMING THE MIND IS ALL ABOUT
WHAT MEDITATION IS FOR
IS TO COOL YOU OUT SO YOU

RE-MEMBER

SO YOU SEE HOW IT ALL IS

TRY SITTING AROUND WHEN YOU'RE FULL OF SELF-PITY
YOU SIT DOWN IN FRONT OF YOUR PUJA TABLE
AND YOU TAKE A PICTURE OF MEHER BABA
AND HE'S SMILING AT YOU LIKE HE'S
THE OTHER MARX BROTHER AND HE'S SAYING:

LET ME HELP YOU

OH, I WISH YOU WOULD, MEHER BABA

IT'S SO HARD

(WOW! DIG THAT SELF-PITY ISN'T THAT EXQUISITE
FULL BLOOM! WHAT AN EXTRAORDINARY COLOR   IT MUST BE A NEW BRAND OF SELF-PITY
A PARTICULARLY FRAGRANT VARIETY I JUST REALLY WANT TO SMELL THAT ONE
TO SIT AND SMELL IT FOR EVER SO LONG. SUCH A GOOD ONE.)

I MEAN: I WISH I COULD HAVE TIME TO GROOVE W/
YOU BUT I'VE GOT TO GET ON W/ LIFE.
I HAVE <u>IMPORTANT</u> THINGS TO DO TODAY.

ALL RIGHT BABA!

I'LL SIT WITH YOU FOR ONE MINUTE.   OKAY?

HERE WE ARE. YOU'VE GOT ONE MINUTE.

DO YOUR THING.   ॐ43 FORTY SECONDS LEFT!

SADHANA

YOUVE GOT TO BE QUIET INSIDE TO DO
THAT KIND OF PHOTOGRAPHY
IT'S VERY EASY TO "PHOTOGRAPH"
'INANIMATE OBJECTS'- LIKE OTHER PEOPLE
BUT : TURN THE LENS RIGHT IN ON
THE VERY STUFF YOURE HIDING IN ~

SHOOT THE CAMERA THIS WAY!
VERY POWERFUL STUFF!
SO ALL I CAN DO ALL THE TIME IS TO
COOL MYSELF OUT...
THAT'S ALL I'M DOING - I DO NOTHING BUT

SADHANA

IF SOMEBODY SAYS: WHAT DO YOU DO, MAN?
I SAY: I DO SADHANA
SURE, BUT DON'T YOU LECTURE?
SURE, LECTURING HAPPENS BUT
I'M DOING MY SADHANA
THIS TRIP IS HELPING ME GET FREE OF MY EGO.
BECAUSE: IF I GET FREE OF MY EGO
WE ALL GET FREE OF OUR EGO
BECAUSE: THAT'S THE WAY THE TRIP WORKS
BECAUSE: WE'RE ALL THE SAME BEING AND
THAT'S THE PROBLEM - WE CAN ONLY MOVE AS
FAST AS WE ALL CAN MOVE....
YOU CAN HEAR THIS MESSAGE ONLY AS PURELY AS
I AM PURE. THAT'S THE WAY IT BOILS DOWN ~
I CAN RESONATE WITH YOU IN THE HIGHEST PLACE
I AM
SO: I CAN DO NOTHING FOR YOU BUT
WORK ON MYSELF.....
YOU CAN DO NOTHING FOR ME BUT
WORK ON YOURSELF!

ॐ 44

OH! I'M GOING TO DO GOOD THINGS FOR MY CHILD. BALONY!
THAT'S ALL EGO. JUST WORK ON YOURSELF
AND: EVERYTIME YOU WORK ON YOURSELF,
YOU GET CALMER
YOU HEAR MORE
YOU SENSE MORE
YOU ARE MORE
YOU'RE MORE PRESENT
WHAT ARE YOU OFFERING A CHILD?
NOT A SET OF SOCIAL ROLES
PASSING IN THE NIGHT....
YOU'RE OFFERING A CHILD HERE AND NOW-NESS

THE TREASURE OF CONSCIOUSNESS
THE TREASURE OF AWARENESS.
IF YOU DON'T HELP OTHER BEINGS CUT
THROUGH THE ILLUS- ION BECAUSE YOU'RE
THROUGH THE ILLUSION
WHAT ELSE ???
WHAT ELSE IS THERE ?

WHAT ARE YOU DOING? DOING MORE OF THE DANCE
WITHIN THE DANCE??? ?
ARE WE ALWAYS GOING TO MEET ON THE STAGE?

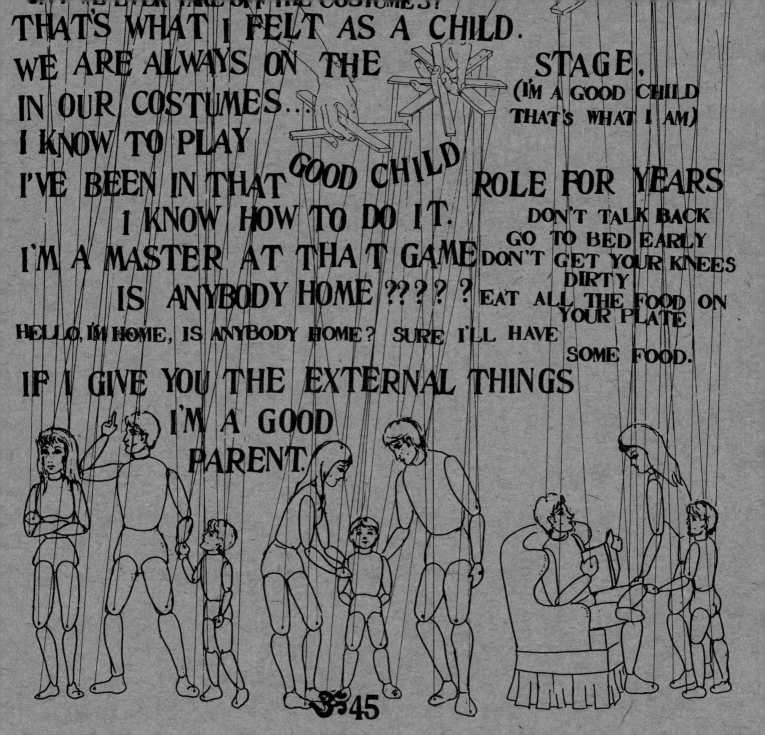

THAT'S WHAT I FELT AS A CHILD.
WE ARE ALWAYS ON THE STAGE,
IN OUR COSTUMES...
(I'M A GOOD CHILD
THAT'S WHAT I AM)
I KNOW TO PLAY
I'VE BEEN IN THAT GOOD CHILD ROLE FOR YEARS
I KNOW HOW TO DO IT.
DON'T TALK BACK
GO TO BED EARLY
I'M A MASTER AT THAT GAME DON'T GET YOUR KNEES DIRTY
IS ANYBODY HOME ????? EAT ALL THE FOOD ON YOUR PLATE
HELLO, I'M HOME, IS ANYBODY HOME? SURE I'LL HAVE
SOME FOOD.

IF I GIVE YOU THE EXTERNAL THINGS
I'M A GOOD
PARENT.

45

YOU AND I CAN ALWAYS STARVE TOGETHER
IF WE'RE BACKSTAGE IN THE HERE & NOW
IF WE'RE NOT IN THE HERE & NOW
NO MATTER HOW MUCH FOOD
WE PUT IN OUR BELLIES
IT'S NEVER GOING TO BE ENOUGH
AND THAT'S THE FEELING OF WESTERN MAN

IT'S NOT ENOUGH

HE'S GOT IT ALL GOING IN
AS FAST AS HE CAN SHOVEL IT
HE'S GOT EVERY SENSUAL GRATIFICATION
HE CAN POSSIBLY DESIRE &

IT'S NOT ENOUGH
BECAUSE THERE'S NO
HERE & NOW-NESS ABOUT IT

HERE & NOW
IS THE DOORWAY TO ALL THAT
ENERGY
BECAUSE IF YOU'RE TRUTHFULLY HERE & NOW
THERE'S NO MORE YOU   THAT'S THE WAY IT WORKS

DID YOU EVER GO THE MOVIES AND GET SO CAUGHT UP
IN THE MOVIE THAT YOU FORGOT WHO YOU WERE
AND THEN THE LIGHTS CAME ON AND
YOU WONDERED..........WHERE AM I?
WHAT'S GOING ON? OH IT'S A MOVIE.

WHAT YOU'VE GOT TO DO IS CREATE IN YOURSELF
AN ABSOLUTELY CALM CENTER WHERE IT'S
ALWAYS RIGHT HERE & NOW IT IS JUST

LIGHT IT IS JUST IS-NESS

GETTING INTO THE TUB

EATING

GETTING INTO BED

GOING TO THE TOILET

UP THE STAIRS

JUST THE IS-NESS

TALKING

3346

RUNNING DOWN THE STREET

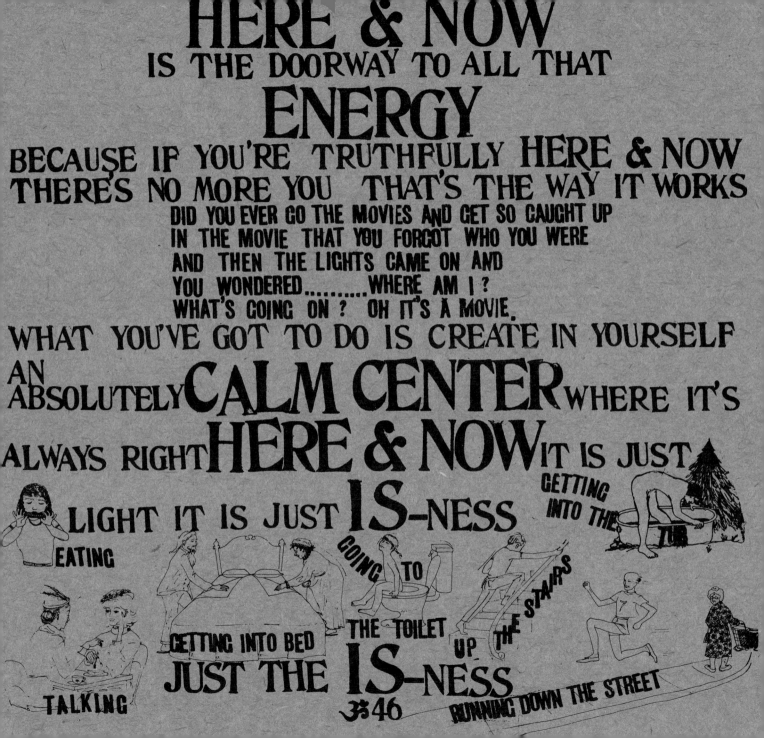

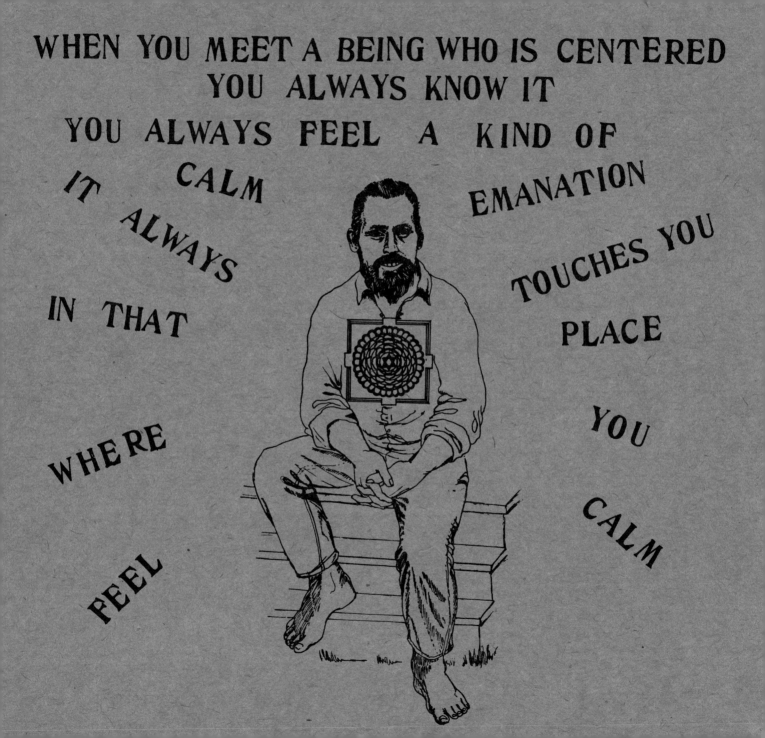

BUT: YOU CAN'T HUSTLE IT
YOU CAN'T MAKE-BELIEVE YOU'RE CALM
WHEN YOU'RE NOT.

IT NEVER WORKS
EVERYBODY KNOWS
YOU KNOW
IT'S HORRIBLE

YOU MUST CENTER

FIND
THAT PLACE

INSIDE
YOURSELF

AND:
WHATEVER
YOUR
DANCE
IS

YOU'RE DOING
IT FROM
THAT PLACE

ALWAYS RIGHT IN

HERE

RIGHT IN
YOUR HRIDAYAM

ॐ47

THE SUBTLE MOTHER

AND EVERY TIME YOU STEP BACK ONE STEP FROM YOUR OWN MELODRAMA THE COSMIC HUMOR GETS HIGHER AND HIGHER OF IT ALL THE EXTREME BEAUTY OF IT ALL!

THE DIVINE MOTHER NATURE!

WHICH IS YOU WHICH IS ALL OF THIS WHICH IS THE WHOLE PHYSICAL PLANE!

3-48

THAT'S ATTACHMENT

CAN'T HAVE HER
CAN'T REJECT HER
CAN'T LIVE WITH HER
CAN'T PUT HER AWAY

JUST HONOR AND HONOR HER

DIVINE MOTHER

YOU'VE GOT TO

WORSHIP HER

ॐ 49

SHE IS THE VEIL
SHE IS SITA

& AT SOME POINT

SITA STANDS ASIDE
ON THE JUNGLE PATH
SO RAM'S BROTHER
CAN SEE RAM
SITA IS RAM'S WIFE
& LAKSAMAN
IS RAM'S BROTHER

RAM IS GOD

& THEY'RE GOING ALONG
A JUNGLE PATH &

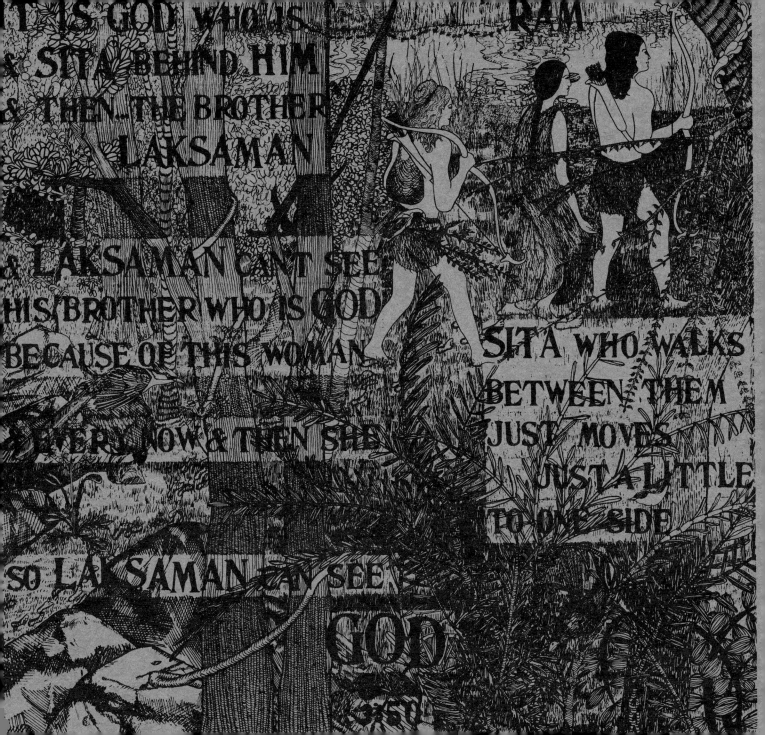

IT IS GOD WHO IS RAM

& SITA BEHIND HIM

& THEN THE BROTHER
LAKSAMAN

& LAKSAMAN CAN'T SEE
HIS BROTHER WHO IS GOD
BECAUSE OF THIS WOMAN

SITA WHO WALKS
BETWEEN THEM
JUST MOVES
JUST A LITTLE
TO ONE SIDE

EVERY NOW & THEN SHE

SO LAKSAMAN CAN SEE

GOD

HER TONGUE DRIPPING BLOOD
A CIRCLE OF SKULLS AROUND HER NECK
A DAGGER IN ONE HAND
GIVING BIRTH IN THE OTHER
THE WHOLE PROCESS OF NATURE

HOW EXQUISITELY SUBTLE

REMEMBER SIDDHARTHA

HIS JOURNEY, AND THE AMOUNT OF TIME HE SPENT IN THE GARDEN OF PLEASURE

WITH A WOMAN WHO HAD MUCH TO TEACH ? SHE ALWAYS HAD A NEW THING

TO TEACH -- SHE WILL ALWAYS HAVE A NEW THING TO TEACH -- ALWAYS

❀   ❀   ❀   ❀   ❀

CAN ANYONE IMAGINE THAT A WOMAN AS FULL
AND SEDUCTIVE AS THAT IS NOT GOING TO
TEACH SOMETHING?
IS NOT GOING TO CONTINUE TO TEACH
SOMETHING?

ॐ 51

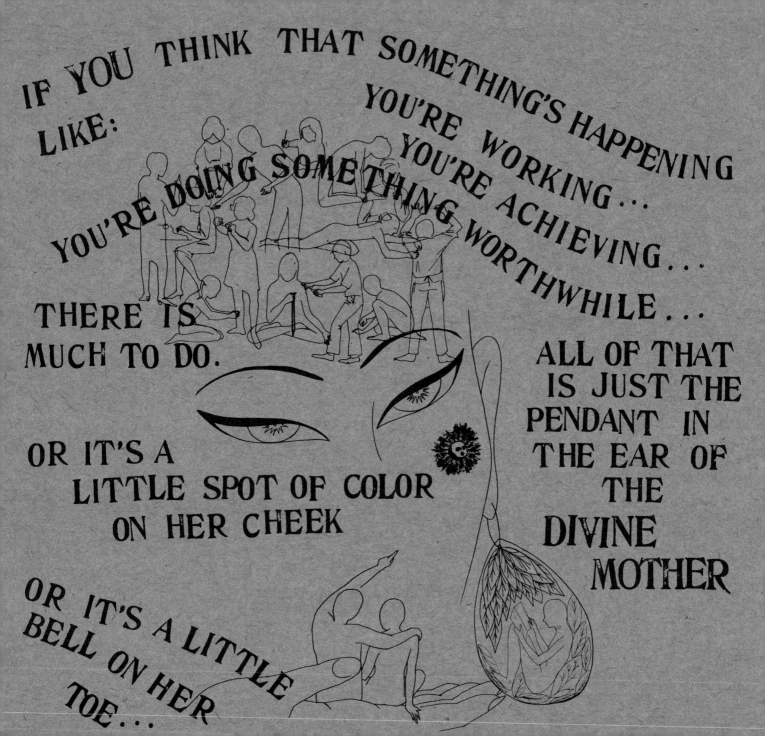

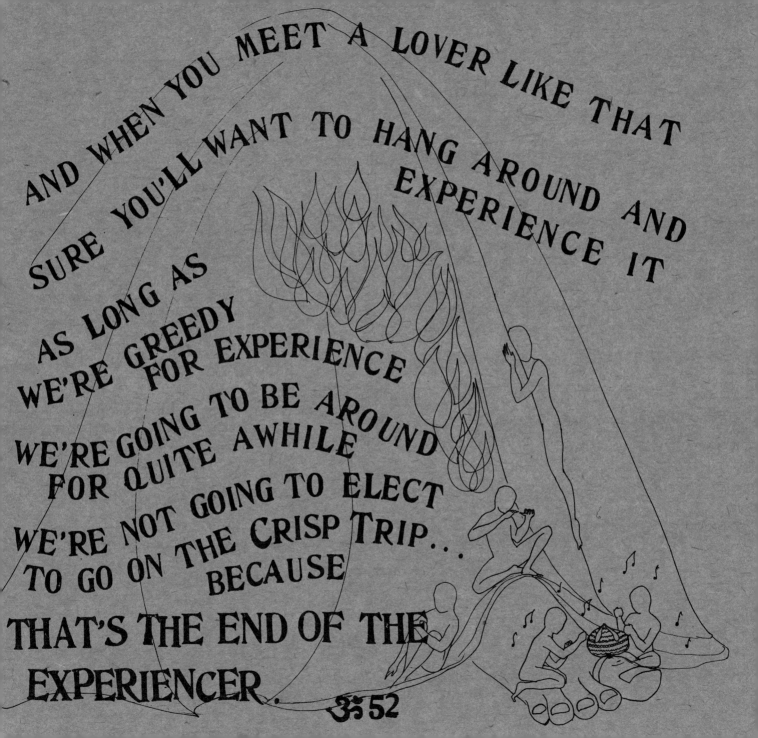

AND WHEN YOU MEET A LOVER LIKE THAT

SURE YOU'LL WANT TO HANG AROUND AND EXPERIENCE IT

AS LONG AS WE'RE GREEDY FOR EXPERIENCE

WE'RE GOING TO BE AROUND FOR QUITE AWHILE

WE'RE NOT GOING TO ELECT TO GO ON THE CRISP TRIP... BECAUSE

THAT'S THE END OF THE EXPERIENCER.

ॐ 52

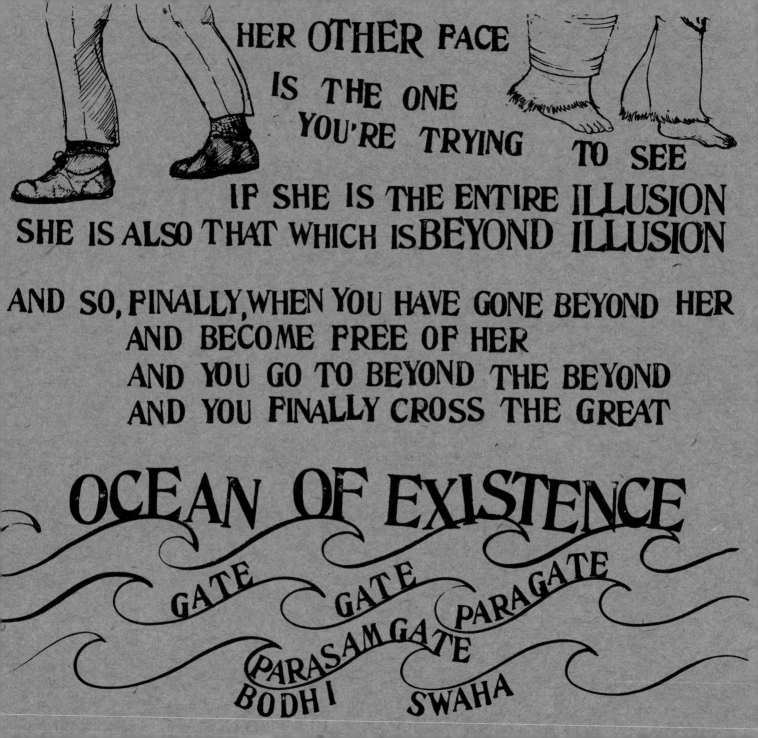

HER OTHER FACE
IS THE ONE
YOU'RE TRYING
TO SEE
IF SHE IS THE ENTIRE ILLUSION
SHE IS ALSO THAT WHICH IS BEYOND ILLUSION

AND SO, FINALLY, WHEN YOU HAVE GONE BEYOND HER
AND BECOME FREE OF HER
AND YOU GO TO BEYOND THE BEYOND
AND YOU FINALLY CROSS THE GREAT

OCEAN OF EXISTENCE

GATE   GATE   PARAGATE
PARASAMGATE
BODHI   SWAHA

AND YOU STAND ON THE OTHER SIDE
AND YOU'RE COMPLETELY FREE
WHO'S THERE? THE DIVINE MOTHER
WELCOMING YOU.

THAT'S THE BODHISATTVA PART OF IT:
YOU HAVE GONE & YOU HAVE GOTTEN THE LIBERATION

&
THEN
YOU
ARE

RIGHT
HERE

CHOPPING WOOD
& CARRYING WATER

ॐ 53

MAKING IT SACRED

THIS (CHOPPING WOOD AND CARRYING WATER)
IS KARMA YOGA... THE YOGA OF DAILY LIFE.
THE WAY TO DO IT IS: DO WHAT YOU DO
BUT DEDICATE THE FRUITS OF THE WORK
TO ME ॐ

THAT'S THE MOST ESOTERIC WAY OF SAYING IT.

ANOTHER WAY OF SAYING IT IS: DO IT WITHOUT ATTACHMENT. ANOTHER WAY OF SAYING IT IS: TOTAL RENUNCIATION!

NOW THAT DOESN'T MEAN YOU GO UP TO A MOUNTAIN AND LIVE IN A CAVE. IT MEANS THAT YOU RENOUNCE ATTACHMENT EVEN TO YOUR OWN DESIRES. IT MEANS YOU DO WHAT YOU DO BECAUSE THAT'S WHAT THE HARMONY OF THE UNIVERSE REQUIRES.

IF I AM A POTTER I MAKE POTS BUT WHO IS MAKING THE POTS? I AM NOT UNDER THE ILLUSION THAT I AM MAKING THE POTS.

POTS ARE.

THE POTTER IS.

I AM A

HOLLOW

BAMBOO

ॐ 54

ॐ ॐ ॐ ॐ ॐ ॐ ॐ ॐ ॐ ॐ ॐ ॐ ॐ

I AM A DOCTOR...A STUDENT...A DROP-OUT....

ALL THE SAME GAME

DON'T LET THAT OFFEND YOU, BUT ... THE
EXTERNAL WORLD IS ALL THE SAME ...
IT'S ALL THE EXTERNAL WORLD!
PEOPLE OFTEN SAY TO ME:

I WOULD REALLY LIKE TO DO SADHANA, BUT... I'M A TEACHER NOW. IF
I COULD ONLY FINISH BEING A TEACHER, I COULD DO SADHANA.

BALONEY! YOU'RE EITHER DOING SADHANA OR
YOU'RE NOT. SADHANA IS A FULL TIME THING
THAT YOU DO BECAUSE THERE IS NOTHING
ELSE TO DO. YOU DO IT WHETHER YOU'RE
TEACHING, OR SITTING IN A MONASTERY...
WHETHER YOU'RE LYING IN BED,
GOING TO THE TOILET, MAKING LOVE,
EATING,
EVERYTHING IS PART OF

WAKING UP.

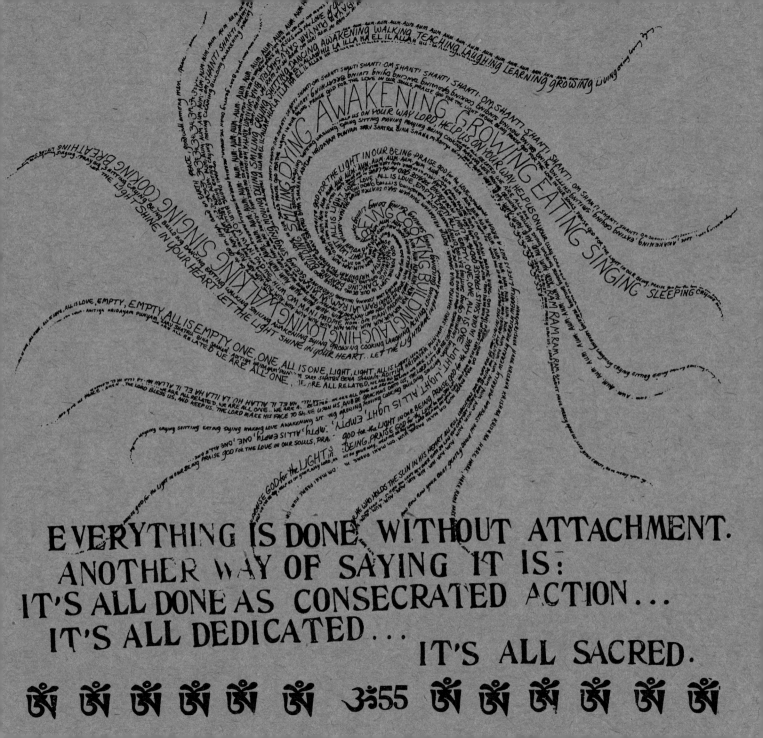

EVERYTHING IS DONE WITHOUT ATTACHMENT.
ANOTHER WAY OF SAYING IT IS:
IT'S ALL DONE AS CONSECRATED ACTION...
IT'S ALL DEDICATED...
IT'S ALL SACRED.

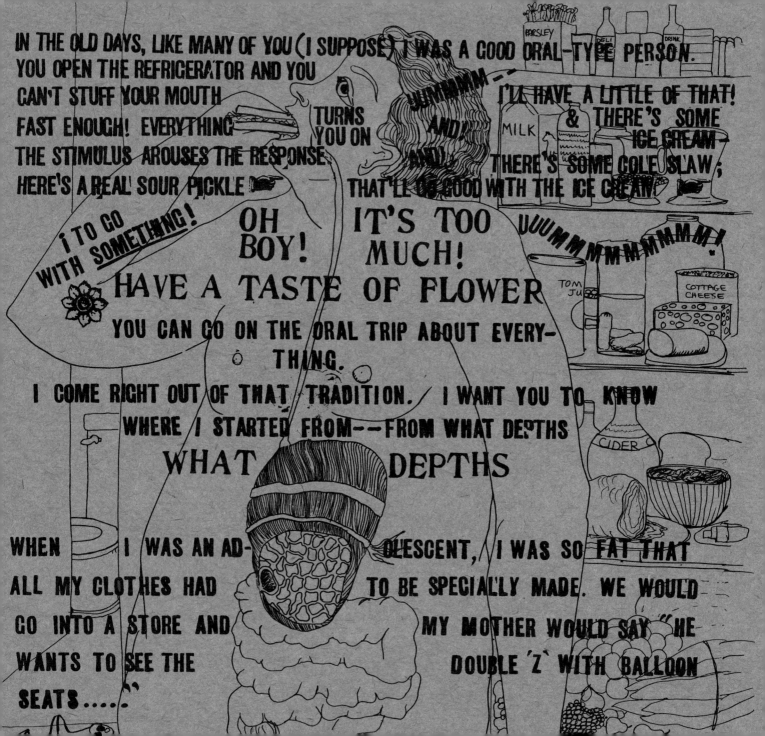

IN THE OLD DAYS, LIKE MANY OF YOU (I SUPPOSE) I WAS A GOOD ORAL-TYPE PERSON. YOU OPEN THE REFRIGERATOR AND YOU CAN'T STUFF YOUR MOUTH FAST ENOUGH! EVERYTHING TURNS YOU ON THE STIMULUS AROUSES THE RESPONSE. HERE'S A REAL SOUR PICKLE

YUMMMM— I'LL HAVE A LITTLE OF THAT! AND! & THERE'S SOME ICE CREAM— AND! THERE'S SOME COLE SLAW; THAT'LL BE GOOD WITH THE ICE CREAM

¡ TO GO WITH SOMETHING!

OH BOY! IT'S TOO MUCH!

UUMMMMMMMM!

HAVE A TASTE OF FLOWER

YOU CAN GO ON THE ORAL TRIP ABOUT EVERY-THING.

I COME RIGHT OUT OF THAT TRADITION. I WANT YOU TO KNOW WHERE I STARTED FROM——FROM WHAT DEPTHS

WHAT DEPTHS

WHEN I WAS AN AD-OLESCENT, I WAS SO FAT THAT ALL MY CLOTHES HAD TO BE SPECIALLY MADE. WE WOULD GO INTO A STORE AND MY MOTHER WOULD SAY "HE WANTS TO SEE THE DOUBLE 'Z' WITH BALLOON SEATS....."

PARSLEY DELI DRINK MILK TOM JU COTTAGE CHEESE CIDER

IT TOOK ME AT LEAST $10,000.00 OF
MY ANALYSIS TO GET RID OF THAT
ONE, I'LL TELL YOU! SO YOU CAN
UNDERSTAND THAT I SPEAK OF
THE ORAL TRIP WITH A CERTAIN
AMOUNT OF EMPATHY

AND NOW SUDDENLY, COMES THIS
NEW RULING SENT DOWN FROM ABOVE

ALL YOUR ACTS WILL BE CONSECRATED ॐ

ALL YOUR ACTS WILL BE
CONSECRATED

ॐ56

WOW, THAT'S GREAT. BUT WHAT ABOUT FOOD? AH...
NOW IN THE WEST WE HAVE A THING. YOU SEE THE
NORMAN ROCKWELL COVER... THANKSGIVING DAY!
THERE'S THE TURKEY & EVERYBODY HAS HIS EYES
CLOSED SAYING GRACE & THE KID'S HAND IS ALREADY
ON THE TURKEY... OKAY! LET'S SAY GRACE &

EAT QUICK!

SO IN INDIA I WAS
TAUGHT THIS THING
TO SAY TO CONSECRATE
THE FOOD & IT WAS
VERY FUNNY.

I'D BEEN TAUGHT IT
BUT I STILL HAD THIS
OLD ORALITY BUSINESS.
SO I WOULD SAY IT BUT... I COULD NOT THINK IT.
AND... I COULD NOT STOP LONG ENUF
TO EXPERIENCE IT.
AT LAST I HAD TO CONFRONT MYSELF
AND SEE WHERE I WASN'T.

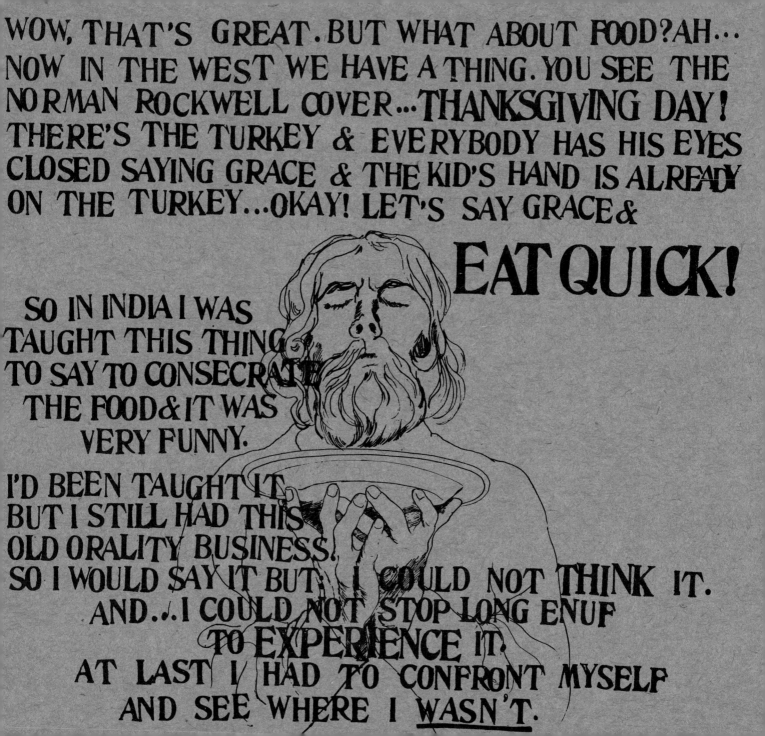

YOU'VE GOT TO GO
AT THE RATE
YOU CAN GO.

YOU WAKE UP
AT THE RATE
YOU WAKE UP.

YOU'RE FINISHED WITH YOUR DESIRES
AT THE RATE
YOU FINISH WITH YOUR DESIRES.

THE DISEQUILIBRIUM
COMES INTO HARMONY
AT THE RATE
IT COMES INTO
HARMONY.

YOU
CAN'T
RIP
THE
SKIN OFF
THE SNAKE. THE SNAKE MUST MOULT
THE SKIN. THAT'S THE RATE IT HAPPENS.

3:57

YOU MEET ANOTHER PERSON & THERE ARE QUALITIES IN THAT PERSONALITY WHICH OFFEND YOU & THERE ARE QUALITIES WHICH ATTRACT YOU— SOME QUALITIES SEDUCE YOU—SOME QUALITIES REPEL YOU—SOME QUALITIES SEXUALLY EXCITE YOU—SOME QUALITIES REVOLT YOU—SOME QUALITIES INTEREST YOU— SOME QUALITIES FASCINATE YOU—SOME QUALITIES BORE YOU. IT'S ONLY WHEN YOU CAN SEE THROUGH ALL THAT VEIL ... THROUGH ALL YOUR OWN DESIRES...

...BEYOND SITA WALKING IN THE PATH THAT YOU CAN SEE BEYOND ALL THAT

TO WHERE THE   OTHER BEING IS

YOU WILL DO THAT WHEN YOU'VE GONE INSIDE
TO SEE WHERE YOU ARE —— BEYOND THE
THINGS IN YOU WHICH ATTRACT YOU AND
SEDUCE YOU AND EXCITE YOU AND REPEL
YOU —— THE JOURNEY ACROSS THE
GREAT OCEAN   OF EXISTENCE

IS A JOURNEY   INWARD

EVER IN DEEPER AND DEEPER
AND THE DEEPER YOU GET IN THE MORE YOU
MEET TRUTH

ॐ58

THE GURU

IT'S HARD TO SPEAK IN WORDS ABOUT
THE GURU .... TO SPEAK OF THE DIF-
FERENCE BETWEEN AN UPA GURU AND
A SAT GURU.

IT'S INTERESTING THAT WHEN I TELL THE
STORY OF MY JOURNEY IN INDIA AND TELL OF THE GURU, I AL-
WAYS SPEAK OF HIS MIRACLES, ALTHOUGH, FROM MY POINT
OF VIEW THEY ARE NOT THE ESSENCE OF THE MATTER AT ALL.

BUT: THEY ARE THAT WHICH IS SPEAKABLE OF...

IT'S A LITTLE LIKE THAT PERSIAN STORY WHERE NASRUDDIN IS
LOOKING FOR HIS HOUSEKEY UNDER THE STREETLAMP AND
OTHERS COME TO HELP HIM AND FINALLY THEY ASK HIM
"WHERE DID YOU LOSE IT?"   AND HE ANSWERS, "IN MY
HOUSE, BUT IT'S DARK IN THERE AND SINCE IT'S LIGHT OUT
HERE THIS IS THE BEST PLACE TO LOOK."

I FIND MYSELF TALKING ABOUT
THINGS THAT ARE TALKABLE ABOUT
WHAT CAN   I SAY ?

ॐ59

CAN I SAY (WITH ANY MEANING)
THAT WHEN I'M WITH THE GURU,
THERE'S NOBODY HOME?   OR:
THAT I LOVE HIM SO THOROUGHLY
THAT I WOULD DO ANYTHING
HE WOULD EVER ASK OF ME AND
THE HIGHEST THING I COULD THINK OF
IS BEING AT HIS FEET AND
AT THE SAME MOMENT
I DON'T CARE IF I NEVER SEE HIM
AGAIN IN THIS LIFE? CAN I SAY THAT?
CAN I SAY THERE IS ABSOLUTELY NOTHING
SPECIAL ABOUT HIM? HE'S JUST A LITTLE
OLD MAN WITH A BLANKET? CAN I SAY
HE'S RIGHT HERE NOW?
WHICH ONE ARE YOU READY TO HEAR?

HEN I WAS AROUND MAHARAJ-JI THERE WAS ALWAYS A CONSTANT STREAM OF DEVOTEES WHO HAVE MUCH REVERENCE (VISHWAS) BUT NOT TOO MUCH FAITH (SHRADDHA) AND THEY WERE ALWAYS ASKING MAHARAJ-JI FOR MIRACLES OR TO GET THEM A JOB, OR THEY WANTED TO USE HIS DIVINATORY POWERS AND TELL THEM ABOUT THE FUTURE.

AND THEN WHEN HE WOULD ASK ME WHAT IT WAS I WANTED, I COULDN'T THINK OF ANYTHING. I JUST FELT HE WAS INSIDE OF ME.

HOW DO YOU ASK YOUR INNER SELF FOR SOMETHING? YOU ARE ALREADY IT. WHAT IS IT THAT YOU COULD GIVE TO YOURSELF? GIVE YOURSELF PRESENTS? IT'S ALL WRONG.

AT FIRST I DIDN'T TRUST IT, SO I'D HAVE TO COME INTO HIS PRESENCE AND THE MINUTE I'D GET THERE I'D FEEL... YEAH... AND I'D LOOK AT HIM AND MY EYES WOULD GET ALL SWIMMING WITH TEARS AND I'D JUST LAUGH AND I'D FEEL SILLY. I WOULD REALLY BE SILLY.

silly (IT'S HARD TO GET ME SPEECHLESS)

ॐ 60

MY TEACHER HARI DASS BABA IS ESSENCE

HE IS PURE

HE IS JUST LIKE A CRYSTAL

HE IS BEAUTIFUL

HE IS READY TO LEARN

HE IS EXQUISITELY ARTICULATED

HE TAUGHT ME EVERYTHING I WAS

EVERYTHING I WAS READY

THE GURU TAUGHT ME NOTHING IN FORM

HE NEVER EXPLAINED ANYTHING
HE'D LAUGH AT ME AND TWIRL MY HAIR
AND HAND ME AN ORANGE AND SAY THINGS LIKE:
YOU MAKE MANY PEOPLE LAUGH IN AMERICA?
AND I'D SAY "YES" AND HE'D SAY "THAT'S GOOD"
THAT DOESN'T TEACH YOU MUCH THAT'S JUST HANGING
OUT. THE TEACHER ON THE OTHER HAND WAS ALL
SPIT AND POLISH..ALL BUSINESS. HE IS A PURE BRAHMIN
AND HE HAS WORK TO DO AND HE IS GOING TO TEACH ME
AND IT WAS ALL NO NONSENSE.
HE WOULD BE MAKING ME A ROPE TO GO AROUND
MY WAIST WITH SEVEN STRANDS
AND HE WOULD BE EXPLAINING EACH STRAND...
AND I HONOR HIM AND LOVE HIM
AND WISH TO SERVE HIM
ONE OF THEM IS IN THE WORLD FOR ME
AND ONE OF THEM IS NOT
THE RELATIONSHIP TO THE GURU
HAS NOTHING TO DO WITH WORLDLINESS
WITH THE 3ॐ61 WORLDLY

BY GURU I DON T MEAN A SPECIFIC GURU
IN MY HEAD THERE IS A UNIVERSAL GURU
A LEVEL OF CONSCIOUSNESS A FREQUENCY OF
VIBRATION A CONNECTION TO ANOTHER PLANE...

I SPENT ALL
LAST WINTER
AND THE YEAR
BEFORE AT THE
TEMPLE JUST
MAKING LOVE
TO MAHARA-JI
IN EVERY WAY
BEING OPENED
WIDER AND WAS
JUST SO AWED
BY THE PURE

HE WAS RIGHT HERE

LAUGHING

AND

BEING

HERE

ALL

NOT MORE THAN
HALF AN HOUR OR
MAYBE AN HOUR
AND MOST OF
THAT WAS SUP
ERFLOUS   I
NEEDED TO SEE
HIM IN THE FLESH
ONLY BECAUSE
MY FAITH WAS
NOT PURE EN
OUGH WHAT

BEING THAT
THERE WAS NO
PLACE FOR MY
PARANOIA YET
EVERYWHERE I
TURNED THERE
IT WAS AND NO
PLACE FOR IT
BECAUSE
I ONLY SAW THE
MAN IN THE
FLESH PROBABLY
EIGHT TIMES
ITS AMAZING
AND ALL BUT
TWO TIMES FOR

PEOPLE WHO
HAVE BEEN
SHARING THIS
JOURNEY WITH
ME THESE PAST
FEW YEARS WHO
HAVE BECAUSE
OF THEIR PURITY
MADE DIRECT
CONTACT WITH
THE GURU IN
THEMSELVES
THROUGH THE
PURITY OF THEIR
LOVE

JESUS SAID

"BECAUSE YOU HAVE SEEN ME
YOU HAVE BELIEVED. BLESSED
ARE THEY THAT HAVE NOT SEEN
AND YET HAVE BELIEVED."

THE WAY BHAKTI WORKS

YOU JUST LOVE

UNTIL

YOU

AND THE

BELOVED

BECOME

ONE

ॐ 63

I'VE REFLECTED ON THE DIFFERENCE
BETWEEN A TEACHER AND THE GURU.

THE GURU **IS** THE WAY

INTO THIS PERFECT CENTER

THE INNER PLACE

THE ATMAN

TO THE WAY

TO THE TAO

THE CLOSER YOU COME

TO GOING

INTO SAMADHI

THE CLOSER YOU COME

TO MAKING CONTACT

WITH THE GURU

IT'S AS IF THE GURU IS AN AIRPLANE HOVERING OVER A LANDING FIELD AND THERE'S JUST TOO MUCH GROUND TRAFFIC FOR THE PLANE TO LAND. CARS ALL OVER THE RUNWAY, LOOKING FOR A GURU. HE JUST CIRCLES AND CIRCLES, DOING A HOLDING PATTERN, WAITING FOR YOU TO CLEAR YOUR RUNWAY SO HE CAN LAND. HE'S SITTING UP THERE (IN HERE) ALL THE TIME.

MAHARAJ-JI IS NOT FURTHER AWAY FROM YOU AT THIS MOMENT THAN THE THOUGHT YOU'RE THINKING NOW AND: IF YOU WERE CAPABLE OF COMPLETELY STOPPING THIS THOUGHT OR: TRANSCENDING IT OR: BEING CENTERED FROM THE INSIDE BEHIND IT HE AND YOU WOULD THEN BE ONE

ॐ 64

YOU DIG THAT MY SPECIAL RELATIONSHIP
TO HIM (IF INDEED, HE IS LIVING IN SAT
CHIT ANANDA) CANNOT CONCEIVABLY BE
SPECIAL. THERE'S NO MEANING TO THAT.
SPECIALNESS CAN ONLY BE IN EACH PERSON'S
KARMA. IT'S NOT AN INTERPERSONAL RELATION-
SHIP-- WITH A BEING THAT IS NOT INTER-
PERSONAL. PEOPLE SAY: YOU'VE GOT SOME-
THING GOING WITH THE GURU. THAT'S ABSURD.
I JUST HAVE WHAT I HAVE GOING WITH MY
OWN KARMA. EACH PERSON IS AS CLOSE TO
THE GURU AT EVERY MOMENT AS HE IS CLOSE
TO THE GURU AT THAT MOMENT. AND PEOPLE
SAY: MAYBE THE GURU WOULD INTERVENE
AND TAKE ON MY KARMA. BUT FROM A
GURU'S POINT OF VIEW

HE JUST UNDERSTANDS

HOW I ALL IS IN

ETERNAL

TIME AND SPACE

ॐ 65

HE HAS NO ATTACHMENT
EITHER TO LIFE, OR DEATH
AND: IF HE TAKES ON YOUR KARMA
IT IS YOUR KARMA THAT HE SHOULD
TAKE ON YOUR KARMA

SIMPLE AS THAT

YOU SEE:

YOU ARE THE GURU

THAT'S WHAT'S SO FAR OUT ~
❀YOU ARE YOUR OWN GURU❀
❀I AM MY OWN GRANDPA❀
AND THAT'S WHAT YOU FINALLY KNOW WHEN
YOU ARE HANGING OUT WITH ONE OF THESE GUYS
YOU HANG OUT WITH YOURSELF

BECAUSE THERE'S NOBODY AT HOME THERE
AT ALL. SO TO THE EXTENT THAT THERE'S
HANGING OUT (IN THE INTERPERSONAL SENSE)
ALL YOU CAN BE SEEING ARE
YOUR OWN DESIRES

HE IS A PERFECT MIRROR

SINCE THERE'S 366 NOBODY HERE

WHEN I MET MY GURU WHO KNEW

EVERYTHING

IN MY HEAD,

I REALIZED

THAT HE KNEW

EVERYTHING

IN MY HEAD

WHETHER "I" LIKED IT OR NOT.

HE KNEW IT.

ॐ 67

AND THERE WOULD BE TIMES AFTER A PARTICULARLY BEAUTIFUL DARSHAN WITH HIM WHEN HE'D SAY TO ME: "OH! YOU GAVE MUCH MONEY TO A LAMA," AND I'D SAY YES AND HE'D SAY: "YOU'RE VERY GOOD. YOU'RE COMING ALONG WITH YOUR SADHANA," AND I FELT SO GOOD AND THEN I'D GO BACK TO THE TEMPLE AND THINK "BOY! I'M GOING TO BE A GREAT YOGI. I'LL HAVE GREAT POWERS. WHAT AM I GOING TO DO WITH THEM?"... AND I'D START TO HAVE THESE HORRIBLE THOUGHTS AND ALL MY IMPURITIES WOULD RISE TO THE SURFACE AND THEY WOULD REALLY BE... AND THEN I'D GO TO BED AND HAVE ALL KINDS OF SEXUAL FANTASIES AND I'D THINK "LOOK YOU'RE BEING A YOGI AND YOU SEE THE ABSURDITY OF THAT SITUATION YOU'RE IN..." BUT I'D STILL HAVE THE THOUGHT. AND THEN, IN THE COURSE OF IT, I'D HAVE A THOUGHT (I'D BE GOING THROUGH MY SHOULDER BAG AND COME ACROSS A NOTE I'D WRITTEN TO MYSELF: "REMEMBER TO VISIT LAMA GOVINDA") AND I'D THINK, "I MUST VISIT LAMA GOVINDA WHILE I'M IN INDIA."

AND THE NEXT MORNING AT 8 O'CLOCK THERE IS THE MESSENGER WITH INSTRUCTIONS: "THE GURU SAID YOU'RE TO GO VISIT LAMA GOVINDA."

NOW! THERE ISN'T A MESSAGE SAYING: "CUT OUT THOSE SEXUAL THOUGHTS," BUT HE MUST OBVIOUSLY KNOW THEM. DO YOU THINK HE JUST PICKED UP ON THE LAMA GOVINDA THING?

CAN I ASSUME THE PROBABILITIES ARE HE ONLY TUNES IN EVERY TIME I HAVE A POSITIVE THOUGHT?

AND THEN I COME BEFORE HIM AND NOW I'M FREAKED BECAUSE I KNOW HE KNOWS IT ALL; AND I WALK IN, AND HE

LOOKS AT ME WITH TOTAL
LOVE

AND I THINK: HOW CAN HE DO IT?
THIS GUY MUST BE NUTS! HE'S LOVING
THIS CORRUPT ... WHY ISN'T HE ... ?
YOU SEE THE PREDICAMENT I WAS IN ?
AND THEN! WHAT I UNDERSTOOD WAS:
HE WAS LOVING THAT IN ME WHICH WAS
BEHIND MY PERSONALITY AND BEHIND
MY BODY.
NOT: "I REALLY LOVE RAM DASS"
IT WASN'T INTERPERSONAL LOVE
IT WASN'T POSSESSIVE LOVE
IT WASN'T NEEDFUL LOVE
IT WAS THE FACT THAT

HE IS   LOVE

ॐ 68

WHERE HE SAW ME
HE LOOKED AT ME   AND HE SAW THAT
                         PLACE IN ME
                         WHICH IS
AND   HERE   WE ARE   LOVE
             IN
             LOVE

THAT'S THE WORLD HE LIVES IN
AND ONCE I APPRECIATED THAT
AND COULD SEE THAT HE
COULD LOOK AT THIS CORRUPT
IMPURE
UGLY

BEING
AND HE COULD LOVE

IT THAT MUCH
NOBODY HAD EVER
DONE THAT
BEFORE
EVERYBODY HAD SAID
I'LL LOVE YOU IF....
AND HE JUST SAID

WHERE YOU
REALLY ARE
AND WHERE I
REALLY AM

WE
ARE
LOVE

AND
WHEN I WAS AROUND HIM
I WAS

IN

LOVE 3469

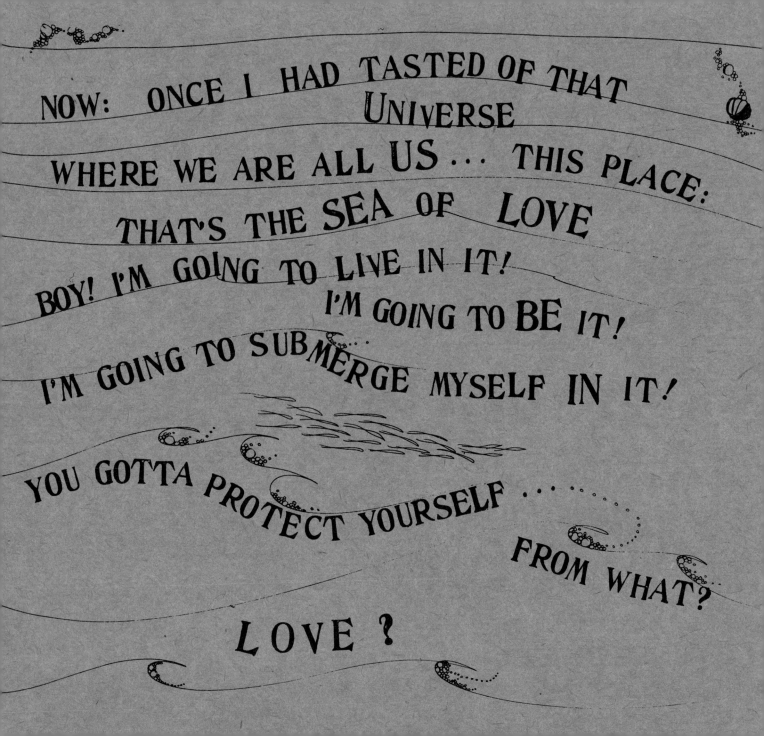

NOW: ONCE I HAD TASTED OF THAT UNIVERSE WHERE WE ARE ALL US ... THIS PLACE: THAT'S THE SEA OF LOVE BOY! I'M GOING TO LIVE IN IT! I'M GOING TO BE IT! I'M GOING TO SUBMERGE MYSELF IN IT!

YOU GOTTA PROTECT YOURSELF ... FROM WHAT?

LOVE ?

ONCE YOU KNOW THERE'S NO PLACE TO HIDE

THEN
YOU WONDER WHO ARE YOU HIDING FROM? ANYWAY

THERE'S A SIKH STORY ABOUT A HOLY MAN WHO GAVE TWO MEN EACH A CHICKEN

AND SAID: "GO KILL THEM WHERE NO ONE CAN SEE."

ONE GUY WENT BEHIND THE FENCE AND KILLED THE CHICKEN.

THE OTHER GUY WALKED AROUND FOR TWO DAYS AND CAME BACK WITH THE CHICKEN.

THE HOLY MAN SAID: YOU DIDN'T KILL THE CHICKEN?"
THE GUY SAID: "WELL, EVERYWHERE I GO, THE CHICKEN SEES."

SAHAJ SAMADHI

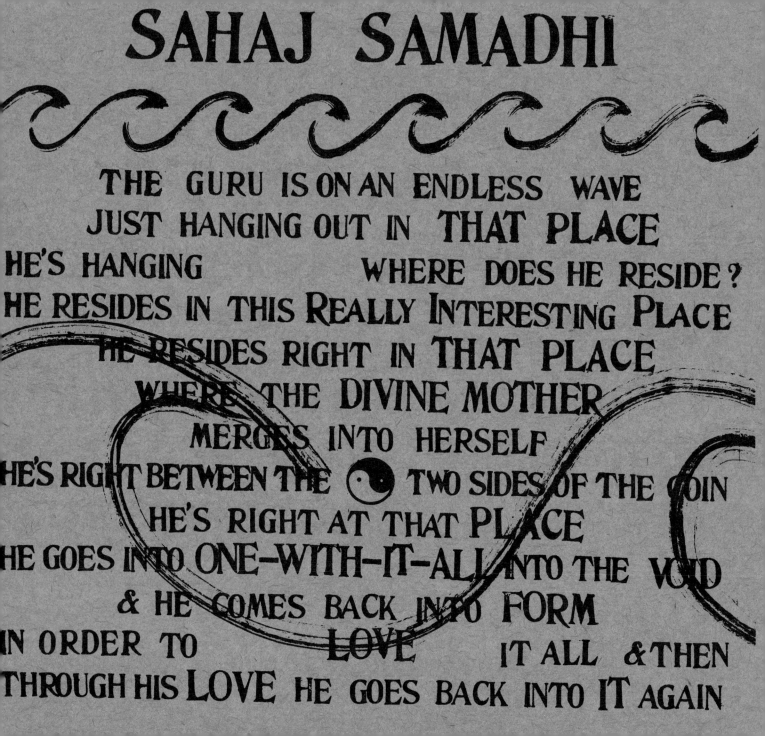

THE GURU IS ON AN ENDLESS WAVE
JUST HANGING OUT IN THAT PLACE
HE'S HANGING   WHERE DOES HE RESIDE?
HE RESIDES IN THIS REALLY INTERESTING PLACE
HE RESIDES RIGHT IN THAT PLACE
WHERE THE DIVINE MOTHER
MERGES INTO HERSELF
HE'S RIGHT BETWEEN THE ☯ TWO SIDES OF THE COIN
HE'S RIGHT AT THAT PLACE
HE GOES INTO ONE-WITH-IT-ALL INTO THE VOID
& HE COMES BACK INTO FORM
IN ORDER TO   LOVE   IT ALL & THEN
THROUGH HIS LOVE HE GOES BACK INTO IT AGAIN

IT'S LIKE MAKING LOVE TO SOME BODY
& YOU PICK YOUR FACE UP FROM
YOUR LOVER IN ORDER TO COME DOWN
TO EXPERIENCE AREN'T WE HAVING A BALL?
& THEN YOU GO BACK INTO ONE-NESS

SUCH A ZEN BEING DOES THAT WITH EVERY BREATH
BETWEEN EACH BREATH——1
& THEN THE BREATH OF——2

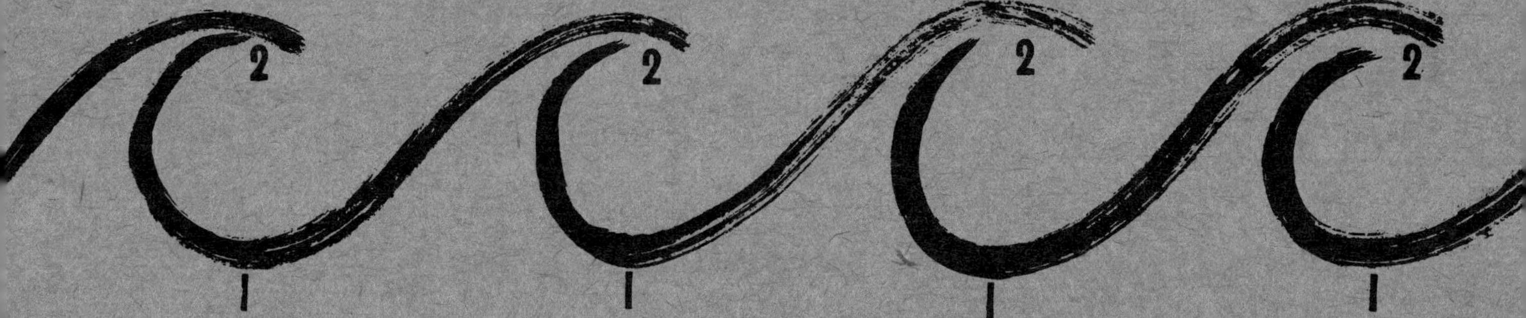

2   2   2   2

HE IS ETERNALLY IN THAT PLACE
HE'S IN WHAT IS KNOWN AS
SAHAJ SAMADHI

ॐ 71

HE'S RIGHT AT THE EDGE
HE STAYS AT THAT EDGE
AND THAT'S WHY HE STAYS
IN HIS BODY . . .   IF HE
JUST STAYED IN THE VOID
THE BODY (AFTER 21 DAYS)
JUST FALLS AWAY
THERE'S NO EGO LEFT
TO HOLD IT TOGETHER
THAT'S THE RULE OF THE GAME
IF YOU'RE WONDERING WHAT HAPPENS.
SOME BEINGS DO THAT
THEY GO INTO SAMADHI
AND THEY'VE FINISHED WITH THEIR
BODIES AND THEY JUST LEAVE THEM.

AND THEN THERE ARE OTHERS
(THERE ARE SOME VERY FAR OUT STORIES IN INDIA)
THERE ARE OTHERS WHO LEAVE A THIN,
VERY, VERY THIN THREAD — OF EGO.

THERE'S ONE BEING WHO FOR TWENTY
YEARS WAS LOCKED UP IN A CAVE:
AND EVERY YEAR HIS DEVOTEES OPENED
THE CAVE. ONCE A YEAR THEY'D GO IN
TO HAVE HIS DARSHAN. THERE WAS
NO FOOD. NOTHING. AND HE LOOKED
LIKE A CORPSE EXCEPT THAT HIS HAIR
KEPT GROWING AND HIS NAILS KEPT GROW-
ING ... FOR TWENTY YEARS ...
HE WAS NOT HANGING OUT WITH MUCH
HE WAS JUST LEAVING A SUBTLE
THREAD TO KEEP

IN CONTACT.

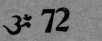

EVERYTHING HE SAID WAS STRAIGHT YOU
UNDERSTAND? ALL THAT STUFF IN THE BIBLE IS
REALLY STRAIGHT. LOOK WHAT HAPPENED TO
SAUL OF TARSUS (FOR GODS SAKE) THERE HE WAS
RIDING ALONG ON THE DESERT ON HIS HORSE OR
CAMEL OR SOMETHING AND A VOICE SAID TO HIM
WHY ARE YOU PERSECUTING ME?
(HE WAS OUT IN THE HOT SUN AND YOU KNOW....) HE FLIPPED OUT
HE WENT FLYING OFF HIS HORSE AND FELL
ON THE GROUND WHAT DO YOU WANT OF ME?"

START MY CHURCH!

"GO TO THE NEXT TOWN AND YOULL BE
INSTRUCTED" THATS WHAT HE HEARD AND HE
WENT THE WHOLE TRIP AND THATS AN ASTRAL
TRIP. A VERY GROOVY ASTRAL TRIP.

3:73

& THAT'S WHAT THE BIBLE IS:
AN ASTRAL STORY
A VERY GROOVY ASTRAL STORY
.....AT ONE LEVEL

I CAN FEEL
THE HORROR IN SOMEBODY
HE'S SAYING.....
HE'S SAYING.....

IT'S A GOOD ASTRAL STORY
BUT ILLUSIONS ARE ILLUSIONS

IT'S
HERE

IN THE SOUND OF THE TAMBOURA
IN SOUND

IN THE BEGINNING WAS

THE
WORD

ॐ74

READY

IT'S A COMBINATION OF THINGS THAT MAKE
YOU READY TO SEE THE GURU. THERE ARE
MANY PEOPLE WHO COME TO SEE MAHARAJ-JI
AND THEY JUST SEE A LITTLE OLD MAN WITH
A BLANKET.
      CAN YOU IMAGINE THE HORROR?
THIS HAPPENED TO TWO PEOPLE WHO HEARD
ME & FIGURED OUT WHERE THE GURU MUST
BE THROUGH LOGICAL DEDUCTION & WENT
TO INDIA & WENT RUSHING TO HIS FEET &
FOUND A LITTLE OLD MAN IN A BLANKET
      WHO THREW THEM OUT
      IMAGINE WHAT THAT MUST FEEL LIKE!
BECAUSE YOU CAN SEE THE DIFFERENCE IN THEIR
MINDS & WHAT IT WAS THEY HAD A MODEL OF—
THE MODEL WAS WHAT THEY SEARCHED FOR
      IT WAS THEIR OWN THOUGHT PRO-
      CESS WHICH KEPT THEM FROM SEEING

ॐ75

TWO THINGS ARE REQUIRED:
ONE IS: VAIRAGYA
THE FALLING A WAY OF WORLDLINESS....
...THE RETURN OF INNOCENCE....

THAT MEANS
YOU'RE STARTING TO HAVE ENOUGH
OF ALL THAT. YOU SEE THAT EVERYTHING YOU'RE
GOING TO EXERIENCE THROUGH YOUR SENSES
AND EVERYTHING YOU'RE GOING TO KNOW THROUGH
YOUR THINKING MIND IS NOT GOING TO BE ENOUGH.
AND WORLDY THINGS BEGIN TO APPEAR
LIKE DROSS INSTEAD OF GOLD...

NOT TOTALLY   JUST
IT BEGINS TO HAPPEN. IT'S FALLING AWAY

MY TEACHER SAID:
THE VEIL FALLS AWAY LIKE THE
                    SKIN OF A SNAKE

    THE EGO THINS LIKE CLOUDS

UNTIL ONLY A TRANSPARENT LAYER REMAINS

THE OTHER THING THAT'S REQUIRED IS THE
            PURE SEEKING

THE PURITY OF THE FAITH

            THERE IS AS MUCH FAITH IN YOU
HERE   IN US   AT THIS MOMENT

        AS ANYWHERE IN INDIA

            ॐ 76

WHERE THERE IS FAITH
THERE IS THE PRESENCE OF
THE GURU
HE
IS
IT ALL
HE IS ALL YOUR IMPURITIES
HE IS ALL YOUR CORRUPTION
THERE HE IS SMILING AT YOU THROUGH THEM
★ SAYING ★
& THIS TOO !
◣ HE SEES ◢
HE UNDERSTANDS
TOTAL COMPASSION
TOTAL COMPASSION MEANS
YOU ARE THE UNIVERSE

YOU ARE ALL FORM
YOU ARE THE BREATH
YOU ARE THE RIVER
YOU ARE THE VOID
YOU ARE THE DESIRE
TO BE ENLIGHTENED
YOU ARE ENLIGHTENED

ॐ71

THAT'S WHO HE IS. THAT'S WHO, WHAT, A GURU IS.
SO ANY CONCEPT YOU CAN HAVE
OF ANY RELATION TO A GURU
OBVIOUSLY IS A HYPE
HOW CAN YOU RELATE TO SOMETHING
WHICH IS ALREADY YOU
& EVERYTHING YOU'VE EVER RELATED TO
OR COULD RELATE TO ....
HOW ARE YOU GOING TO TALK ABOUT IT ?
I MET HIM   WHO ? WHAT ?
I'M GOING TO LOOK FOR THE GURU
HOW ABSURD !

YOU ARE IT

IT'S REALLY JUST ANOTHER COP-OUT
TO BE SEARCHING FOR THE GURU

HE'S YOUR
JUST BITE YOUR   FINGERNAIL
& YOU'RE EATING   FINGERNAIL
                    HIM ALIVE

WHEN YOU KNOW
HOW TO LISTEN

EVERYBODY
IS
THE GURU

SPEAKING TO YOU
IT'S RIGHT HERE.... ALWAYS

ॐ78

HERE & NOW

I KEEP DOING TH[...] BECAUSE I DON'T
THINK PEOPLE [...] THOROUGHLY GROK
THE FACT THAT [...] IS WHERE IT ALL
IS. AFTER YOU [...] FINISH THE WHOLE
THING & YOU'VE [...] VIBRATED YOUR SPINE
FOR YEARS & DON[...] YOUR PRANAYAM &
MEDITATED FOR [...] YEARS & YEARS &
SAT IN A CAVE & [...] ANTS HAVE EATEN
YOUR ARMS & LEGS [...] YOU ARE.

YOU'RE RIGHT **HERE** AGAIN ....&

WHAT BLOWS YOUR MIND IS

YOU WERE **HERE** ALL THE TIME

& IT'S SUCH A COSMIC JOKE

IT'S SO FUNNY YOUR STRUGGL-

ING SO TO GET **HERE**

AT THIS MOMENT IF YOU SET THE ALARM
TO GET UP AT 3:47 THIS MORNING AND WHEN
THE ALARM RINGS AND YOU GET UP AND TURN
IT OFF AND SAY: WHAT TIME IS IT? YOU'D
SAY: NOW HERE!
NOW WHERE AM I? HERE!

❀ THEN GO BACK TO SLEEP ❀❀❀
GET UP AT 9:00 TOMORROW. WHERE AM I??

HERE! WHAT TIME IS IT? NOW!
TRY 4:32 THREE WEEKS FROM NEXT THURS.

BY GOD
IT IS — THERE'S NO GETTING AWAY FROM IT —
THAT'S THE WAY IT IS
THAT'S THE
ETERNAL PRESENT

YOU FINALLY FIGURE OUT THAT IT'S
ONLY THE CLOCK THATS GOING AROUND ....
IT'S DOING ITS THING BUT YOU — YOU'RE SITTING

HERE
RIGHT NOW
ALWAYS

ॐ80

NOBODY IS GOING ANYWHERE
NOBODY IS COMING FROM ANYWHERE
WE'RE ALL HERE
WE'RE ALL HERE
IN ETERNAL TIME & SPACE
WE'RE ALWAYS GOING TO BE HERE
WE'RE JUST DOING LILA RASA
THE DIVINE DANCE WE'RE DANCING

& DANCING & DANCING
DANCE AFTER
DANCE
IN ONE BODY
IN ANOTHER BODY
& WE'RE ALL HERE
WE'RE ALL STAYING RIGHT HERE
3 · 81

NOTHING TO DO

THERE
IS
NOWHERE
TO
GO

&

THERE
IS
NOTHING
TO
DO

& WE'RE GOING TO KEEP COMING
TO KNOW ONE ANOTHER
MORE & MORE FREE OF BEING IDENTIFIED WITH ANY VEIL
WE'RE GOING TO SEE
MORE & MORE OF OTHER BEINGS
LESS IDENTIFIED WITH THEIR VEILS
AS YOU FIND THE LIGHT IN YOU, YOU BEGIN TO SEE THE
LIGHT IN EVERYONE ELSE
AS YOU FIND GOD IN YOURSELF THERE IS GOD EVERYWHERE

SUCH A SIMPLE OBVIOUS SEQUENCE OF STUFF TO DO

SOMEBODY SAYS OH I TRY MEDITATING & I CAN'T & I JUST...

I'M AFRAID I'M NOT READY & I'VE GOT TO GO...

GREAT ☆ SURE MAN ☆ GO ☆ GO AHEAD ☆ OF COURSE

WHAT ELSE IS THERE TO DO?

GOING BACK INTO THE WORLD IT'S CALLED

IT'S A GOOD STEP

AM I GOING BACKWARD OR FORWARD?

I CAN'T DO EITHER OF THEM ☆ I CAN'T GO BACKWARD & I CAN'T GO FORWARD

AND I CAN'T STAND STILL 382 ALL OF IT IS IRRELEVANT

WE'RE ALL JUST CAUGHT IN THE DELUSION
ALL OF US CAUGHT IN THE
ILLUSION
BEING AWARE OF IT AS ILLUSION
AND YET SO MUCH IN IT !

IF YOU HAVE EVER WATCHED A BEAUTIFUL ZEN MONK ,
A VERY OLD MONK WHO IS
REALLY THERE,
OR HERE,
REALLY HERE , WHICHEVER...
YOU WATCH HIM.....
HE'S COOKING FOOD
HE'S LIFTING STONES
HE'S MOVING
YOU WATCH HIM WALK AND ITS LIKE
NOBODY'S WALKING...

THE LEGS ARE GOING,
AND THE WHOLE THING IS HAPPENING BUT

NOTHING IS HAPPENING
NO MATTER
WHAT
IS HAPPENING!

AND THATS WHAT BLOWS YOUR MIND WHEN WE GET OUT
OF THE KINDS OF HEADS WE'VE GOT GOING THAT
DON'T ALLOW US TO
REALLY UNDERSTAND
HOW THIS CAN BE.
ॐ83

RETURN TO THE ROOTS

YOU LIVE OUT YOUR KARMA.

THE BEST I CAN TELL YOU ABOUT KARMA IS:

IF YOU ARE

PURE SPIRIT

YOU ARE <u>NOT</u> MATTER! .... YOU ARE THAT

ETERNAL SPIRIT...

WELL :

IF EACH OF US IS THAT VERY OLD BEING..

AND NOT THIS YOUNG BODY,

OR THIS BODY THAT IS GOING

THROUGH THIS LIFE...

WHY DON'T WE

REMEMBER?

WHY DON'T WE REMEMBER IT ALL ??

WHY CAN'T WE READ

THE ENTIRE AKASHIC RECORD ??

• BECAUSE OF OUR ATTACHMENTS TO

THE PHYSICAL PLANE OF REALITY...

• BECAUSE OF THE POWER OF OUR IDENTIFICATION

WITH OUR OWN BODY-SENSES

3:84 AND THOUGHTS.

IF YOU COULD GO INTO A MEDITATION ROOM
CLOSE UP YOUR EARS · SIT DOWN · CENTER
GO · IN · IN · IN · IN
FURTHER IN·OH MUCH FURTHER IN·OH YOU'VE JUST BEGUN
KEEP GOING BACK IN
DON'T LINGER TO SMELL THE PRETTY SUNFLOWER
DON'T LINGER TO HOLD ON TO THE ECSTACY OF BLISS
KEEP GOING IN BEHIND THE SENSES·BEHIND YOUR THOUGHTS
AND IF YOU CAN GO BACK IN FAR ENOUGH YOU WILL SEE
EVERYTHING YOU'VE IDENTIFIED WITH "HIM"
YOU WILL SEE .... YOUR OWN PERSONALITY·YOUR OWN BODY
YOUR OWN LIFE DRAMA.....IT'S VERY AWESOME

THE POINT IS WE HAVE GONE OUT & OUT & OUT

& WE HAVE SOUGHT & SOUGHT & FOUND MUCH

BUT IT HASN'T BEEN ENOUGH !

& NOW BY MERELY TURNING THE PROCESS INWARD

YOU GO IN & IN & IN

UNTIL YOU COME TO THE PLACE WHERE

GURU RIMPOCHE SITS

ॐ 85

AND WHAT IS THIS PLACE?
HINDUS CALL IT THE ATMAN
AND WHAT IS THE ATMAN?

THE BHAGAVADAM, ONE OF THE HOLY BOOKS OF INDIA
SAYS:

THE ATMAN OR DIVINE SELF
IS SEPARATE FROM THE BODY
IT IS ONE
WITHOUT A SECOND
PURE, SELF-LUMINOUS
WITHOUT ATTRIBUTES
FREE
ALL-PERVADING
IT IS THE ETERNAL WITNESS
BLESSED IS HE WHO KNOWS THIS ATMAN
FOR, THOUGH AN EMBODIED BEING
HE SHALL BE FREE
FROM THE CHANGES AND QUALITIES

PERTAINING TO THE BODY
HE ALONE IS EVER UNITED WITH ME

THIS IS THE PLACE OF PURE BEING
THAT INNER PLACE WHERE YOU DWELL
YOU JUST BE. THERE IS NOTHING TO BE
DONE IN THAT PLACE. FROM THAT PLACE
THEN, IT ALL HAPPENS, IT MANIFESTS IN
PERFECT HARMONY WITH THE UNIVERSE.
BECAUSE YOU ARE THE LAWS OF THE UNIVERSE
YOU ARE THE LAWS OF THE UNIVERSE!

ॐ 86

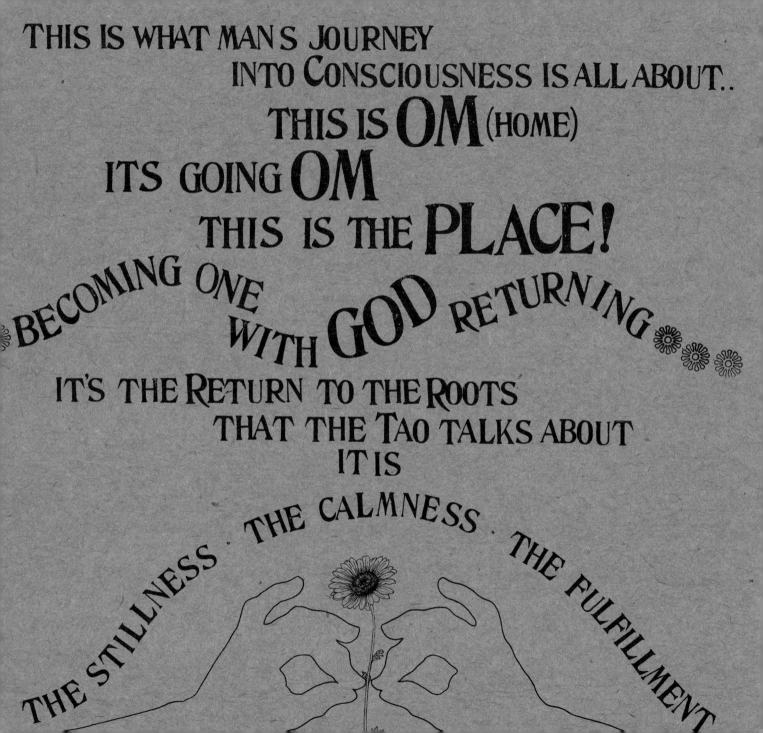

THIS IS WHAT MAN'S JOURNEY
INTO CONSCIOUSNESS IS ALL ABOUT..
THIS IS OM (HOME)
IT'S GOING OM
THIS IS THE PLACE!
BECOMING ONE WITH GOD RETURNING
IT'S THE RETURN TO THE ROOTS
THAT THE TAO TALKS ABOUT
IT IS
THE STILLNESS · THE CALMNESS · THE FULFILLMENT

WHEN YOU MAKE LOVE AND EXPERIENCE
THE ECSTACY OF UNITY...

THAT'S THE PLACE!

WHEN YOU EXPERIENCE A GREAT ACHIEVEMENT,
AND YOU FEEL A MOMENT OF EXHILARATION...

THAT'S THE PLACE!

WHEN YOU SEE A MOMENT OF POETRY IN A FLOWER
OR IN WORDS ◦ OR IN ART ◦ THE WAY ITS SUPPOSED TO BE..

THIS IS THE PLACE!

RIGHT HERE!

❀ IT'S BUDDHA CONSCIOUSNESS ❀

❀ IT'S CHRIST CONSCIOUSNESS ❀

JESUS SAYS:

I AND MY FATHER ARE ONE

WHEN BUDDHA SAYS:
YOU GIVE UP ATTACHMENT AND
YOU FINISH WITH THE ILLUSION

THIS IS THE PLACE!

ॐ·87

STILL
YOU DO YOUR THING
LIVE YOUR LIFE IN THE WORLD
THE WATER GOES ON DOWN THE STREAM
YOU CHOP THE WOOD AND CARRY THE WATER
YOU DO YOUR THING   YOUR MIND DOES ITS THING
YOUR SENSES THEIR THING BUT
YOU

ARE NOT ATTACHED
BECAUSE YOU SAT IN FRONT OF THE CANDLE FLAME
UNTIL THERE WAS JUST YOU AND THE CANDLE FLAME
& THEN FINALLY
YOU EXTRICATED YOURSELF FROM THE ATTACHMENT
TO YOUR OWN THOUGHTS
TO THE TYRANNY OF THE "DRUNKEN MONKEY"
EVEN TO THE THOUGHTS OF I & CANDLE FLAME

NOT SO THAT YOU WOULD NEVER THINK AGAIN

I MEAN FEW PEOPLE WHO KNOW ME

DON'T APPRECIATE THE FACT THAT I THINK

& HAVE KEEN DISCRIMINATION & I HAVE NOT LOST MY MIND

& I AM A SOPHISTICATED AWARE BEING

& YET

BEHIND EVERY WORD

& BEHIND IT ALL

IS A MANTRA

GOING INSIDE MY HEAD

IN WHICH I AM SITTING

CALMLY WATCHING THIS 3:88 WHOLE DRAMA UNFOLD

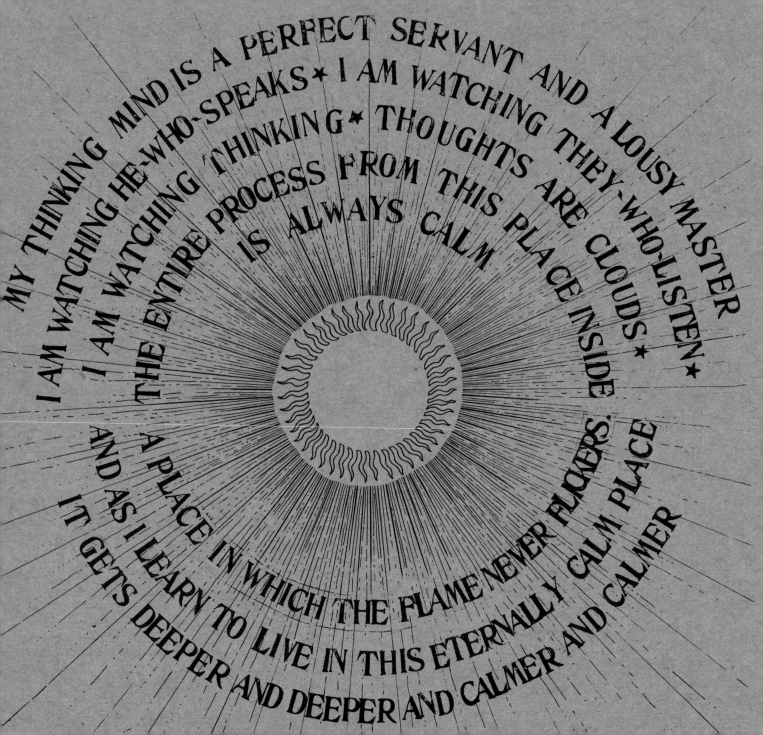

MY THINKING MIND IS A PERFECT SERVANT AND A LOUSY MASTER * I AM WATCHING THEY-WHO-LISTEN * I AM WATCHING HE-WHO-SPEAKS * I AM WATCHING THINKING * THOUGHTS ARE CLOUDS * I AM WATCHING THINKING * THOUGHTS ARE CLOUDS * THE ENTIRE PROCESS FROM THIS PLACE INSIDE IS ALWAYS CALM

A PLACE IN WHICH THE FLAME NEVER FLICKERS * AND AS I LEARN TO LIVE IN THIS ETERNALLY CALM PLACE IT GETS DEEPER AND DEEPER AND CALMER AND CALMER

AND WISER AND WISER
AND LIGHTER AND LIGHTER
AND I AM MORE LOVE AND I BECOME MORE AND MORE

LIKE THE SUN

JUST THE PROCESS OF
CALMING, CENTERING
CENTERING, CALMING
EXTRICATING MYSELF FROM THE DRAMA *

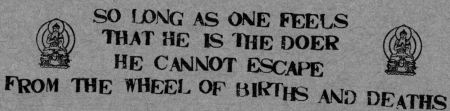

SO LONG AS ONE FEELS
THAT HE IS THE DOER
HE CANNOT ESCAPE
FROM THE WHEEL OF BIRTHS AND DEATHS

THIS DOESN'T MEAN THAT I'M LYING IN
BED DOING NOTHING * THAT'S DRAMA
* AS MUCH AS THIS BOOK IS DRAMA ***
ॐ 89

DRAMA IS DRAMA IS DRAMA IS DRAMA
DESIRE IS DRAMA   BREATHING IS DRAMA
THOUGHT IS DRAMA   EMOTIONS ARE DRAMA
                          ALL FORM IS DRAMA

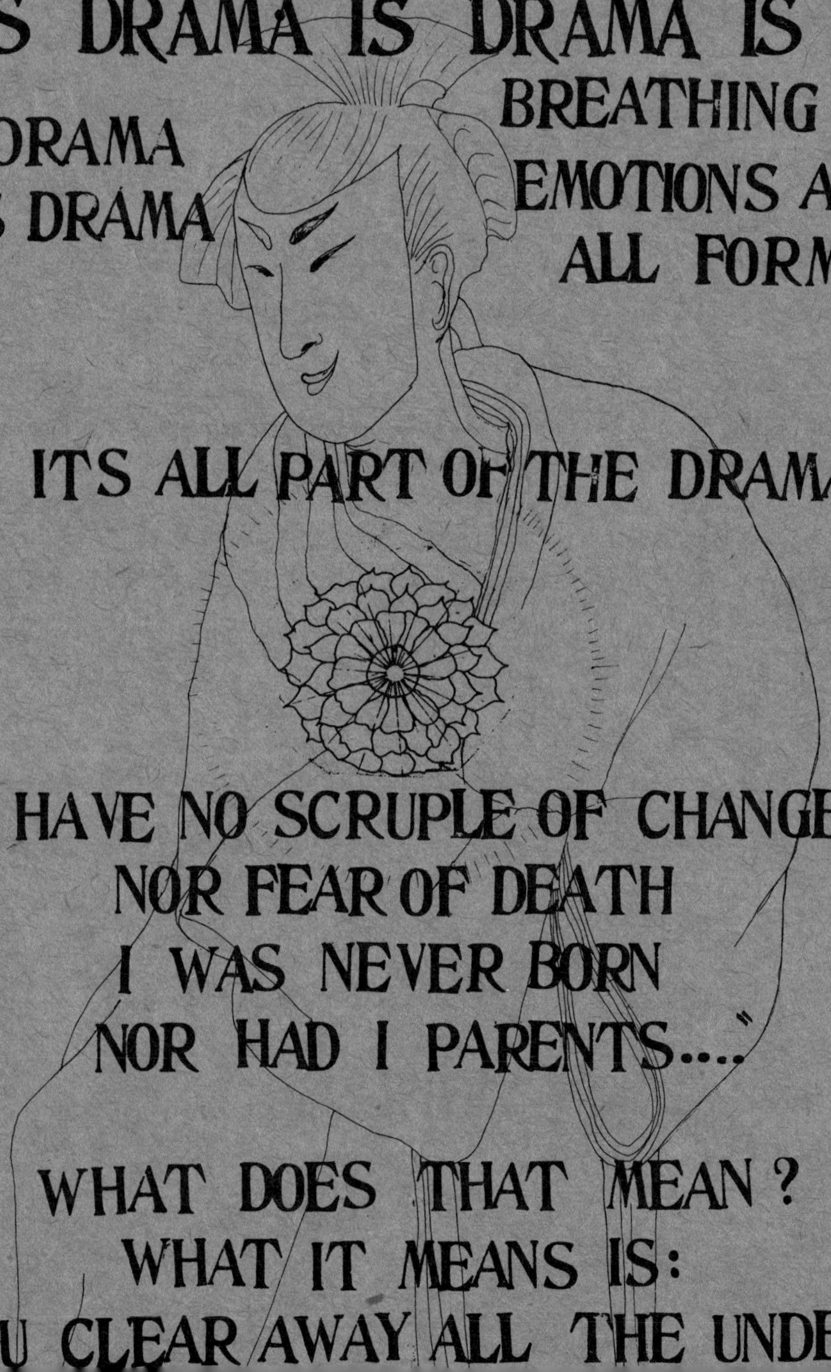

ITS ALL PART OF THE DRAMA

"I HAVE NO SCRUPLE OF CHANGE
NOR FEAR OF DEATH
I WAS NEVER BORN
NOR HAD I PARENTS...."

WHAT DOES THAT MEAN ?
WHAT IT MEANS IS:
WHEN YOU CLEAR AWAY ALL THE UNDERBRUSH

WHEN YOU GO BACK AND BACK
NOT FOR THE FUN OF IT
OR FOR THE POWERS INVOLVED
BUT TO GO BACK TO BE WHO YOU REALLY ARE

WHO YOU ARE TURNS OUT TO BE SPIRIT

TURNS OUT NOT TO BE MATTER AT ALL

NO MATTER
NEVER MIND
NO MIND
NEVER MATTER
EITHER WAY IT WORKS
ॐ 90

ROUND TRIP

MIND CREATES MAT
TER. THE CAUSAL
PLANE IS   THE
WORLD OF IDEAS
THAT CREATES
THE UNIVERSE
RIGHT AT THE TOP
OF THE CAUSAL
PLANE IS WHAT WE CALL THE GODHEAD ITS THE FIRST
PLACE INTO THE UNIVERSE OF FORM ITS THE FIRST
WORLD OF FORM ITS THE PLACE WHERE THE MIND
THAT S GOD MANIFESTED INTO THE UNIVERSE HIS

THOUGHT MANIFESTED INTO ALL THE LOWER LEVEL
OF THE CAUSAL PLANE ALL THE ASTRAL PLANES AND THE
PHYSICAL PLANE AND WHEN YOU GO BACK BACK BACK
YOU GO TO THAT PLACE WHERE YOU BECOME ONE WITH THE
GODHEAD YOU ARE
GOD YOU ARE THE ID
EA THAT LIES BEHIND
THE UNIVERSE YOU
ARE LITERALLY IT
YOU'RE NOT MAKING
BELIEVE YOU'RE IT
YOU ARE IT

AND THE FUNNY THING IS
YOU'RE STILL NOT FINISHED
AND AS FAR AS THE BUDDHIST IS CONCERNED
YOU HAVEN'T EVEN BEGUN THE TRIP
YOU'RE STILL HUNG UP ON FORM

BECAUSE HE SAYS
BABY
IT'S ALL ILLUSION
NO MATTER HOW
GROOVY IT GETS
THE PHYSICAL PLANE
IS OBVIOUSLY
AN ILLUSION
ALL A DREAM
YOU GO TO BED
AT NIGHT
AND DREAM

YOU NOTICE
ABOUT YOUR DREAMS
THEY'RE VERY REAL
AND YET THEY DON'T
HAVE ANY SUBSTANCE
ON THE
PHYSICAL PLANE
THAT'S THE
ASTRAL PLANE
YOU'RE DREAMING
ON THE ASTRAL PLANE

AT THE POINT
OF PURE IDEAS
SOMETIMES VERY HIGH
PHYSICISTS OR POETS
TOUCH PURE IDEA
SOMETIMES MUSIC, ART,
A VASE, A HEIROGLYPH
OR SOMETHING
GETS SO ESSENCY
YOU FEEL
YOU ARE TOUCHING
GOD

BY BEING
IN CONNECTION WITH
THAT PIECE OF ART
BECAUSE IT'S PURE IDEA
IT'S THE IDEA
OF VASENESS
IT'S CAUSAL PLANE
THE MIND
AT THE CAUSAL PLANE
CREATED THAT VASE
THAT PLACE OF PURE
IDEA

IT'S THE PLACE WHERE YIN AND YANG MANIFEST
IT'S THE PLACE WHERE DUALITY EXISTS THE FIRST PLACE
INTO FORM FROM THE IMMANENT DUALITY IN THE UNMANIFEST
FROM THE FORMLESS YOU COME INTO THAT PLACE WHERE
THERE IS ENERGY BECOMING FORM
ॐ 92

IN ORDER TO BECOME
A FULLY REALIZED BEING
YOU MUST DELIGHT IN THE EXQUISITENESS
AT EVERY SINGLE LEVEL
YOU MUST TAKE JOY
IN YOUR MALENESS
OR FEMALENESS
AT THE SAME MOMENT THAT YOU REALIZE
THAT YOU ARE BOTH MALE & FEMALE
IT'S THAT FAR OUT!

BUT THEN YOU GO THROUGH
THE FINAL DOOR
AND YOU GO FROM

FORM
INTO

THE
FORMLESS

INTO THE VOID
INTO THE BEYOND THE BEYOND
WHEN YOU HAVE CROSSED
THE OCEAN OF SAMSKARA
THE OCEAN OF ILLUSION
THE OCEAN OF ATTACHMENT
CALL IT WHAT YOU WILL
IT'S THE SAME OCEAN
WHEN YOU HAVE CROSSED
THROUGH ALL FORM
YOU ENTER THE STATE OF

FORMLESSNESS

IT IS ETERNALLY QUIET
IT IS ETERNALLY QUIET
IT NEVER WAS

ॐ93

"PUSH FAR ENOUGH INTO THE VOID
HOLD FAST ENOUGH TO QUIETNESS
AND OF THE TEN THOUSAND THINGS
NON BUT CAN BE WORKED ON BY YOU
I HAVE BEHELD THEM WITHER THEY GO BACK
SEE ALL THINGS HOWSOEVER THEY FLOURISH
RETURN TO THE ROOTS FROM WHICH THEY GREW

THIS RETURN TO THE ROOTS IS CALLED
QUIETNESS
QUIETNESS IS CALLED
SUBMISSION TO FATE
WHAT HAS SUBMITTED TO FATE
BECOMES PART OF THE
ALWAYS SO
TO KNOW THE ALWAYS SO IS TO BE
ILLUMINED
NOT TO KNOW IT
MEANS TO GO BLINDLY TO DISASTER"

SO SAYS LAO TZU IN THE TAO TE CHING

U GO YOU'VE GOT TO GO THE WHOLE TRIP
ALL THE WAY TO THE BACK
BEFORE YOU GET TO THE PLACE
WHERE YOU SEE THAT BEHIND ALL THIS
THERE IS ALL THIS IN ITS

OM

IN ITS UNMANIFEST FORM
ALWAYS
ETERNALLY
YOU PERCEIVE THAT
NOTHING
IS REALLY HAPPENING AT ALL
NOTHING
EVER HAPPENS
NOTHING
IS GOING TO HAPPEN
THERE'S
NOTHING
YOU'VE GOT TO DO
THERE'S NO DOER
TO DO IT ANYWAY
3·94

AND THEN: YOU'RE IN THE VOID
        THEN THE BUDDHA NATURE SEES
THERE ARE MANY BEINGS WHOSE VEILS
ARE VERY THIN AND YOU CAN COME BACK
AND TEACH THEM THROUGH YOUR BEING
THAT'S THE BODHISATTVA ROLE. BECAUSE
YOU FINALLY UNDERSTAND THAT: THOUGH
IT IS ALL ILLUSION...IT NEVER WAS AND
NEVER WILL BE...AT EVERY LEVEL AT WHICH
YOU EXIST YOU'RE PART OF EVERYBODY ELSE.
BECAUSE: IT'S ALL   ONE BEING

    REALLY !
THAT'S THE BODHISATTVA PROBLEM.
SO: WHAT HAPPENS IS:
    YOU GO ALL THE WAY OUT
    AND THEN YOU COME BACK TO
          HERE

"HE WHO CLINGS TO THE VOID AND NEGLECTS COMPASSION DOES NOT REACH THE HIGHEST STAGE. BUT HE WHO PRACTICES ONLY COMPASSION DOES NOT GAIN RELEASE FROM THE TOILS OF EXISTENCE. HE HOWEVER WHO IS STRONG IN THE PRACTICE OF BOTH REMAINS NEITHER IN SAMSARA NOR IN NIRVANA. HE NEITHER REMAINS IN THE VOID NOR IN THE WORLD."

ॐ 95

THE FINAL PLACE THAT THE GAME LEADS TO IS:

WHERE YOU LIVE CONSCIOUSLY
IN ALL OF IT

WHICH IS IN NOTHING

YOU ARE ETERNAL

YOU HAVE FINISHED PERISHING

THERE IS NO FEAR OF DEATH BECAUSE

THERE IS NO DEATH

IT S JUST A TRANSFORMATION

AN ILLUSION

AND YET, SEEING ALL THAT, YOU STILL
CHOP WOOD AND CARRY WATER .

YOU STILL DO YOUR THING .

YOU FLOW IN HARMONY WITH THE UNIVERSE.

YOU ARE BEYOND MORALITY
AND YET YOUR ACTIONS ARE TOTALLY MORAL
BECAUSE THAT'S THE HARMONY OF THE UNIVERSE.
YOU SEE THAT TO DO ANYTHING WITH ATTACHMENT.
WITH DESIRE...WITH ANGER..GREED..LUST...FEAR...
IS ONLY CREATING MORE KARMA, WHICH IS
KEEPING YOU IN THE GAME... ON THE WHEEL
OF BIRTH AND DEATH

ONCE YOU SEE THROUGH THAT...

DESIRES CAN'T HELP BUT FALL AWAY

BUT AT FIRST WHEN YOU
SEE—
YOU WANT TO RUN DOWN THE STREETS
SHOUTING—
SPREADING THE GOOD NEWS—
RUN DOWN THE AISLES OF CHURCHES
YELLING:

LISTEN TO THOSE WORDS YOU'RE SINGING!!

IT'S REALLY HERE! THEY'RE ALL TRUE!
YOU'RE SINGING ABOUT IT ALL
"JUST LIKE THE BOOK SAYS"!

DON'T BE PSYCHOTIC: WATCH IT. WATCH IT.
ॐ 97

THAT PSYCHOSIS BUSINESS IS AN INTERESTING BUSINESS
IF YOU GO THROUGH THE   DOORWAY TOO FAST
AND YOU'RE NOT READY
FOR IT YOU'RE BOUND HAND
AND FOOT AND THROWN INTO
OUTER DARKNESS☀

YOU MAY LAND ANYWHERE AND
LOTS OF PEOPLE END UP IN
MENTAL HOSPITALS☀
 THE REASON THEY DO IS:

THEY WENT THROUGH THE DOOR
WITH THE ▮▮▮ CO ON   AND:

NOW! I'VE BEEN INVITED TO THE WEDDING FEAST

I MEAN DIG ME! SAM JONES!

THEY DON'T UNDERSTAND THAT YOU GOTTA DIE TO BE BORN

THAT ONLY WHEN YOU HAVE BEEN BORN AGAIN DO YOU ENTER THE KINGDOM OF HEAVEN SO, THEY'VE GONE IN ON THE FIRST ROUND AND WHAT HAPPENS IS THEY GO ON A HUGE EGO TRIP AND IT'S CALLED: THE MESSIANIC COMPLEX IT'S CALLED: PARANOIA DELUSIONS OF GRANDEUR

SAM JONES IN HEAVEN! SAM JONES STANDING ON THE RIGHT SIDE OF THE LORD THERE'S THE LORD AND THERE'S GABRIEL AND THERE'S SAM JONES

98

I HAVE A RELATIVE WHO IS IN A MENTAL
HOSPITAL HE THINKS HE IS CHRIST
WELL, THAT'S GROOVY I AM CHRIST ALSO
BUT HE DOESN'T THINK I AM CHRIST HE
THINKS HE IS CHRIST BECAUSE IT HAP-
PENED TO HIM AND HE TOOK HIS EGO WITH
HIM SO HE SAYS: I'M SPECIAL AND WHEN
I SAY TO HIM: SURE MAN YOU'RE CHRIST
AND I'M CHRIST TOO HE SAYS: YOU DON'T
UNDERSTAND AND WHEN HE'S OUT HE STEALS
CARS AND THINGS LIKE THAT BECAUSE HE
NEEDS THEM BECAUSE HE'S CHRIST AND THAT'S
ALL RIGHT SO THEY LOCK HIM UP HE SAY'S:
I DON'T KNOW... ME... I'M A RESPONSIBLE
MEMBER OF SOCIETY I GO TO CHURCH ME
THEY PUT IN A MENTAL HOSPITAL YOU'RE
FREE YOU'VE GOT A BEARD YOU WEAR A
DRESS YOU

AS LONG AS THERE IS AN UP DOWN IN YOUR

HEAD: **OUTER DARKNESS**

AS LONG AS YOU'RE IN THE WORLD OF YIN YANG ☯

OUTER DARKNESS

T TAKES A LOT OF PURIFICATION

PURIFICATION OF WHAT?

PURIFICATION OF THOUGHT

PURIFICATION OF BODY

FREEDOM FROM ATTACHMENT

AND AFTER A LONG TIME OF GOING UP AND DOWN WITH-

OUT UNDERSTANDING WHY I WAS GOING UP AND DOWN

OR HOW TO STOP IT

SLOWLY . . . SLOWLY . . . IT DAWNED ON ME

NOW WHY DID I KEEP TRYING?

THE ANSWER IS VERY SIMPLE AND ALMOST ALL
OF YOU KNOW THE ANSWER ALREADY
THE ANSWER IS: ONCE THE SEED HAS
BEEN PLANTED
ONCE YOU HAVE BEEN BORN AGAIN

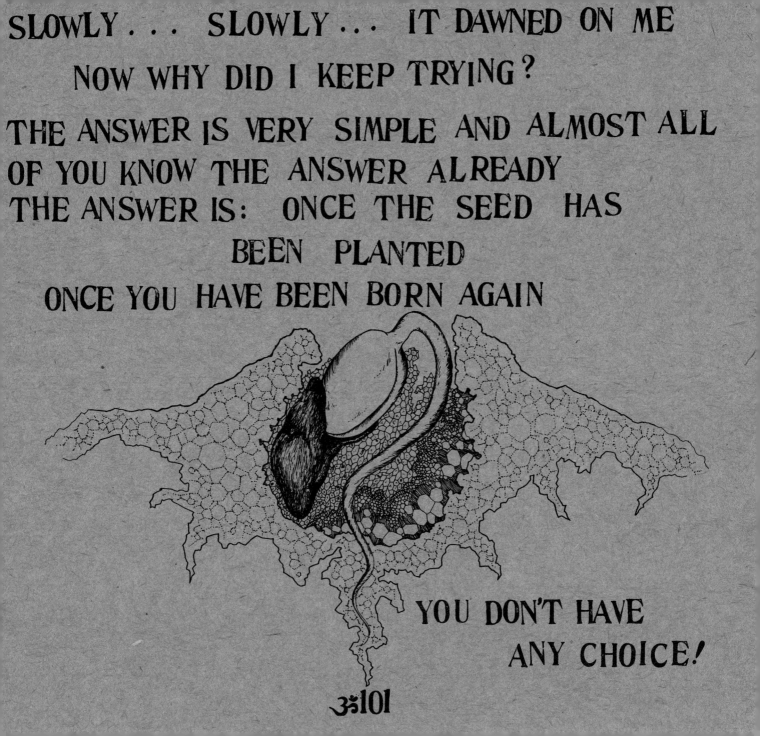

YOU DON'T HAVE
ANY CHOICE!

ॐ101

THE NEXT MESSAGE

IS WHERE YOU ARE WHEN YOU HEAR THE NEXT MESSAGE. WHENEVER YOU'RE READY YOU'LL HEAR THE NEXT MESSAGE.
THE INTERESTING THING IS THERES ALWAYS A NEXT MESSAGE AND ITS ALWAYS AVAILABLE TO YOU. NOW! THATS A HARD ONE!
THE HANDWRITING IS ALWAYS ON THE WALL SAYING:

MAGIC THEATRE
FOR MADMEN ONLY
PRICE OF ADMISSION
YOUR MIND

ALWAYS THERE.
QUESTION IS: CAN YOU SEE IT ?
3:102

FUNNY THING ABOUT ALL THE SECRETS OF THE EAST OR THE SECRETS OF MYSTICISM...

THEY'RE NOT SECRET!

NOBODY'S SAYING "DON'T TELL HIM". THEY'RE TELLING YOU. THEY'RE YELLING IT. THEY'RE SAYING: "EXCEPT YE BE CONVERTED AND BECOME AS LITTLE CHILDREN, YE SHALL NOT ENTER THE KINGDOM OF HEAVEN."
THAT'S A SECRET?

THINK OF HOW MANY TIMES YOU'VE HEARD THAT AND YOU SAY: "YEAH, THAT'S REALLY INTERESTING. THAT'S GREAT. THAT'S THE MINISTER TALKING. HE'S DOING HIS THING. HE'S GOT A LIVING TO EARN. HE'S A GOOD GUY."

THE SECRET IS A SECRET TO YOU BECAUSE OF WHERE YOUR HEAD IS AT.

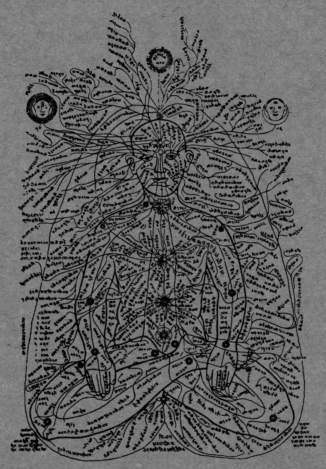

YOUR RECEIVING MECHANISM ISN'T TUNED
FOR THAT PARTICULAR FREQUENCY

ॐ103

IN MY CASE I KEPT
READING THE BOOKS BUT
I DIDN'T UNDERSTAND
THEM. THEY WERE
YELLING THE SECRETS
BUT I COULDN'T HEAR
THEM BECAUSE I WAS
LOOKING AT THEM FROM
THE WRONG ! PLACE !
THAT WAS MY PROBLEM
AND I COULDN'T GET MY
HEAD INTO THE RIGHT PLACE
I STILL WANTED TO KNOW
I KNEW. SEE ? I WAS STILL
WESTERN RATIONAL MAN

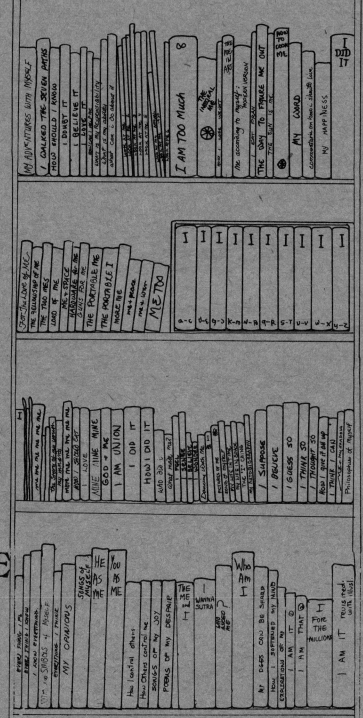

SO I WENT AND I LOOKED
AND LOOKED AND LOOKED
AND AS LONG AS I LOOKED
LIKE A RATIONAL MAN
LOOKING I DIDNT FIND
ANYTHING. I JUST FOUND
MY OWN S H A D O W
ALL THE TIME THATS
ALL YOU EVER FIND:
YOURSELF
YOU ONLY READ TO YOURSELF
YOU ONLY TALK TO YOURSELF
YOU ONLY EVER KNOW YOURSELF
THATS ALL THERE IS !
STRANGELY
ENOUGH !

I SAW THAT MY WHOLE GAME DIDN'T WORK.
IT GAVE ME ALL THE REWARDS THAT SEEMED
TO BE OFFERED BUT IT DIDN'T WORK. THERE
WAS A PLACE IN ME THAT KNEW IT WASN'T
WORKING. I KNEW THERE WAS SOMETHING ELSE
BUT I COULDN'T GET TO IT. AT THAT POINT
I GAVE UP. AND THEN I WAS READY FOR THE
NEXT MESSAGE

WHEN I WENT THROUGH THE DOORWAY I THOUGHT: WOW! IT ISN'T LIKE I THOUGHT AT ALL. I MEAN: IF I AM GOING TO THROUGH A SET OF POWER GAMES AND SENSUAL GRATIFICATIONS WHAT'S THE PAYOFF? THE END IS THAT IT'S GOING TO

SPEND MY LIFE
MANIPULATING
THIS PUNY EGO

END ANYWAY
BECAUSE IT'S ALL
IN TIME

AND SUDDENLY I DIG WHO I AM AT THAT
MOMENT WHEN I M STONED! HIGH! I AM
OUT OF TIME!
I AM   OUT OF SPACE!
BUT BOY! DOES IT FEEL VALID!   DOES IT
FEEL REAL! IT FEELS LIKE THE FIRST
REAL THING THAT'S EVER HAPPENED TO ME!
EVERYTHING ELSE HAD A CERTAIN HUSTLE
LIKE QUALITY TO IT
EXCEPT MY SUFFERING

AM I HE?

I WAS REALLY INTO MY SUFFERING
YOU CAN REALLY GET INTO YOUR SUFFERING
SELF-PITY...THAT'S REAL!
EVERYTHING ELSE MAY GO
BUT BOY! YOU'VE GOT TO SUFFER!
IT'S THE SAME FOR ALL OF US
WE'RE JUST COMING OUT OF THE
DARK NIGHT OF THE PROTESTANT ETHIC

SUFFER BABY!

THAT'S THE ONLY WAY YOU'LL BE GOOD
IT FEELS SO GOOD TO HURT SO BAD!

WE'VE ALL BEEN ON THAT TRIP:
SUFFERING IS GREAT.
IT'S LIKE STRAIGHTENING-BY-FIRE
IT'S PURIFYING
IT'S VERY GOOD
A FUNNY THING...WANT ANOTHER PARADOX?

THIS TRIP
REQUIRES
TOTAL
SUFFERING
BUT:

IT'S GOT TO BE SUFFERING

THAT IS NO SUFFERING

YOU'VE GOT TO GO THE WHOLE SUFFERING TRIP

BUT:

YOU CAN'T BE THE GUY WHO IS SUFFERING.

3:106

DO YOU THINK
THAT WHEN CHRIST IS LYING THERE
AND THEY'RE NAILING THE NAILS IN
HE'S SAYING,"OH MAN, DOES THAT HURT!"? HE'S
PROBABLY LOOKING AT THE GUY WHO'S NAILING HIM
WITH

ABSOLUTE COMPASSION

HE DIGS WHY THE CAT'S DOING IT.
WHAT HE'S STUCK IN
HOW MUCH DUST COVERS HIS EYES
WHY HE'S GOT TO BE DOING IT
THAT'S THE WAY IT IS
HE SAID THE NIGHT BEFORE:
"WELL, TOMORROW IS THE BIG TRIP.
YEAH-RIGHT-THESE ARE THE NAILS
WOW! LOOK AT THAT!"

AM I HE WHO IS BEING PAINED

NO! THAT'S THE THING. ONCE YOU KNOW THAT
THEN: PLEASURE & PAIN
LOSS & GAIN
FAME & SHAME
ARE ALL THE SAME
THEY'RE ALL JUST HAPPENING
ॐ CVII

YOU'RE STANDING

ON A BRIDGE

WATCHING

YOURSELF

GO BY

WOW! LOOK AT THAT!

108

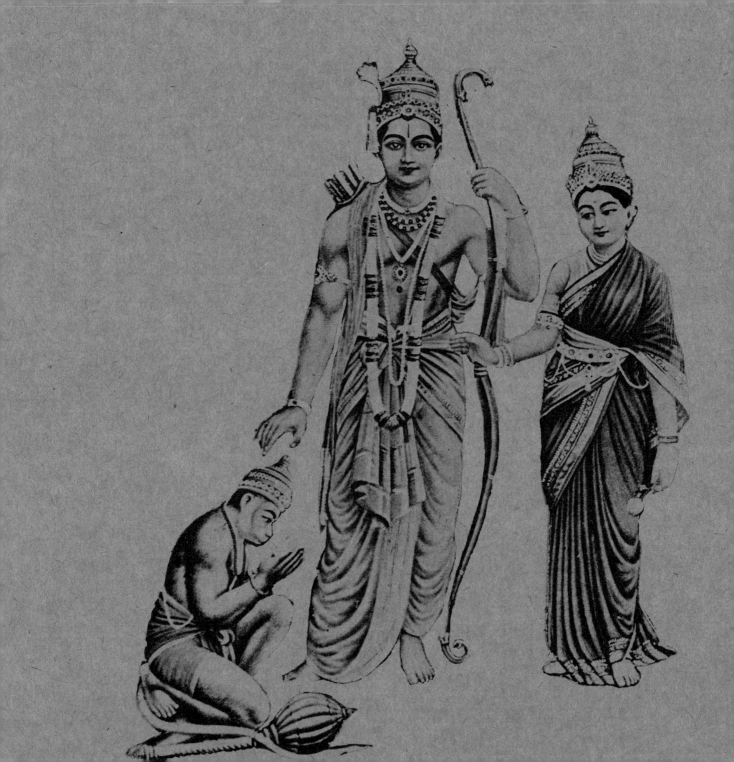

mmmm.....

THIS ONE
IS
DEDICATED
TO
THE ONE EYE
LOVE

INGREDIENTS

Introduction

Readiness 2
Guru and Teacher 4
Renunciation 9
Tapasya 11
Sleeping 15
Eating 17
Study 21
Asanas 23
Mantra 32
Transmuting Energy 39
Pranayam 43
Sexual Energy 46
Siddhis 50
Satsang 52
Getting Straight 54
Truth 57
Drop Out/Cop Out 58
Money and Right Livelihood 63
Karma Yoga 65
Bhakti Yoga 72
Dance 77
Meditation 80
The Rational Mind 85
Time and Space 90
Psychedelics as an Upaya 92
The Course of Sadhana 96
Setting 99
Family Sadhana 109
Sadhana If You Live Alone 113
Dying 114
Glossary

COOKBOOK FOR A SACRED LIFE

Dedicated to those who wish to get on with it. . .

INTRODUCTION

We offer this book with humility and a compassionate awareness of our own predicament—and yours. We are all on the journey towards enlightenment and at each stage must share what has been discovered with those who will listen. The sharing is part of the work. The listening is part of the work. We are all on the path.

"The journey of a thousand miles begins with one step."—Lao Tzu

BUT WHERE DO WE BEGIN? The answer is simple: you begin just where you are.

"If thou but settest foot on this Path,
thou shalt see it everywhere . . ."—Hermes Trismegistus

Then you become aware of the inevitable process of the evolution of consciousness . . . that daily, slowly, the cloud of illusion becomes thinner and thinner . . . until, at last, there is light.

This manual concerns no more or no less than the living of daily life. At first you "do" *sadhana* (work on the spiritual path) within certain time and space boundaries, such as going to church on Sunday mornings, or getting high on Saturday nights, or meditating each morning. Eventually, it turns out that *SADHANA* IS EVERYTHING YOU DO.

"WARNING: if you don't have room in your livingroom for an elephant—don't make friends with the elephant trainer . . ."—Sufi mystic

This manual contains a wide variety of techniques. Everyone's needs are different and everyone is at a different stage along the path. But, as with any recipe book, you choose what suits you. If you listen to your own inner voice, it will tell you where you are now, and which method will work best for you in your evolution towards the light.

"May the longtime
sun shine 'pon you
All love surround you
and the pure light within you
Guide your way home."—The Incredible String Band

READINESS

Potent Quotes

"To everything there is a season, and a time to every purpose under the heaven."—*Ecclesiastes*

"Who hath ears, let him hear."—Jesus

"Dislodging a green nut from a shell is almost impossible, but let it dry and the lightest tap will do it."—Ramakrishna

"Is it then not a mistake to precipitate the time of awakening? He himself has given the answer: he wants to know. As to the rest of the way, not the greatest master can go even one step for his disciple; in himself he must experience each stage of developing consciousness. Therefore he will know nothing for which he is not ripe."—de Lubicz

"You can't teach a hunter it is wrong to kill."—Hari Dass Baba

"I found that the chief difficulty for most people was to realize that they had really heard 'new things': that is, things that they had never heard before. They kept translating what they heard into their habitual language. They had ceased to hope and believe there might be anything new."—Ouspensky

"But the natural man receiveth not the things of the Spirit of God: for they are foolishness unto him. Neither can he know them, because they are spiritually discerned."—Paul of Tarsus

"If he wants to work on himself, he must destroy his peace. To have them both is in no way possible. A man must make a choice. But when chosing the result is very often deceit, that is to say, a man tries to deceive himself. In words he choses work but in reality he does not want to lose his peace.

Such submission is the most difficult thing there can be for a man who thinks that he is capable of deciding anything."—Ouspensky

"I wish I could join the Solitaries instead of being Superior and having to write books. But I don't wish to have what I wish, of course."—Abbot John Chapman

"It can be said that there is one general rule for everybody. In order to approach this system seriously, people must be **disappointed,** first of all in themselves, that is to say, in their powers, and secondly in all the old ways . . . A man . . . if he is a scientist should be disappointed in his science. If he is a religious man he should be disappointed in his religion. If he is a politician he should be disappointed in philosophy. If he is a theosophist he should be disappointed in theosophy. If he is an occultist he should be disappointed in occultism. And so on."—Gurdjieff, by Ouspensky

"It is time now for us to rise from sleep."—St. Benedict

"The eternal world or the external life is not a valley of suffering for those who enjoy it, but only for those who know of a higher life. The animal enjoys animal life; the intellect the intellectual realm; but he who has entered into regeneration recognizes his terrestrial existence as a burden and prison. With this recognition he takes upon himself the cross of Christ."—Jacob Boehme

"Most truly I say unto you, unless anyone is born again, he cannot see the kingdom of God . . . Unless anyone is born from water and spirit, he cannot enter into the kingdom of God. What has been born from the flesh is flesh, and what has been born from the spirit is spirit."—Jesus

"We are born into the world of nature; our second birth is into the world of spirit."—*Bhagavad Gita*

"Except ye be converted and become as little children, ye shall not enter into the kingdom of heaven."—Jesus

"I have brought you this far, and I have been your leader. Right here I'll take off the cap of authority, which was a crown of thorns for the person I remember myself to be. Far within me, where the memory of what I am is still unclouded, a little child is waking up and making an old man's mask weep. A little child looking for mother and father, looking with you for protection and help—protection from his pleasures and his dreams, and help in order to become what he is without imitating anyone."—Daumal

"But I had seen myself, that is, I had seen things in myself that I had never seen before. There could be no doubt about it and although I afterwards became the same as I had been before, I could not help **knowing** that this had been and I could forget nothing."—Ouspensky

"As soon as a man is fully disposed to be alone with God, he is alone with God no matter where he may be . . . in the country, the monastery, the woods or the city. The lightning flashes from East to West, illuminating the whole horizon and striking where it pleases and at the same instant the infinite liberty of God flashes in the depths of that man's soul, and he is illumined. At that moment he sees that though he seems to be in the middle of his journey, he has already arrived at the end. For the life of Grace on earth is the beginning of the life of Glory. Although he is a traveler in time, he has opened his eyes for a moment in eternity."—Merton

"Ask, and it shall be given to you; seek, and ye shall find; knock and it shall be opened unto you: For everyone that asketh receiveth; and he that seeketh findeth; and to him that knocketh it shall be opened."—Jesus

3

GURU AND TEACHER

Question: I have read in many holy books that you need to have a **guru,** a spiritual guide, to realize an enlightened state. If this is true, how do I go about finding one?

Answer: At certain stages in the spiritual journey, there is a quickening of the spirit which is brought about through the grace of a **guru.** When you are at one of the stages where you need this catalyst, it will be forthcoming. There is really nothing **you** can do about **gurus.** It doesn't work that way. If you go looking for a **guru** and you are not ready to find one, you will not find what you are looking for. On the other hand, when you are ready the **guru** will be exactly where you are at the appropriate moment.

All you can do is purify yourself in body and mind. Each stage of purification will make you sensitive to new levels of perception. Finally you arrive at a level where the **guru** is. There

4

is **no one** who is ready for the grace of the **guru** who does not receive it at that very moment.

Question: Does everyone have a **guru?**

Answer: Yes. However, you may or may not meet your **guru** on the physical plane in this lifetime. It isn't necessary. Since the relation between a **guru** and *chela* (disciple) is not on the physical plane, the **guru** can act upon you from within yourself. You may meet him through dreams or visions or merely sense his presence. However, it is only after much purification that you will honor these meetings rather than rejecting them in favor of the more gross manifestations. There have been many saints who realized enlightenment without ever meeting their **guru** in a physical manifestation.

Question: How will I know how to purify myself without the guidance of a **guru?**

Answer: Relax. You are being guided. In fact, the next message you need in the treasure hunt is **exactly where you are** when you need it. The message may be in the form of a teacher or a lover or an enemy or a pet or a rock or a chemical or a book or a feeling of great despair or a physical illness or the eyes of a person you pass on the street.

Question: What is the difference between a teacher and a **guru?**

Answer: A teacher points the way. A **guru** is the Way. In the course of your awakening you will have thousands of teachers. Throughout all of this teaching, the **guru** waits, beckoning from beyond.

Question: There are many beings who profess to be **gurus.** Should I follow one of them? How do I choose from among them?

Answer: You can't choose to follow a **guru.** It doesn't work that way. If you are in doubt, don't. When the correct manifestation of the guru for you appears, you'll know it with **all your heart.** It is surrender which is no surrender. It is inevitable and totally compelling.

Now, it is possible that a being who is ultimately to be known to you as your **guru** comes forward and says, "I am your Guru." And you hold back. That's because you are not yet ready. You can't honestly do otherwise. Don't worry. When you are ready, he'll be back. Just relax and trust the process.

Question: What kind of teachers should I study with?

Answer: Listen to your inner being. If you are at the point where you sense you need instruction in calming your mind or getting your body in shape, then you will become sensitized to available teachers who can instruct you concerning the specific practices required. Often you will find a teacher who knows the specific information although he doesn't elicit in you a great love or trust. Honor him as your teacher, learn what you can, and then move on. Trust the messages coming from your heart and intuition.

This journey is an inner journey. The charisma of an impure being such as a Hitler would not be of influence on another person were that person totally honest with himself and totally true to his inner voice. There is a place in each human being where at all times he knows exactly "where it is at." So, if in doubt about the next step, just listen. And if still in doubt, wait. When it's time to move, you'll know.

Exercises

1. Purification Exercise with Guru Rimpoche

Consider a being of pure light and love (whom you can name Padmasambhava, the Lotus-evolved One, if you would like), who is sitting in the midst of a lake on a lotus flower in front of you. He is seen as being in front of you and slightly above you . . . so that you look up to him at about a thirty degree angle. He will come into your heart when you have sufficiently purified yourself.

1. Closing your left nostril, breathe three deep breaths out of your right nostril. Visualize the air being ejected as dark red and consider it to be all of your bodily diseases and attachments.

2. Close your right nostril. Now breathe out three deep breaths through your left nostril. Visualize the air being ejected as a blue-grey and consider it to be all your mental obstacles and anger.

3. Now breathe out three deep breaths through your mouth. Visualize this air as purple and consider it as the sloth that impedes your progress . . . the inertia . . . breathe it out.

4. Now visualize that from the *ajna* (the point between the eyebrows) of Padmasambhava directly to your *ajna* there is a piercing beam of white light which, as it burns into you, rids you of bodily sins and wrongs (the sound connected with this is **OM**).

5. Now visualize a red beam from the throat *chakra* (point of energy) of Padmasambhava directly to your throat center. This beam rids you of lapses of speech, of untruths (the sound connected with this is **AH**).

6. Now visualize a blue beam of light coming from the heart of Padmasambhava to your heart. This beam purifies you of wrongs done in ignorance, wrong thoughts (i.e., thoughts which maintain the illusion). (The sound associated with this beam is **HUM**.)

7. Now allow that blue beam to become a broad blue avenue of light. Then you will see Padmasambhava come down that avenue and come directly into your heart. Here he will sit in your *hridayam* (spiritual heart). His mantra is: *Om Ah Hum Vajra Guru Padma Siddhi Hum*. This means three-in-one (the unmanifest, imminent manifestation, and manifestation) lightning- bolt **Guru** of unbearable compassion and infinite power who resides in my heart. To say his *mantra* is to keep Him in your heart . . . until finally you and He become One.

2. The Four Bodhisattva Vows (say three times)

1. I resolve to become enlightened for the sake of all living beings.
2. I will cut the roots of all delusive passions.
3. I will penetrate the farthest gate of *Dharma*.
4. I will realize the supreme way of Buddha.

Potent Quotes

"Guru, God, and Self are One."—Ramana Maharshi

"Silence thy thoughts and fix thy whole attention on thy Master, whom thou dost not see, but whom thou feelest."—Blavatsky

"The influence of the Guru is obstructed by mental activity, by reliance on one's own exertions and by every kind of self-consciousness and self-exertion."—Sathya Sai Baba

"What is the nature of Guru's grace?
It is beyond thought and word.
Then how can it be said that the devotee realizes his true
Being by virtue of the Guru's grace?
It is like an elephant waking up on seeing a lion in a dream.
Just as the appearance of the dream lion is enough to wake the
elephant so also the glance of grace from the master is enough to
waken the devotee from the sleep of ignorance to the Knowledge of
the Real. It is sure and certain."—Ramana Maharshi

Disembodied **guru** to disciple: "Child you must meditate more. Your gaze is not yet faultless. I was fairly extinguished in the ether by the agitation of your restless mind."—Babaji

"I beseeched him fervently thus: 'It is my great desire that I should actually experience your gracious wisdom. Kindly fulfill my desire.' In those days Sri Ramana was not speaking much. Still he spoke kindly as follows: 'Is it the body in front of me which desires to obtain my grace? Or is the awareness within it? If it is the awareness, is it not now looking upon itself as the body and making this request? If so let the awareness first of all know its real nature. It will then automatically know God and my grace. The truth of this can be realized even now and here.' "—Ramana Maharshi magazine

"Rain water falling upon the roof of a house flows down to the ground through spouts shaped grotesquely like a tiger's head. One gets the impression that the water comes from the tiger's mouth, but in reality it descends from the sky. In the same way the holy teachings that come from the mouths of godly men seem to be uttered by those men themselves, while in reality they proceed from God."—Ramakrishna

"The Grace of the Guru is like an ocean. If one comes with a cup he will only get a cupful. It is no use complaining of the niggardliness of the ocean. The bigger the vessel the more one will be able to carry. It is entirely up to him."—Ramana Maharshi

RENUNCIATION

You might think of renunciation in terms of some external act like a New Year's resolution, or leaving family and friends to go off to a cave. But renunciation is much more subtle than that—and much harder—and much much more continuing. On the spiritual journey, renunciation means **non-attachment**.

To become free of attachment means to break the link identifying you with your desires. The desires continue; they are part of the dance of nature. But a renunciate no longer thinks that he **is** his desires.

"What is the necessity of giving up the world altogether. It is enough to give up the attachment to it."—Ramakrishna

A *sadhak* (someone doing *sadhana*) sees clearly that his craving is creating his own veil of illusion. At this point desires start to fall away of themselves. This process is called the onset of *vairag* (the falling away of worldly desires). As each one falls away, more subtle forms of desire arise. These too must be given up. Eventually the only desire is for bliss. Then that one must be thrown away . . .

As long as any desire pulls or pushes you, you are like a flame which flickers in the winds. But as you come to your center, as you break the identification with desire, you become calm, like a candle in a niche where no wind comes.

Remember you can't do away with desire or give it up or try to get rid of it. However, with increased wisdom and preoccupation with your *sadhana*, desires will just fall away.

"You can't rip the skin from the snake. It will shed its skin when it is ready."—Hari Dass Baba

And as you extricate yourself from your attachments and become quiet, you will be able to know more and more clearly how it all is . . . The Way. And the more clearly you hear, the more your actions will be in harmony with the Way . . . with His Will. Then you will truly understand:

Not my but Thy will, O Lord.

Potent Quotes

"Desire is a trap
Desirelessness is MOXA (liberation)
Desire is the world

9

Desire is the creator

Desire is the destroyer."—Hari Dass Baba

"Lay not up for yourselves treasures upon earth, where moth and rust doth corrupt, and where thieves break through and steal: but lay up for yourselves treasures in heaven, where neither moth nor rust doth corrupt, and where thieves do not break through nor steal; for where your treasure is, there will your heart be also."—Jesus

"If a pickpocket meets a Holy Man, he will see only His pockets."—Hari Dass Baba

"Everywhere I look I see only my own desires."—Hari Dass Baba

"Wheresoever the body is, thither will the eagles be gathered together."—Jesus

"On the hat of poverty three renouncements are inscribed: Quit this world, quit the next world, quit quitting."—Sufi poet

"When you got nothing, you got nothing to lose. You're invisible now, you got no secrets to conceal."—Bob Dylan

"The fly that touches honey cannot use its wings; so the soul that clings to spiritual sweetness ruins its freedom and hinders contemplation."—Aurobindo

"He consciously moves with the cosmic current. In moving he loses nothing but his limitations. He can take with him in essence all the experiences and understanding that he has gained."—Collins

"The essence of civilization consists not in the multiplication of wants but in their deliberate and voluntary renunciation."—Gandhi

"Lay it down, drop it, let go, sing it out, throw it out. Going all the Way is holy but alas some linger on the path to see and smell the pretty golden sunflower or hold hands with Eternity or practice Ecstasy Bliss or circulate the light or reach neither perception nor non-perception but lingering anywhere you might . . . get stuck for Kalpas . . . You can't go forwards or backwards or stand still. Move! Move! Mu . . ."—Bhagavan Dass

"Therefore I say unto you, Take no thought for your life, what ye shall eat, or what ye shall drink; nor yet for your body, what ye shall put on. Is not the life more than meat, and the body than raiment?"—Jesus

"He that loveth father or mother more than me is not worthy of me."—Jesus

"By letting it go it all gets done

The world is won by those who let it go.

But when you try and try

The world is then beyond the winning."—*Tao Te Ching*

TAPASYA

The simplest and most direct type of renunciation would seem to be to just give up the satisfying of one's desires. That is, if one is preoccupied with eating and oral gratifications, just fast. If one is obsessed with sexual concerns, just give up sex. And so on. This technique is known as *tapasya* or "straightening by fire."

"If a man gives way to all his desires, or panders to them, there will be no inner struggle in him, no 'friction,' no fire. But if, for the sake of attaining a definite aim, he struggles with the desires that hinder him, he will then create a fire which will gradually transform his inner world into a single whole."—Ouspensky

The struggle that comes through imposing austerities upon oneself as a systematic part of one's *sadhana* is a powerful form of inner confrontation. It certainly shows you where you are not. For example, if you usually get up at 8 a.m. as everyone else does, try getting up at 4 a.m. every morning. (Buddha and other high beings have noted that the best time of day to work on oneself is between 4 and 7.) Or perhaps you like sleeping in a really comfortable bed . . . start sleeping on a thin mat on the floor.

But there are two warnings to be kept in mind with regard to any austerities:

1. Austerities can be performed in ways to enhance or strengthen the ego. Pride in how much one is suffering and masochism, are two examples.
"Another thing that people must sacrifice is their suffering. No one who has not sacrificed his suffering can work. Nothing can be attained without suffering but at the same time one must begin by sacrificing suffering."—Ouspensky
2. Austerities that are excessive (in relation to the degree of spiritual development of the individual) are merely demonstrations of ego will and as such can harm the body or the mind in such a way as to make further *sadhana* in this lifetime difficult or even impossible.
"And even in his corrections, let him act with prudence, and not go too far, lest while he seeketh too eagerly to scrape off the rust, the vessel be broken."
Rule for the Abbot, Ch. 64

Two examples:

There is a method of meditation in which a *sadhak* sits in the lotus position in the desert and looks directly into the sun without blinking from sunrise to sunset. Now it is obvious that if most people were to try this they would blind themselves through burning their retina. This particular exercise is only safe to do when one has evolved to such a point that his mind is totally one-pointed and thus he can keep his eyes open and directed at the sun without ever even once "looking" at the sun.

Pranayam, which utilizes control of breath in order to control *pran* or life force, involves in its advanced forms the stopping of the breath for extended periods of time. One arrives at these very delicate forms of *pranayam* only after considerable purification of body and mind for they require that the breath stop although the *sadhak* feels no experience of holding his breath. One over-zealous aspirant injected chemical agents to strengthen "his will" and override his body's warning system . . . and then forced himself into deeper and deeper *pranayam*. He died. And leaving the body this way entails ego and is thus a subtle form of suicide which leaves him with more work to do, but no body to do it in . . . until next time.

Such warnings make a person really want a nice, wise, paternal type teacher to impose discipline. But waiting for such a teacher is usually a cop-out, for at this point practically everything a teacher would say to us we already know. There are many ways on our own that we can "get on with it." (Later, when we have progressed on the path of purification and really need a teacher, he will appear.)

In undertaking any *tapasya*, one is usually overwhelmed by the amount of ego that creeps in. Pride, self-pity, wanting to stop because it all seems meaningless or confusing or is too slow . . . all of these ego demons and many more drop around to foil any such undertaking. A thousand times they will succeed and you will give up your program in disgust. But a thousand and one times you will return to your efforts because you see how it all is. That's just the way it is. As many times as you trip and fall, i.e., give in to a desire—just get up. There is a tendency when we fall for many of us to sit around and feel guilty and wallow in self-recrimination.

"However sinful a person may be, if he would stop wailing inconsolably: 'Alas! I am a sinner, how shall I attain liberation?' and, casting away even the thought that he is a sinner, if he would zealously carry on . . . he would most assuredly get reformed."—Ramana Maharshi

Such self-recrimination is just more of the ego dance. Let it go by and get on with it. After all, if you were finished, you wouldn't need to begin. Just accept where you are in the here and now and proceed full speed.

And so for those who can undertake austerities without feeling that they are too austere, perhaps even proceed joyfully, here are some suggested exercises.

Exercises

1. Get in the habit of remaining silent for a few hours a day. This is most easily done when one is at home or around people who understand what you are trying to do. (In India if

you are silent everyone immediately says, "Ah, *Mouna*" and honors you. In the West people either interpret silence as a sign of your hostility towards them or as a physical illness about which they feel pity. Either of these reactions makes your work more difficult.) At first you may want to remain by yourself during these few hours. Later you will be able to be around people comfortably without having to speak.

Soon you may feel that you are ready to undertake one day of silence a week. Some spiritual communities have incorporated a day of silence into their program for the entire group. Many communities take meals in silence.

2. If you wish to undertake longer periods of silence you may wish to work with a chalk board. A piece of light slate about 4" by 5" can be worn on a piece of twine or rope around the neck. With a piece of chalk also attached to the twine, you can convey any necessary messages of practical import. This device, although somewhat cumbersome, is an excellent technique for showing a person his own verbosity. To have to write down every communication quickly leads one to convey the essence of the communication without all the redundancies and amplifications. With such a device, Hari Dass Baba has carried on much worldly work for fifteen years without speaking.

The effects of this very modest *tapasya* will very quickly be manifested in the forms of more calmness of mind and more energy and the ability to hear more around you.

Other exercises of *tapasya* are included in other sections of this cookbook.

Potent Quotes

"Conserve your powers. Daily renewed sense yearnings sap your inner peace; they are like openings in a reservoir that allow vital waters to be wasted in the desert soil of materialism.

The forceful activating impulse of wrong desire is the greatest enemy to the happiness of man. Roam in the world as a lion of self control; don't let the frogs of sense weakness kick you around."—Sri Yukteswar

"I realized in this place that people feared silence more than anything else, that our tendency to talk arises from self-defense and is always based upon a reluctance to see something, a reluctance to confess something to oneself.

Directly a person is quiet himself, that is, awakes a little, he hears the different intonations and begins to distinguish other people's lies."—Ouspensky

13

"The more you talk about it, the more you think about it, the further from it you go;
STOP TALKING, STOP THINKING, AND THERE IS NOTHING YOU WILL
NOT UNDERSTAND."—Seng-ts'an

"Drown all sound in My Silence to hear My Word of words."—Meher Baba

"The whole world is tormented by words
And there is no one who does without words.
But in so far as one is free from words
Does one really understand words."— Saraha, *Treasury of Songs,* v. 88

"To reconnect consciousness with the unconscious, to make consciousness symbolical is
to reconnect words with silence; to let the silence in. If consciousness is all words and no
silence, the unconscious remains unconscious."—N.O. Brown

"I said I will take heed to my ways, that I sin not with my tongue, I have placed a watch
over my mouth; I became dumb and was silent, and held my peace even from good
things."—St. Benedict

"Quietness is master of the dead."—*Tao Te Ching*

"Those who know do not talk
And talkers do not know."—*Tao Te Ching*

"He who tells the truth says almost nothing."—Porchia

"Do not squander your treasure. Exuberance is a good stimulus towards action, but the
inner light grows in silence and concentration."

"Ephrem the Syrian says, 'Good speech is silver, but silence is pure gold.' "—*Way of a
Pilgrim*

"I did not eat so they said I was fasting;
I did not speak so they said I was mouni."—Ramana Maharshi

"Oh Lord, Thou shalt open my lips, and my mouth shall declare Thy praise."—*Bible*

SLEEPING

Exercises

As you get further on the path you will need less and less sleep. Start from where you are. Get as much sleep as you seem to need. However, it is helpful in facilitating your transformation to:

(a) Go to bed early and get up early. Most people in the West fill their evenings with activity and stimulation. As you get into a yogic way of life, those activities such as "hanging out," movies, TV, "making out," etc., cease to exert such a strong influence over you. Then the change in schedule becomes easy. If you have the opportunity to live away from electricity for a period of time, it is easier to notice the sunset and sunrise and to adapt your schedule to the natural order of things. If you think you are matinal or nocturnal don't worry about it . . . just slowly bring your schedule into harmony.

(b) Sleep on a firm surface—perhaps a mat on the floor or a thick mattress. At first this may be uncomfortable if you are unaccumstomed to it, but quickly you adapt and find that the patterns and nature of your sleep change markedly as you change the surface upon which you sleep.

(c) It is good to sleep on your back or upon your side. (The left side is often recommended for reasons concerning which nostril it is most useful to breathe through during the night. Most of the time you breathe through one nostril dominantly. There is an evolved science in yoga concerning the effects of breathing through one nostril or the other. The nostril opposite the side you are sleeping on stays open.)

(d) Sleep without a pillow or with a small pillow under your neck. It is good to keep your spine as straight as possible.

(e) Meditate for a few minutes before lying down to go to sleep.

Patterns of Sleep

When you first lie down, relax your body progressively from feet to top of head. Experience the relaxation at each point along the way. Get out of the habit of "thinking about things" when you are going into sleep. Clear your mind. If you work with *mantra*, it is good to repeat your *mantra* and let all else fall away. As your *sadhana* proceeds you will be able to remain more conscious through the period of transition from your normal waking

15

state into the states of sleep. You will witness these transitions in planes of consciousness from the vantage point of the calm niche created by your *mantra* (witnessing vantage point).

During the first part of your sleep you will be in a state of deep sleep. This is a dreamless state in which you merge once again into the unity of the One. Through this re-uniting you tune in on much *pran* and become refreshed. (Parallels are often made between this state and *Nirvikalp Samadhi* and the First *Bardo*.) Only when you have evolved far along the path will you remain conscious throughout the period of deep sleep. At that stage you no longer sleep but merely pass the night by going into deeper states of *samadhi*.

Once your being has been sufficiently refreshed through deep sleep, you begin to re-enter through various planes of consciousness—finally coming to the physical plane at which point you usually say that you have "awakened." The various planes you pass through prior to returning to the physical plane are generally referred to by most laymen in the West as the "dream state." Actually, what we refer to as "dreams" are merely experiences which we are having on planes other than the physical plane. Such experiences are going on all the time but usually our awareness is attached to the physical plane and we are oblivious of any other information coming from these other planes.

Most of us have had the experience of being awakened by an alarm clock and being in the middle of a dream. Sometimes we are able to finish the dream without "going back to sleep." That is, we keep in mind that the alarm has gone off, but we stay in the state of half awake/half asleep in order to finish the dream. Many people are trained to do this in psychoanalysis. It is possible almost immediately upon embarking on one's *sadhana* to become aware in the same way during the process of dreaming.

Once you know how to center through *mantra*, witness, etc., it is easy to observe your dreams running on. With very little practice you will find that by sleeping on a hard surface you sleep more lightly, which allows you to awaken into your dreams almost immediately upon coming out of deep sleep. It is useful to keep a *mantra* going while the dreams pass. Although you may be an actor in your dream, if you identify with your *mantra* or witness, you can still watch your dreams in the same way as you might watch a movie—watching yourself as one of the actors.

This is a technique for learning a great deal about who you are on planes other than the one with which you are familiar. The major advantage of some familiarity with other than the physical plane of consciousness is that it helps you to see that what you call your "waking state" is little more than another plane of consciousness . . . no more and no less. Once you know this and live this knowledge from moment to moment, then such exercises with dreams are unnecessary for they merely clutter your head with more illusion. At that stage it is good as soon as you come out of deep sleep and become aware again to get up immediately and go into meditation . . . keeping as free from any thoughts as possible.

EATING

Our body is our temple where we live and where we do the work of becoming enlightened. Just as certain external environments are more conducive to increased awareness than others (at least in the early stages of awakening), so it is with the inner environment—the body itself. It can be a "clean, well-lighted place."

"We are what we eat" may be an oversimplification, but it contains a grain of truth. What we eat affects the nature of the body cells and organs and the way they function. At another level, you could say that the vibrations of anything you put into the organism modifies the vibrations of the total organism.

At the outset of *sadhana*, you cannot radically change your eating pattern without damage to the physical body. But what you can do is to attend to what and how you eat. Basically, there is a program of diet for the *sadhak*:

1. Don't eat too much. The traditional way of saying this is that at the conclusion of a meal, a yogi's stomach should be half full of food, one-quarter full of water and one-quarter full of air.

2. Eat light, healthy, unadulterated foods which are easily digestable. It would be desirable if we could find one agreed-upon diet that would be optimal for *sadhana*. But it is apparent from the many controversies that rage concerning which foods are "good" and which are "bad," that no single diet is universally considered desirable.

Such a welter of conflicting information may confuse a beginner. But such confusion may be constructive if it precipitates closer scrutiny of diet and a search for what is the essence of the matter behind all diets. Much of the controversy is the result of a failure to realize that a *sadhak* needs different kinds of foods at different stages of his journey. When he is first shedding his habitual meat diet he may wish to substitute whole grains, such as brown rice and whole wheat, along with vegetables, some fish, fruit, honey instead of sugar, nuts and dairy products. Later, he may find as he further purifies his body that certain of these foods interfere with his *sadhana* by producing mucus or vibrations which made meditation more difficult. He may eventually find, if he is leading a contemplative life, that fruit and nuts are enough.

17

Even such a sparse diet as that is merely a step upon the path. At the conclusion, one is capable of living **upon light alone**.

We, as separate entities, could be characterized as energy transformers. We take in energy (*pran*) in certain forms, transform this energy and then emit it in other forms. Beings whose consciousness is totally attached to the physical plane consider food, water and air as the major sources of their energy. As a being progresses along the path, he comes to understand that there are other sources of energy available to him. Finally he arrives at the stage where he is able to transmute everything in the Universe into useful energy. In modern Western science, the relationship between mass and energy as set forth by Einstein reflects this truth:

"That is, what appears to us to be mass is merely huge amounts of bound energy. If and when the mass can be broken down there is a release of energies. From this came the splitting of the atom."

3. Abstain as much as possible from strong (hot, spicy or pungent) foods. Also go light on stimulants such as coffee, tea and "spirits." Certain spices are useful in digestion and these may be used in moderation.

In order to go the spice trip, you have to alter your model of why you eat. Most Westerners are very sensual and spend large amounts of time in titillating their palates with variety and subtlety in tastes. The gourmet represents the epitome of such a value. The *sadhak*, however, realizes that all sense gratification is merely perpetuating the enslavement to desire so he attempts, early on, to surrender the taste trip in favor of his spiritual goal. But this is not necessarily required. At the early stages of work, it is useful to simplify one's diet (even to the taking of the same menu every day), making it as tasty as possible with mild and healthful spices. This repetition and blandness may be distasteful at first, but soon one develops new sensitivities in taste and new feelings of lightness in mind and body which more than compensate for what has been "given up."

4. Be concerned with the vibrations associated with the source, preparation and eating of foods. Most of us are so gross in our sensitivity that we can hardly even appreciate this point. But those of us who have been doing *sadhana* for a period of time, or who have lived with very pure beings, find these rules to be obvious:

(a) Any food which entails violence (killing) in its source is not to be taken. At one end of the continuum is meat—the preparation of which obviously includes the killing of an animal which has a rudimentary self-consciousness. It thus experiences fear and releases into its system adrenalin and other chemicals from the endocrine glands which are not helpful for meditation. At the other end of this continuum are fruits which fall from trees—given as a gift for our needs. Which of the foods in the middle of the continuum involve some violence

18

to the natural order of things in order to obtain them (e.g., vegetables, milk) is a much debated question. In this manual we can only recognize the existence of such a continuum and bring it to your attention.

(b) Food which entails cooking in its preparation should only be eaten when it has been cooked with *mantra* and/or love. The vibrations of the person preparing the food enter into food cooked over fire. A Sanskrit *mantra* which can be used for preparing food is:

OM ANNAM BRAHMA RASO BISHNUR BHOKTA DEBO JANARDANAHI AWARM GYANTWA TO YO BHUNKT ANN DOSHORN LIPYATE

which means: Food is *Brahma*. Its *rasa* (juice) is *Vishnu*. The whole world (Life Being) is its user. Having this thought makes ineffective the evils connected with this food.

(c) There is a state of mind suitable for taking of food—calmness. There is a *Sufi* saying:

"If a person eats with anger, the food turns to poison."

5. Finally, consecrate the food you take. Such food is called *prasad*. Consecrating food means to offer the food up. Another way of saying this is that the taking of the food should be considered as part of one's spiritual work or *sadhana*. In the West we sometimes say grace before meals. This is one form of consecrating the food. All you have to do now is continue to say grace, but now **listen to it.**

A Sanskrit consecration of food taken from the *Gita* is as follows:

BRAHMAPANAM - BRAHMA HAVIRE
BRAHMAGNI - BRAHMANA HOTA
BRAHMAI - TAN - GANTABYAM
BRAHMA - KARMA - SAMADHINAH
GURU BRAHMA - GURU VISHNU - GURU
    DAWVO MAHISH WARA
GURU SAKSHAT
PARAM BRAHMA TUS MAEE
SHRI GURU VEY NA MA HA
OM SHANTI SHANTI SHANTI

Translation: This ritual is *Brahma*. The food is *Brahma*. He who offers the food is *Brahma*. The fire (hunger) is also *Brahma*. All *karma* is *Brahma*. He who knows this may go to *Brahma*. I offer this food to the **Guru** who is the creator, the preserver, and the agent of change. To the **Guru** who is also all energy and who is the Sun beyond all. I touch the lotus feet of the **Guru.** *OM,* Peace, Peace, Peace. (Just before *OM, SHANTI, SHANTI, SHANTI . . .* you may wish to inject silently some additional beings whom you wish to honor by offering the food.)

19

It is true that food offered with a pure heart is received in essence.

In a short story by J.D. Salinger called "Teddy," a young boy who is a very high being describes how he first realized in this lifetime how it all was:

"I was about six years old and was watching my little sister in her highchair drinking milk. Suddenly I saw it was like pouring God into God if you know what I mean."

Perhaps you would find it a meaningful *mantra* to merely think upon pouring God into God, if you know what I mean.

Potent Quotes

"AND GOD SAID, 'Behold I have given you every plant yielding seed which is on the face of all the earth and every tree yielding seed in its fruit; you shall have them for food. And to every beast of the earth, and to every bird of the air, and to everything that creeps on the earth, everything that has the breath of life, I have given every green plant for food'."—*Genesis*

"When you are at table, speak to none, keep your eyes lowered and think of the heavenly table, of the food that is served thereon, which food is God Himself, and of the guests at this table, who are the angels."—St. Teresa of Avila

"Complaint of the Stomach:

One day there had been feasting at the Ashram. Many had been upset by the large quantity of rich food. Someone quoted the following complaint about the stomach by the Tamil poet Avvayar:

'You will not go without food even for one day, nor will you take enough for two days at a time. You have no idea of the trouble I have on your account, Oh wretched stomach! It is impossible to get on with you!'

Bhagavan immediately replied with a parody giving the stomach's complaint against the ego:

'You will not give even an hour's rest to me, your stomach. Day after day, every hour, you keep on eating. You have no idea how I suffer, Oh trouble-making ego! It is impossible to get on with you'."—Osborne

"Ravana's gigantic brother, Khumba-karn, obtained as a boon from *Brahma* that whenever he had satisfied his voracious appetite the slumber of repletion might be the longest and deepest, and he might only wake to eat again."—*Ramayana*

STUDY

Study, like *mantra*, is a technique for bringing you close to the higher (more conscious) ideas of higher beings. As a member of a culture which dotes on collecting knowledge, you may first set out on the path wanting to read what is written about higher consciousness. You might get books about the history of mysticism, the lives of the prophets of the great religions, the curricula of obscure schools of thought, the writings and sayings of great mystics, the implications of mysticism for modern man, and books on methods. This reading provides a context for your personal experiences. It demonstrates that throughout the history of man there have always been mystics, that what can be said about the mystical experience from an external observer's point of view is relatively trivial, and that though the words differ from one mystic to another, the communality of experience is amazing.

There are four categories into which these writings can be placed (in terms of the author's own state of development):

1. Realized or enlightened beings. For the most part they have written very little; often their words (e.g., Gospels) have been recorded by disciples.)

2. Spiritual seekers who are very much on the path and are sharing their insights, methods, etc.

3. *Pandits,* intellectuals, scientists who evolve highly intellectually sophisticated subtle models and explanations of the mystical experience. (The veil for many of these writers is still heavy, though often they have had some mystical experience of their own on which to anchor their writings.)

4. Professional writers who write objective, superficial, and quite external accounts of mysticism. They seek the "facts."

After you have completed the first superficial reading overview, it becomes apparent that if you are to change your way of thinking about the universe, it would be a good idea to "hang out with"

(a) those who know, and
(b) those who are seriously working on themselves.

Thus your reading quickly narrows to the first two categories of authors listed above.

The second stage of study is often called **reflection.** It is described in the following passage from *Autobiography of a Yogi,* by Yogananda.

"The scene was a forest hermitage in Eastern Bengal . . . Dabru Ballav had gathered his disciples around him in the sylvan solitudes. The holy *Bhagavad Gita* was open before them. Steadfastly they looked at one passage for half an hour, then closed their eyes.

Another half hour slipped away. The master gave a brief comment. Motionless they meditated again for an hour. Finally the Guru spoke.

'Do you now understand the stanza?'

'Yes, Sir.' One of the group ventured his assertion.

'No, not fully. Seek the spiritual vitality that has given these words the power to rejuvenate India century after century.'

Another hour passed in silence.''

Daily Exercise

Working with one of the books containing the words of a realized being (e.g., the *Bhagavad Gita,* the *Tao Te Ching,* the words of Jesus in the Gospels, *Sayings of Ramana Maharshi* or Ramakrishna, the *I Ching,* etc.), take one passage—perhaps a phrase—certainly no more than a page. Read and re-read and re-re-read it. Then let your thoughts work around it. Paraphrase it. See how it applies to others and to yourself. Note if and how it differs from the way in which you usually think about things . . . different assumptions, etc. What are its implications regarding your own journey? Read it again. What laws of nature is it reflecting? Then, sitting quietly, let your mind associate to the passage. And then be quiet. Certainly a half hour a day is not too long to spend on this exercise.

ASANAS

"Let a man though living in the body, so treat his body that, with right effort, right watchfulness and right concentration he will overcome the sorrow that is produced by the sensations that arise in the body."—Dhamnapada

The word *asana* is sometimes translated as "easy, comfortable" and sometimes as "seat." It concerns a comfortable seat in which one can remain for long periods of time.

"To remain motionless for a long time without effort is an asana."—Yoga Darshana

"The aim of the bodily posture is secured when 'the physical reactions of the body are eliminated and the mind dissolves into the Infinite.'"—Danielou, quoting from Yoga Darshana

You work with your body for some very obvious reasons. First, it is the environment in which you dwell in this incarnation on the physical plane. Second, unless you can cool out your body, it keeps on capturing your attention over and over again and thus distracts you from the one-pointedness of mind that you are seeking.

Third, to work with body energies and to be able to move such energies up the spine requires sensitization to nerves in the body of which most people are unaware. Until you can hear your body, you cannot bring it under voluntary control in such a way that it helps you rather than interferes with your *sadhana*. And fourth, a *yogi* realizes that the message of his being is reflected in all his manifestations and he seeks the power of the one-pointedness that comes from having his body as well as his thoughts directed towards the state of realization. Just as bringing the hands together in prayer or challenging someone with a raised fist have associated with them various thoughts and feelings, so it is with the total body. At any moment it is making its statement, and as you come to hear such statements you bring the messages of your body in line with the messages of your heart and head. For a realized being, every movement is a perfect statement.

It is well in undertaking work with the body (*hatha yoga*) to keep in mind these reasons. If in your head you undertake *hatha yoga* as a form of exercise or body building, you will end up with just what you reached for . . . a more beautiful body. On the other hand, if you undertake *hatha yoga* as a form of *yoga* then it will, in a relatively short time, bring about a profound metamorphosis in your body calmness, sensitivity, and lightness . . . all of which will facilitate your *sadhana*.

In undertaking *asanas* it is desirable to have a teacher who can demonstrate the correct positions and correct any bad habits that develop in your performance of the *asanas*. It is useful at the beginning to take an introductory course or set of lessons in *hatha yoga* if it is available to you. These lessons will start you on the right path. Even if a qualified teacher is not available, a friend who has had a teacher can point out errors in your *asanas* which will help you.

A note of caution, however. Teachers of *hatha yoga* who teach **only** *hatha yoga* often mistake the shadow for the substance. Although they may be able to point out correct postures and procedures, many of these teachers do not themselves comprehend the implications of the term *yoga* . . . that is, they are not doing *asanas* as a means of union with the One. A student who works with such teachers runs the risk of profaning the undertaking in the very beginning by developing a poor mental set towards this work. With this caution in mind, however, it is possible for you, if you understand the reasons (especially the one concerning the use of body positions as a form of prayer) for doing *asanas*, to learn specific methodology from a teacher who himself does not understand these reasons.

If a teacher is not available it is still possible for you to undertake the regular practice of *asanas* profitably. Under these conditions, however, you must move slowly and gently . . . don't force your body . . . listen very carefully to the information that your body gives you. By proper centering you will, in fact, be calling upon an inner teacher who will guide you.

Asanas are positions. Once you have gotten into the position and made the statement connected with that position you are there. You become a statue in each *asana*.

The statue image is a useful one. No matter how unusual the position of the *asana* may seem to you, once you are in the position then you become totally centered in that position. It—your body—comes to be a position of rest . . . as if you were always in that position, as a statue.

Your state of mind is of paramount importance in *asanas*. Don't identify with the ego who is **doing** the *asanas*. Merely watch the body move into the appropriate position. Stay in a place inside yourself where nothing is happening at all.

When the body has gotten into the *asana* as perfectly as it is able without forcing (just firm pressure) . . . then go into "neutral" with the body so that it becomes perfectly relaxed and stable in the position of the *asana*.

There are 84 main *asanas* which an advanced *yogi* works with. Of these about 12 or 15 are sufficient until one arrives at a very advanced stage of *sadhana*. The following are a set of instructions for carrying out these simple *asanas*:

1. Find a quiet place to work. It is best to be alone. The surface on which you work should be flat. A blanket or thin mat on the floor is suitable.

2. Your clothing should be light and very flexible (leotards) or very loose. *Asanas* may be done naked although men sometimes find a loin cloth or athletic supporter preferable.

3. Success of *asanas* is dependent upon your being relaxed and calm and centered. It's

going to start by relaxing yourself, just with breathing. Spread your arms wide, take in a breath, and then bring your arms across your chest and let the breath out. Let the breathing happen naturally, becoming deeper as you relax your arm movements more. Arms across your chest and then out, and then across your chest and then out. Breath through your nose. Continue for a minute or two.

Another relaxing exercise is the turning, twisting of the body. Stand straight with arms extended straight out to the sides from your shoulders. Now twist the upper part of your body to the left so that your right arm comes out in front and the left arm is behind. At the same time, throw your left leg over to the right in front of your right leg. This forces the lower part of your body to turn in the opposite direction from the upper part. Then reverse the whole process . . . so that the left arm and right leg are extended out in front across your body. Do this in a relaxed swinging fashion to limber up your body.

Now lie down on your back for another loosening-up exercise. Pull your knees up to your chest and embrace them with your arms. Then roll back and forth with great relaxation just as if your're a ball, and with abandon—total abandon—just roll. Roll, back and forth, side to side. This is just to relax your back and loosen you up.

4. Breathing pointers: when your head comes forward towards your feet (your body jack-knifes), you let out air. When your body straightens out or stretches backwards you take in air. It's like a bellows. When you have gotten into an *asana* that involves bending or stretching, and you wish to go into it a little further, use small breaths to help. If the *asana* requires forward bending, take in a little breath and then as you let it out, let your body go just a bit further forward . . . and then another tiny breath, and so forth.

5. Do *asanas* at your own rate . . . calmly maintaining your center throughout the entire session.

I. SAVASANA (Corpse Position):

Lie flat on your back and relax. Legs out straight, feet together and your hands by your sides. Relax your feet, calves, thighs, pelvis, abdomen, chest, arms, neck and head.

II. PASHIMATASANA (Head-Knee Position):

Extend your arms very slowly over your head until they are stretched out straight behind you. Slowly sit up, bringing your arms and head up together and keeping your heels on the ground. Bend at the waist.

Smoothly proceed forward until you touch your toes. Keep your legs straight. If you can, hold your feet with your hands, pulling your feet towards you and bending your elbows until they are touching the ground on either side of your legs.

ASANAS

CORPSE

HEAD-KNEE I

HEAD-KNEE II

HEAD-KNEE III

COBRA

FISH

26

SPINAL TWIST II

LION

TRIANGLE

SPINAL TWIST I

WHOLE-BODY

BOW

PLOW

CORPSE

Make sure you are bending from as low in your back as possible. Don't strain. Get into the *asana* as far as possible. Then take small breaths and with each exhalation go a little further.

Now stop and become aware of your entire body . . . note the pains and the stretching muscles and the tight places. Just BE for a moment. Now gently raise your arms and return to a prone position (inhaling as you do).

Work up daily until you are doing about thirty of these. Some may be started from a sitting position with hands extended over your head. Remember to avoid thinking "I am **doing** an *asana*." Just experience the *asana* happening. Working with your eyes closed will help.

III. JANU-SIRASANA (Head-Knee Position):

Sit up with your legs stretched out in front of you. Now bend your left leg and place the sole of your left foot against the inside of the thigh of your right leg (which is still straight). Maintain that position. Raise your arms over your head and bring them slowly down towards your right foot. Bend as low in the back as possible.

Bring your head down until it is just to the left of your right knee. Then after a pause for the eternal moment, gently raise the upper part of your body until your hands are once again extended over your head. Work up daily until you are doing thirty of these.

IV. JANU-SIRASANA (Head-Knee Position):

Now change legs so that the left leg is extended and the right is bent. Repeat the *asana* as above.

You may also modify these two *asanas* by putting the foot on top of the thigh instead of next to it.

During the first few weeks you will probably experience pains and aches as well as the presence of muscles you never knew you had. Just be gently persistent. You will also notice dramatic improvement at first. Don't get hung up measuring improvement. Just quietly and calmly do your *asanas* each day. Work at your own rate.

V. BHUJANGASANA (Cobra Position):

Roll over on your stomach and lie flat with your legs together and your hands by your sides. Bend your arms until your hands are flat on the floor next to your chest. Very gently start to push up with your forearms, thus raising the upper part of your body. Raise your head first, then your neck, and then slowly raise lower and lower parts of your spine.

At the same time you are raising the upper part of your body, press down into the ground with your pelvis. When the *asana* is done properly, you will finally feel the pressure at the tip of your spine.

Keep your head up. It is helpful to keep your eyes open and to keep trying to look further and further over your head.

When you have reached the point that you can reach comfortably, stop and remain in that position for about 15 seconds and then gently starting at the base of your spine, lower the upper part of your body to the ground. The head touches down last.

Remember your breathing. As you go up, breath in; as you return, breathe out. Do about three of these.

You can also work with the "moving cobra." Proceed as above until you have raised yourself as far as possible. Then, instead of returning to the ground, bend your knees until you are sitting back on your calves with your arms still stretched out before you. This forces you to curve your back towards the ground. Then keeping your head and upper part of your body very close to the ground, glide along the ground until you are again out straight and then start to raise the head and on down the spine. This moving cobra is one continuous serpentine movement.

VI. MATSYASANA (Fish Position):

Sit up and cross your legs. If you are able to get into the lotus position (that is, with the top of the foot resting upon the opposite thigh) do so. Don't strain. You can adopt any cross-legged position that is comfortable.

Place your hands behind you and slowly let yourself back down until you are resting on your elbows. Then lower your head until the top of your head touches the ground. Arch your back. Rest the upper part of your body on the top of your head and the lower part of your body on your cross-legged seat. Now place your hands lightly on top of your thighs (or feet if you are in the lotus position). Remain in the position for about 15 to 30 seconds and then slowly return to a sitting position.

If you wish, at this point you can continue forward until your head is on the floor and your shoulders are resting on your thighs (or feet if you are in the lotus position). Then holding the wrist of one arm with the hand of the other behind your back, slowly raise your arms behind you as high as you can. Then bring them down and relax.

VII. DHANURASANA (Bow Position):

Roll over on your stomach. Behind your back take hold of your ankles with your hands, firmly. Now push away with your feet (attempt to extend your legs). This will bring your head and chest up. Keep lifting in this fashion until your thighs are fully off the ground. Look straight ahead. When you have gotten up as far as you can without strain, then remain in that position calmly for 15 to 30 seconds. Gently return to the ground. Do this *asana* three times. If you wish, when you are in the *asana* you can rock back and forth like a rocking chair.

VIII. ARDHA-HATSYENDRASANA (Twist Position):

Sit up straight with your legs out straight before you on the floor. Bend your left knee and put your left leg under your right leg so that the left heel is to the right of (and pressed firmly against) your right buttock. Now bring your right leg up by bending it at the knee and place the right foot flat on the ground to the left of the left knee.

Raise your left arm and twist the upper part of the body to the right until your left armpit is directly over your right thigh. Now turn your left forearm in such a fashion that you can pass it back through the triangle made by the bend in your right knee. At this point your left armpit is almost resting on top of the right thigh.

Reach around behind you with your right arm until your right and left hands can grip each other. Turn your head so that you are looking behind you over your right shoulder. Without straining, twist as far as possible. Then hold the position for about 15 to 30 seconds and return to a straight sitting position.

Now do the twist to the left, reversing all the above instructions.

IX. SIMHASANA (Lion Position):

Assume a kneeling position. Place your hands on your knees so that your fingers are extended outwards and you are leaning slightly forward.

Extend the tongue outward as far as possible and turn the eyes upward and towards the middle of the forehead. Exhale the breath as much as possible and contract the throat muscles. Make the entire body as taut as possible—as if you were a lion about to spring. Stop, return, and then relax. Repeat this *asana* about four times.

X. TOLANGULASANA (Balance Position):

Lie on your back. Raise your legs off the ground and spread them, keeping them straight. Then raise the upper part of your body to form a V with the point of contact with the ground being the tip of your spine. Stretch your arms forward between your spread legs. Remain in this position for 30 seconds. Don't strain. Return to a relaxed position.

XI. SARVANGASANA (Neck Stand):

Lie flat on your back. Very gently, in one smooth movement, lift your legs off the ground (keeping them straight) and raise them until they are at a 90° angle to your torso. Then placing your hands behind your back, slowly left your hips off the ground and more and more of your back, until only your head and neck are on the ground. Your back is supported by your hands, which should be as high up (close to the neck) on your back as possible. Elbows are on the ground. Remain with legs and body straight up for two minutes.

XII. HALASAN (Plough Position):

Starting from the neck stand, gently bring legs over head, still keeping them straight, until your toes touch the ground behind your head. Keeping your legs straight, attempt to bring your heels to the ground and to walk in towards your head. When you have gotten as close as possible without straining, then stop for 10 seconds.

XIII. KARNA PEEDASAN (Ear-Knee Position):

Starting from last position, now bend your knees until they touch the floor next to your ears. Remain in that position for ten seconds. Then gently retrace your steps, one by one, until you are back on the ground resting on your back. You can sense how limber your spine is as you come down from the neck stand. As you lower your body, press each vertebrae against the ground from the neck down. You should hear clicks along the way.

XIV. SAVASANA (Corpse Position):

Return to Corpse position and remain there for five minutes.

OM TAT SAT

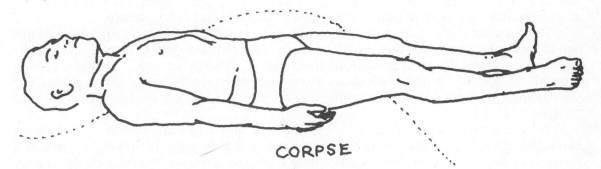

CORPSE

31

MANTRA

The major obstacle at every stage of the path of enlightenment is our own thoughts. Thoughts keep us separate. Even the thought of Unity is far different from Unity. And the thoughts keep coming; each one making its bid for our attention and identification.

Are all thoughts part of the illusion? Yes.

Are some thoughts better than others? Just diving into the water is aided by a spring board, and crossing the great ocean is aided by a raft, so certain thoughts are useful along the way. At the final moment, of course, even these thoughts must be transcended.

What are the steps of the process of calming the mind? Think of a lake in whose depths lies hidden what you seek. You try to see down into the lake, but you can't because the surface is covered with waves going in all directions . . . choppy water . . . thoughts coming from all directions . . . from your senses, from your memory . . . habits of thought learned unconsciously, running off mechanically . . . the causes of which are too subtle for your analytic mind to grasp.

Now, create an artificial wave . . . consciously add a new component . . . choose a single thought . . . and **consciously** set about making that thought dominant . . . so that a continuous sequence of even waves all coming from one direction overrides all the choppy water, as an ocean wave absorbs all the eddying waters at the shoreline. Now each wave is that same thought over and over again . . . no other thought can capture your attention which remains fixed upon the single thought.

Does this mean that other thoughts stop? No. Thoughts continue as a natural process in nature, but you run them through on automatic (base brain)—the same way most people drive an automobile, that is, without attending to each movement of the accelerator or steering wheel. We function under the fallacy *(cogito ergo sum)* that we are our thoughts and therefore must attend to them in order for them to be realized.

To break your identification with your own thoughts is to achieve inner freedom.

So you identify with this new thought you have added, until you and that thought become one and all other thoughts are passing just like clouds in the sky.

When you have arrived at the point where that one thought is the dominant one for you at all times . . . when going to sleep or waking . . . when walking or sitting . . . when talking or eating . . . then all of your life is on automatic. Then you are free of all but that one thought . . . and then . . . through deep meditation . . . you leave that thought aside too.

Which thoughts are useful to repeat? There are different kinds of *mantras* (phrases). Different *mantras* take you to different planes. Some seed *(beej) mantras* resonate within in such a way as to open one of your *chakras* (energy centers). There are power *mantras* to strengthen your will, and other *mantras* to open your heart in such a way as to deepen your compassion. For example:

"With a beam of love I touch the heart of my brother (sister, father, mother, beloved)." —Herman Rednick

ADITYA HRIDAYAM PUNYAM
SARV SHATRU BENA SHENAM

(All evil vanishes from life for him who keeps the sun in his heart.)—Ramayana

Some *mantras* are useful to help you accept the Divine Plan without feeling you have to act or do anything about it. For example:

"Let It Be"—McCartney
And That Too
TAT TWAM ASI (That thou art)

Also helpful in getting you to listen carefully in order to understand the part you play in the sacred dance is the *mantra:*

Not my but Thy will, O Lord.

Then there are special *mantras* used at special times of the day or for certain acts: for taking showers, toileting, washing clothes, cooking. The use of such special *mantras* is to help you see the act you are performing or about to perform in such a way as to prevent your identifying with the do-er of the act. Example:

When taking a shower you place water in your left hand. Then with your right fourth finger you touch the water and then touch in succession your mouth, nose, eyes, ears, forehead, and heart.

The simple mantra is:

OM VISHNU OM VISHNU OM VISHNU

OM WAK (mouth) *OM PRAN* (nose) *OM SHAKSHU*

OM SROTRAM OM SHIRAH OM HRIDAYAM

OM OM OM

and then continue to chant OM during the entire shower. This *mantra* reminds you that ALL is part of the ONE.

A *mantra* to be used while going to the toilet:

UTTISH THANTU SURAH SERUE YEX

GANDHARV KINNERAH PISACHA-GUHYAKASH

CHEV MAL MOOTRAM KAROMYA HAM

And a *mantra* for taking dope:

OM SHIVA SHANKARA

HARI HARI GANGA

You can make up other *mantras* for other daily acts to bring to consciousness your center so that you break the identification with an ego who is performing the act.

And then finally there are general *mantras* . . . *mantras* which can be used by anyone . . . and which move you from whatever stage you are at to the next stage, until you finally arrive at the doorway at which even *mantra* must go. For example:

OM

RAMA

HARI KRISHNA

GATE GATE PARAGATE

PARASAMGATE BODHI SWAHA

(Beyond, beyond, beyond the beyond. To thee, homage!)

OM MANI PADME HUM

(See Lama Govinda's *Foundations of Tibetan Mysticism* for discussion of this
 mantra)

OM TAT SAT

OM NAMAH SHIVAYA (To Siva, I bow)

Does a *mantra* have to be invested for it to work? Not in the usual sense . . . that is, not necessarily on the physical plane. Investing of a *mantra* means that it is passed in the Spirit. That is, if I am working with a *mantra* and the *mantra* is so deep within me that when I repeat it, it takes me into the Spirit, then I can hand it on to someone else. Whether he will be able to use it will depend upon how much faith he brings to it. If he brings little faith or commitment to it, then he will get little return; if he brings much faith he will get the highest returns. Many teachers who invest *mantras* will do so only when they know the student to be "ready" to receive the *mantra,* having sufficient faith to use the *mantra* profitably. *Mantras* which are purchased or which come from a source in which the student does not have full trust do not work unless the student is so advanced that he can transmute negative energy.

"The power and the effect of a *mantra* depend on the spiritual attitude, the knowledge and the responsiveness of the individual. The *sabda* or sound of the *mantra* is not a physical sound (though it may be accompanied by such a one) but a spiritual one. It cannot be heard by the ears but only by the heart, and it cannot be uttered by the mouth but only by the mind."—Lama Govinda

Can I use a *mantra* that I read in a book? If you feel that the author of the book is pure in his intent in transmitting the information, and if you sense that the book is in the spirit (i.e., it gets you high to read it), then you can find profit in working with the *mantra*. Get high, and then start working with it. An excellent book is *The Way of a Pilgrim* (translated from Russian), in which the *mantra* is "the Jesus prayer" (Lord Jesus Christ, have mercy on me.) used by the Greek Orthodox Christian mystics.

Why are we using *mantras* that are in the Sanskrit language? Wouldn't it be better to use English? No. Sanskrit is the root of the Indo-Aryan languages of which English is a part. It is a language that was evolved consciously, i.e., each sound syllable resonates in a specific *chakra*. Thus use of a Sanskrit *mantra* not only affects the user through the rational medium—the meaning of the *mantra*—but through the sound of the *mantra* as well. Often the investing of a *mantra* includes the pronunciation as well. However, if a person works with a *mantra* with sufficient purity to be able to "hear," he will come to hear the *mantra* outside/inside of himself (in the *akash,* or ether) and he will come to say the *mantra* in unison with these voices which he hears.

What is *Japa? Japa* is *mantra* which is the name of God. RAMA is such a *mantra*. To repeat the name of God over and over brings you closer to Oneness with the Divine.

How do you do *mantra?* Don't **do** *mantra*. Let it happen to you. For example, if you feel the desire to work with the *mantra* RAMA:

(1) Consider who Ram was historically. Ram was the *Avatar* in the *Sat Yuga*—the purest period. At that time most of the people in the world were in the Spirit so they

35

recognized and honored the Avatar. The story of the *Ramayana* tells of the life of Ram. He is pictured as the perfect son, husband, brother, father, king—that is, a perfect *karma yogi*. He represents living daily life as an act of worship.

He is a beautiful dark being of great light, love and compassion, wisdom and power—in perfect harmony. Ram is the essence of who you are when you realize your true Self (the *Atman*).

(2) Consider Ram as a Spiritual Being. He is another statement of Eternal Perfection reflected in the form of a human being. He is pure light, love, energy, compassion, wisdom, power. Like the sun, he emits light and warmth and life force. He is as Real at this moment as you have faith to allow him to be.

(3) Start to pronounce His name silently. It is two syllables: Ra and Ma. However, the "a" of Ma is sounded silently. Listen inside until you can hear the name and then begin to let it come outside, as if you were speaking along with the inside voice which is whispering it. Then keep saying it.

(4) After some time you will notice that though you are still repeating it with your tongue, the *mantra* is moving, perhaps first to a sub-vocal point and then to your brain. Finally, if you have done the *mantra* long enough, it will start to sound in your heart.

(5) You should keep doing it consciously until it has become a strong habit. Take a walk and say the *mantra* all the time you are walking. Notice everything but keep the *mantra* going. Keep realizing that God is It All . . . and therefore everything you look at is part of Ram. Everyone you meet is Ram who has come to teach you something. You are continually meeting and merging into perfection.

(6) Make yourself like Hanuman (the monkey in the *Ramayana*)—the perfect servant and lover of Ram.

(7) If you wish to use an external aid to help keep the *mantra* in your awareness, you might obtain a *mala*. This is a string of 108 prayer beads plus a **guru** bead. In the West it is usually called a rosary. These beads you can pass between the thumb and fourth or third finger (the index finger is not used because in India it is used for pointing in accusation) of your right hand, bead by bead, repeating the name of Ram with each bead. In using a *mala* you proceed up to the **guru** bead and then turn the beads and go the other way. You do not complete the circle. The beads are moved towards you. After a period of usage your beads will begin to have an investment of the *pran* or Spiritual Force which your doing of *Japa* has brought to them.

(8) Get in the habit of coming out of sleep into *mantra*.

(9) Get in the habit of having every strong emotion—positive or negative—serve as a reminder to bring you back to your *mantra*.

36

(10) Get in the habit of cutting through your own thought prisons by just dissolving it all back into the *mantra*.

(11) Do *mantra* with others who are in the spirit. Do *mantra* when you are high.

(12) Do not discuss the *mantra* with anyone who is less into the spirit than you. If you can't make that discrimination, then don't discuss it with anyone. For everytime you run your *mantra* through the head of someone who doubts or is cynical their doubt or cynicism will resonate with the places in you where your own faith is not enough. That is why *mantras* are often invested secretly.

(13) Some practices with *mantra* require that at the outset one work with the *mantra* only about 15 minutes in the morning and 15 minutes in the evening. If you prefer you may follow this system and then let the *mantra* expand out into your life as it naturally will. If you "try" to make the *mantra* work—or force it as an act of egoic will—then you will lose it (though it can be regained). So it is good to keep in mind that in truth the *mantra* is doing you. You are not doing the *mantra*. Let it pull you towards itself as you are ready. Be a passive instrument in its hands.

Potent Quotes

"When the mind perceives an object it is transformed into the shape of that object. So the mind which thinks of the Divinity which it worships *(Ista-devata)* is at length, through continued devotion, transformed into the likeness of that Devata. By allowing the Devata thus to occupy the mind for long it becomes as pure as the Devata. This is the fundamental principle of Tantric Sadhana or religious practice."—Woodroffe

"World comes into play only when one forgets the Lord. By constant remembrance of God, one while living in the world among friends and relations is yet not of the world."—Persian Divine

"I do not feel that I am walking at all. I am only aware of the fact that I am saying the prayer. When the bitter cold pierces me, I begin to say my prayer more earnestly and I quickly get warm all over. When hunger begins to overcome me I call more often on the name of Jesus and I forget my wish for food . . . I have become a sort of half-conscious person. I have no cares and no interests. The fussy business of the world I would not give a glance to. The one thing I wish for is to be alone, and all by myself to pray, to pray without ceasing: and doing this I am filled with joy."—*Way of a Pilgrim*

"After no great lapse of time I had the feeling that the Prayer had, so to speak, by its own action passed from my lips to my heart. Further, there came into my heart a gracious warmtn.—*Way of a Pilgrim*

"None of these things made me feel at all cast down. It was as though they happened to someone else, and I merely watched them. The prayer brought sweetness into my heart and made me unaware, so to speak, of everything else." —*Way of a Pilgrim*

"If the enemy cannot turn us from prayer by means of vain thoughts and sinful ideas, then he brings back into our minds good things we have been taught, and fills us with beautiful ideas, so that one way or another he may lure us away from prayer, which is a thing he cannot bear. It is called 'a theft from the right hand side.'

He taught me therefore not to admit during times of prayer even the most lofty of spiritual thoughts. And if I saw that in the course of the day time had been spent more in improving thought and talk than in actual prayer of the heart then I was to think of it as a loss of the sense of proportion or a sign of spiritual greed." —*Way of a Pilgrim*

"Everywhere, wherever you may find yourself, you can set up an altar to God in your mind by means of prayer . . ." —*Way of a Pilgrim*

"Free from sensual passions and absorbed in devout affection to Rama the soul disports itself like a fish in the ambrosial lake of his beloved name." —Tulsi Das

"Place the name of Rama as a jewelled lamp at the door of your lips and there will be light, as you will, both inside and out." —Tulsi Das

"Any wretch who invokes his name is able to cross the vast and boundless ocean of existence, and you are his messengers; have then no fear, but with Rama's image impressed upon your soul, concert your plans." —Tulsi Das

"Devi, imagine the Sanskrit letters in these honey-filled foci of awareness, first as letters, then more subtly as sounds, then as most subtle feeling. Then leaving them aside, be **free**." —Reps

TRANSMUTING ENERGY

The entire cosmos, at every plane and in every form, is energy. This energy is known as *pran*. Your body is a form of *pran*, so is your thought and feeling, and so is light. These forms of *pran* differ from one another in terms of the rate and amplitude of their vibrations. Solids are *pran* in a grosser form; light, in a finer form. The finest form of *pran*, the tiniest quantum of energy, is the Universe . . . the highest plane of form (as opposed to formless), from which all other planes are derived, is the Clear White Light: a homogeneous light field which includes everything. Every quantum of energy is interchangeable with every other one, and there is continuous change: continuous transformation of energy from one form to another. Thus everything in the universe is interrelated.

At the level at which there is only pure *pran*, a number of labels are interchangeable. This plane could also be called pure light or pure consciousness as well as pure *pran*. The implications of this are far reaching. For it means that the universe **is** consciousness. It follows that when you have succeeded in fully breaking the identification with your body, senses, and thoughts, then you merge into pure consciousness—Universal Consciousness. What you thought was "your" consciousness turns out to be only a part of a Consciousness caught in the illusion of separateness. A person who has severed all attachments and has thus become one with Consciousness is said to be in *SAT CHIT ANANDA*: total existence, total knowledge, total bliss. This is the highest form of *samadhi*. Short of this state, however, there are many intermediate steps in which you become free of attachments to the grosser forms of *pran* and function in more rarified planes.

Input of energy:

Until the final state of *Sat Chit Ananda*, an individual keeps his separate identity. And this separate "being" is a conduit through which energy passes. This separate entity is able to receive *pran* at a vibration similar to the plane at which there is still attachment. Thus, if you are attached to your body, you receive *pran* in the grossest form, that is, through food, water, and air. Some of this *pran* is expended in gross muscle activity and reproduction, while another part of the *pran* is transformed into a finer form which is usable as thought, feelings, or, in the highest form, as the experience of the Spirit or pure consciousness. This highest form of *pran* is called *ojas*, the lower form is known as *bindu*.

For a person who has broken his identification on the gross physical plane, *pran* is available to him at a higher vibration. He is able to transform this *pran* which can come from thoughts, sights, etc. into finer vibrations as before, or into more gross vibrations. Thus, he is able, as was Theresa Neumann, to feed his body directly with Light, alleviating the necessity for taking in food. Such powers are of course unnecessary in most cases. It is more usual to evolve to the point where one eats what one needs with enjoyment, though without attachment. The sun emits the higher vibrational forms of *pran* which most of us can only use when it has gone through a vibrational step-down through the medium of plants, etc.

If you have broken your attachments at the physical plane, then you have available to you energy at a vibrational rate of a subtle or astral plane as well as the gross physical energy to which you are accustomed. Therefore, as you proceed with purification, you experience considerably greater energy. Of course, the end of the path is the point at which you become ALL energy. However, even at the early stages of the journey, the additional energy poses certain problems. All of your habits of reaction are based on your usual input of energy. As you feed in more energy, it is like feeding in a 220 current into a home that is wired for 110. Unless the electrical fixtures in the home are suitably adapted, you will burn out all the appliances. You might try to "carry on business as usual" . . . only with greater intensity and duration . . . physical activity, sexual activity, talking, etc. . . . but you soon find that these channels are not adequate.

What you must do is develop a framework of new habits of thought as to (a) who you are, and (b) how to use energy. There are two strategies that you can pursue once you realize this. The first is to avoid the fulfilling of the still-active desires, using the energy instead for specific acts of purification. The second alternative is to use the energy to fulfill the desire once again, but simultaneously to be conscious of the entire process, that is, use the experience to get finished with the desire. This second method, called *ban marg*, or the left-handed path, is very risky. Most people who attempt to use it are not successful and succeed only in creating more *karma*. However, it is such a seductive route that most Westerners prefer it and wrap their subsequent failure in layers of rationalization.

What is required is the surrender of the model of a finite ego. But that model dies hard, for it is the model that keeps the dance of nature mechanically proceeding. And the ego would be only too happy to have under its control all this additional energy to gratify its own desires. Such use, however, turns out to be short-lived, for using powers in the service of the ego creates new *karma* and new attachment which ultimately lead to the loss of the power. That is, one gets re-attached at the grosser plane and loses the new resource of energy.

However, the using of increased amounts of energy to fulfill old desires has another effect. One finally uses up the desire. It's like having a craving for peanut butter and then getting a large amount and eating it directly out of the jar. Finally you arrive at the point where the desire for peanut butter is satiated. If you keep eating it beyond satiation—because you are still living out the old thought pattern "I desire peanut butter"—you ultimately

40

arrive at a point where the experience is so negative that you may permanently lose desire for peanut butter.

As this happens with more and more desires, that is, as they fall away, you at first experience loss, emptiness and despair in your life . . . a deadened meaninglessness. At that point you may try to resurrect old desires, but it really doesn't work. It's at this point of despair that you are truly ripe to begin to tune in to the next level of consciousness.

Now you can see the pros and cons of using the new energy to fulfill old desires. On the one hand you are satiating and finishing with these desires. On the other hand you are getting more deeply enmeshed because every time you satisfy a desire you strengthen the habits connected with it. And every desire, no matter how perverse it may seem, is an attempt to get to the light. (The Devil knows not for whom he works.)

Further clarification:
Here is another way of stating your predicament: you have some activity going on in the first four *chakras* (centers). Survival, sex, power, and compassionate oneness with other beings all bid as motivators of your perceptions and behaviors. If all of your energy were localized in the second *chakra*, for example, your life would be relatively simple. You would be primarily motivated and preoccupied with sexual gratification. You would notice and be attracted to possible sexual partners and your actions with these people would all be directed towards sexual gratification. If your energy were all localized in the third *chakra*, then it would still be simple . . . all power. You would see each person only in terms of whether that person could be used to enhance your ego. You would experience fear and hatred of those who held power over you. Your behavior would be subservient or officious or benignly paternalistic. You would be unable to see another human being as a peer but only as superior or inferior to you in one dimension or another. In those dimensions where you are equal, you would not notice the other person.

If you had crossed the first great barrier (between the third and fourth *chakras*) so completely that all your energy were localized in the fourth *chakra*, then you would experience only the compassionate feelings of the brotherhood of the Spirit with all other beings. Whether in a sexual embrace or in a business or social contact, the only feeling towards the other person would be one of "us-ness," of brotherhood. Since you would no longer have any investment in yourself as a separate entity, all of your actions would be in perfect harmony with all the forces acting in the field at that moment. You would be living in the *Tao*.

But your predicament is that you are simultaneously involved in all of these *chakras*. So if you try to seduce someone as if the second *chakra* is what it's **all** about, you suddenly find your sexual desires fluctuating as you experience waves of compassionate love interspersed

41

with lust. Or if you join with someone in prayer or singing the praises of God, you become aware of sexual desires towards that person or desires to control him. Many of the relationships to spiritual teachers have components of power and sex in them.

At the outset, it is necessary to acknowledge where you are in your development. All of these forces are present. Denial will not help. What will help?

As you come to understand fully that you will be finished with human suffering only when you are living in the fourth *chakra* (or higher), and you become strongly committed to "getting on with it," then the method is straightforward. Keep converting every relationship into one of compassion. Keep a compassionate model uppermost in your consciousness at all times. Every time you slip back into one of the lower *chakras,* don't pity yourself or damn yourself. Merely redefine the situation in terms of the fourth *chakra* . . . in terms of compassionate love for all beings. If you find you are in a relationship with someone which is gratifying to him, you because of the power you have over them, consider that you and he are both manifestations of the One . . . look him in the eye until you both see clearly where power stops and where love begins. Once you have seen through that veil, then you have transmuted the energy from the third to the fourth *chakra*. This is the Divine Work: making the profane sacred.

What is the risk? By working with energies associated with the lower *chakras* you are arousing all the habits which keep you stuck in those *chakras*. If your will is not strong enough (i.e., your desire to get on with it), you may end up just strengthening the illusion and increasing your *karma*. The safest strategy is to keep as far away from the fires of the lower *chakras* as possible. When you have to get near them, then transmute the energy. The riskiest strategy is to seek out stimuli which arouse the lower *chakra* energies and then attempt to transmute those energies. Keep in mind that most people who attempt this high-risk strategy stay caught in the illusion of separateness for their entire lifetime.

Between these two extremes is the path that most Westerners who are on the path follow. They design their life in such a way as not to be inundated by stimuli connected with the lower *chakras*. At the same time they do not avoid such stimuli. When one comes along, they do their best to transmute the energy. They accept their own limitations, feel no guilt about getting caught again, and yet slowly and gently they learn to transmute the energy. This is the middle path: living life joyfully and as consciously as possible.

42

PRANAYAM

Exercises

One of the manifestations of *pran*, or life force, in the human body is breathing. By working with your breath you are able to tune in to the larger energies of the universe. Furthermore, there is an intimate relationship between thought and breath. When you calm your breath, there is simultaneous calming of the mind. When you succeed either in stopping the breath altogether or in stopping all thought, then you are in a state of *samadhi* or super-consciousness. The two are so intimately related that to stop one is to stop the other also.

Pranayam is the control of vital force or energy or *pran* through a series of disciplined breathing exercises. The actual stopping of the breath is only possible for advanced *yogis* who have done much *sadhana*. However, there are some beginning exercises which are almost immediately effective in calming you down. In addition, these exercises are preparatory to the more advanced breathing retention exercises by which the *kundalini* is aroused (energy moving up the spinal column to the head). For the advanced exercises, supervision is important.

In addition to bringing about a calmness and a sense of peacefulness throughout the day, these exercises also alter the constitution of the blood through oxygen exchange, and lead to more shallow breathing throughout the day. You will notice that advanced *yogis* all have very gentle breath and never get "out of breath."

These breathing exercises can be done anywhere from one to four times in twenty-four hours, depending upon the intensity of your *sadhana*. They must be done on an empty stomach (at least three hours after taking food and one hour after taking liquid). Most people will find that doing *pranayam* as part of the early morning purification is ideal. A second suitable time is at sunset before the evening meal.

While it is good to learn deep breathing, these particular exercises limit breath to the thoracic cavity rather than the abdominal cavity. During the remainder of the day you should be using deep breathing, that is, breathing which involves the lower abdominal cavity as well as the upper thoracic cavity.

1. Sit upright. If you can sit in the lotus position do so. On the other hand you can sit in a chair as long as you keep your head, neck, and chest in a straight line.

2. Close the *muhlbandh*. This means to pull in and up on the anal sphincter and genitals. At first you will find this very difficult to maintain. With a little practice, however, it will become easy to retain this closed position during the entire set of exercises. If you wish you

43

can make a small ball of cloth about the size of a golf ball and sit on it so that it presses up on a spot midway between the anus and the genitals. This will help.

3. Pull in slightly on the *udyanabandh*. That is, pull in your gut . . . slightly contract your abdominal muscles. Keep them that way throughout these exercises. Do not raise your shoulders or tighten your body when doing these exercises.

Exercise 1: *SHEETLI* (also called *sitali)*

Extend the tongue out of the mouth as far as possible. Form it into a "U" shape with the sides high and middle low (like a trough). If you don't think you can do this, look into a mirror and get as close to that position as possible. Then breathe in through the mouth as deeply as is comfortable with the abdominal muscles slightly contracted. Then retract the tongue into the mouth and breathe out through the nose.

During the inhalation, imagine that you are bringing into your body pure *pran* or life force or light or consciousness. Throughout the exercise focus on the point between the eyebrows so that you experience bringing the *pran* to that point. As you breathe out, imagine breathing out impurities of body and mind.

Initially do five of these the first day. Increase by one each day until you are doing fifty a day. Continue at that rate.

Exercise 2: *BHASTRIKA* (also called *kapalabhati* or bellows)

This breathing involves a rhythmic shallow breathing through the nose only. There is no pause between inhalation and exhalation. You start slowly in order to keep the in-breath and out-breath of equal intensity and duration. Once you have equated them, then you can increase the rate and intensity. Ultimately the breath is short and staccato in nature with a definite feeling of impact at the points between the in-breath and the out-breath and in-breath.

During this exercise focus on the inside of the tip of the nose at the point where the air hits the nasal passage during exhalation.

Do this exercise for about thirty seconds. Stop. Rest. Then do it again for about thirty seconds. Later, if you wish, you can increase the number of these thirty second units to three or four at a sitting.

If you are doing it properly, at the end of two to four weeks you will notice that at the end of this exercise you smell a new and pleasantly sweet smell at the tip of your nose at the completion of this exercise.

Exercise 3: *NARI SODHAN*

Place the right hand so that the third finger is resting between the eyebrows, the thumb is by the right nostril, and the fourth finger is by the left nostril. Close the right nostril with the thumb and inhale slowly and evenly through the left nostril (about 4 seconds). Then hold the nose by closing both nostrils for about 2 seconds. Then remove the thumb and exhale slowly and evenly through the right nostril (about 8 seconds). Then after a second or two, inhale through the right nostril (4 seconds), hold (2 seconds) and exhale through the left nostril (8 seconds). In other words, you change nostrils before each exhalation.

As you take in the breath through your left nostril, imagine a charge of energy going down the *ida* (a nerve on the left side of your spine). As you then hold the breath for the two seconds, imagine that charge of energy crossing from the left to the right side at the base of your spine. Then as you exhale through the right nostril, imagine that charge of energy coming up the *pingala* (a nerve on the right side of the spine). As your total purification program proceeds, these imaginings will be replaced by actual sensations in your spinal column.

Start with five of this exercise on the first day and increase to fifty a day and continue at that rate.

If you experience hiccoughs or pain from doing these exercises, stop at once and concentrate on other forms of *yoga* for a year or two before attempting *pranayam* again.

Potent Quotes

"Human endeavor must always remain short of perfection; besides no one will ever weed out the tendencies innate in his particular nature; the point is to change their force into life power."—Ouspensky

"Just as hunger, not greed, has a legitimate purpose . . . so the sexual instinct has been implanted by nature solely for the propagation of the species, not for the kindling of insatiable longings. Destroy wrong desires now; otherwise they will remain with you after the astral body has been separated from its physical casing. Even when the flesh is weak, the mind should be constantly resistant. If temptation assails you with cruel force, overcome it by impersonal analysis and indomitable will. Every natural passion can be mastered."—Sri Yukteswar

"Fire animates man; a sexual fire reproduces him. These two fires are one at their source. Man can either drain this fire for his pleasure, or he can sublimate it into a divine force . . ." de Lubiz

45

SEXUAL ENERGY

There are seven focal points of psychic energy in the body. These points are called *chakras*. Each center is associated with a different vibrational expression of the energy—from the first *chakra* which works with the grossest form of this energy to the seventh *chakra* which works with the energy in its finest form. Just as a personality profile can describe an individual's dominant personality characteristics, so a person can be described in terms of the *chakras* in which his energy is received and dissipated.

There are certain labels which can be affixed to these *chakras* to define the dominant concern of an individual whose primary energy expression is fixed at that particular level. Thus the first *chakra* is associated with survival, a jungle or animal mentality. The second *chakra* is associated with reproduction and sexual gratification. The third *chakra* concerns power and mastery. These three *chakras* are the focal points for most of the energy presently used by man in his worldly endeavors. These three *chakras* are primarily concerned with the use of energy for the maintenance and enhancement of the ego.

It is only when we arrive at the fourth *chakra*, the heart *chakra*, that we enter into a realm which starts to transcend the ego. This fourth *chakra* is primarily concerned with compassion. The fifth is concerned with the seeking of God. The sixth (located between the eyebrows) is concerned with wisdom (the third eye); and the seventh, with full enlightenment or union.

The spiritual path can be conceived, from an energy point of view, as the path up the spine . . . that is, the movement and transformation of energy from the lower to the higher *chakras* . . . the purification of energy. With this definition in mind, it is apparent that any use of energy which further strengthens the hold, or intensity, of the lower *chakras* interferes with the spiritual progress.

The experience and habits associated with lust are the domain of the second *chakra*. Freud was the master spokesman of the person who is fixated in the second *chakra*, just as Adler was the spokesman for the third *chakra*, and perhaps Jung the spokesman of the fourth.

In our Western culture there has been such an investment in the models of man associated with the second and third *chakra* (sex and power) that we have developed strong and deeply held habits of perceiving the inner and outer universe in these terms. Though we may realize intellectually that the spiritual journey requires the transformation of energy from these preoccupations to higher centers, we find it difficult to override these strong habits which seem to be reinforced by the vibration of the culture in which we live.

Thus it seems "normal" to have certain ego needs with regard to sex and power. It is difficult for us to comprehend that what is normal for a second-*chakra* preoccupied person is hardly normal for a fourth-*chakra* person.

A second-*chakra* person, as so well described by Freud, thinks of everything as sexual in nature . . . a pencil is phallic, political power is sexual potency, etc. Freud describes religion as sublimated sexuality. A third-*chakra* person sees it all in terms of power or mastery. Even his sexual activity is seen in that light.

All "takes" of the Universe in terms of the first, second and third *chakra* are profane. That is, they maintain and enhance man's illusion of separateness. Every time you live out an act in terms (habits of thought) of a lower *chakra,* you strengthen the hold of that *chakra*.

There are two strategies with regard to the very powerful energies localized at the level of the second or sexual *chakra* in human beings. You can avoid arousing these energies and simultaneously work from within to transmute these latent forces into spiritual energy. This

47

requires sexual continence and is called *brahmacharya*. The alternative is to continue to arouse the second *chakra* energies and to attempt to direct these now manifest energies into spiritual realms. This technique is known as sexual *tantra*.

Brahmacharya

Brahamacharya—sexual continence—is a specific process of taking energy you might otherwise use in second *chakra* acts and moving the energy up the spine into the higher *chakras*. The purpose is to generate or collect energy which you can use in the service of becoming enlightened. Most *brahmacharyas* are converting and moving the energy up to the higher centers so effectively that they experience little of the sexual frustration that someone who is "celibate" in the usual sense might. They experience higher energy of the specific nature that is useful in breaking through in meditation into the state of *Sat Chit Ananda*. The techniques involved include primarily *pranayam, mantra*, diet, and the avoidance of second *chakra* stimuli.

From a habitual Western vantage point it looks as if such a person is giving up something and must be suffering. But the true *brahmacharya* is not only **not** suffering, but is often experiencing far higher and more permanent states of bliss than can be experienced through the lower *chakras*.

Sexual Tantra

In *bhakti yoga*—the *yoga* of devotion—the highest form of the method (as reflected in the story of Krishna and the Gopis) is the relation of devotee to God as lover to beloved. The *gopis* (milkmaids) are in love with Krishna—the young handsome boy with the flute. On autumn evenings by the full moon he would play his flute by the river bank and call the *gopis* to him. And there he would manifest himself in 16,000 forms—one for each *gopi*—and proceed to make love to each in the way most desired by her. This brought all the energy contained in the desire for merging that exists between a lover and the beloved (as two, i.e., dualism) into the service of union in total love with God.

Krishna says in the *Bhagavad Gita*, "Do what you do but dedicate the fruits of your acts to me"—all acts, and the act of sex is no exception.

To practice sexual *tantra*, **total truth and total trust are required.** You and your partner must both consciously understand that you are working together as an act of purification to burn away all impurities so that you may become ONE. You have agreed to share *karma*. This has nothing to do with any specific acts either now or later, it only implies that there is no holding back or unwillingness to accept how it is at this moment.

48

It is totally Here and Now. All fantasies are shared and brought to the Here and Now. Thoughts must be openly, fully openly, shared until the paranoia attendant to lust has been replaced by the luxurious warmth of love.

The practice starts with meditation together and after perhaps the sharing of a cardamon seed. Slowly the dance evolves . . . the dance in which every breath . . . touch . . . movement . . . even thought . . . is totally savoured (compassionately understood) by the one consciousness that you are sharing. You are both man and you are both woman . . . and there is an act in which two bodies are involved, but the act (like two hands clapping) is a unity experienced by a single consciousness.

The body of the partner becomes the body of Ram or the Divine Mother. Each touch or kiss is an act of devotion to that sacred being. The entire experience is the act of worship and the orgasm itself ceases to be of paramount importance.

The difficulty with this method, of course, is the tendency to get lost in the personal sensual gratification which draws you and your partner apart and casts you back into a second *chakra* dance which merely once again perpetuates the illusion of separateness. There are numerous specific techniques which reduce the risk of losing your center. An example is the *mathuna* position in which the woman sits astride the man. This position slows down the arousal process and the orgasm, thus allowing the partners to remain conscious throughout the entire practice.

None of us who are collaborating in the preparation of this manuscript are sufficiently evolved in the use of this method to present this section in a more definitive fashion at this time.

A woman once came to Mahatma Gandhi with her little boy. She asked, "Mahatma-ji, tell my little boy to stop eating sugar."

"Come back in three days," said Gandhi.

In three days the woman and the little boy returned and Mahatma Gandhi said to the little boy, "Stop eating sugar."

The woman asked, "Why was it necessary for us to return only after three days for you to tell my little boy that?"

The Mahatma replied: "Three days ago I had not stopped eating sugar."

SIDDHIS

"And in the fourth watch of the night Jesus went unto them, walking on the sea. And when the disciples saw him walking on the sea, they were troubled, saying, It is a spirit; and they cried out for fear. But straightaway Jesus spake unto them, saying, Be of good cheer; It is I; be not afraid.

And Peter answered him and said, Lord, if it be thou, bid me come unto thee on the water. And he said, Come. And when Peter was come down out of the ship, he walked on the water to go to Jesus.

But when he saw the wind boisterous, he was afraid; and beginning to sink he cried, Lord, save me.

And immediately Jesus stretched forth his hand, and caught him, and said unto him, O thou of little faith, wherefore didst thou doubt?

And when they were come into the ship, the wind ceased."—Matthew

Levitation? Astral travel? Mind-reading? Parting the Red Sea? Withering the fig tree? Moving mountains?

What role do powers play in the spiritual journey?

As one purifies one's mind and body, i.e., increases the one-pointedness of mind, one gains more and more powers (*siddhis*). At each stage there is the option to use or not to use a newly gained power.

If you are interested in powers, you'll get them. That's the trouble! Along with each step of purification, i.e., with increasing ability to bring the mind to one-pointedness, all of the powers you've either read about or thought about become available to you. These are like the lions at the gates of each successive inner temple. The lions become more and more ferocious.

If you have a desire other than the desire for enlightenment, at each stage of your work you become increasingly capable of gratifying that desire. If you want wealth, wealth will be yours. If you want a beautiful lover, why, a beautiful lover will be yours. The problem of course is that everytime you direct your attention to the gratification of a specific desire, you create more thoughts about that desire and thus strengthen its hold over you. Thus, you slow down your own journey into the light. Since you already realize that the gratification of that desire is going to be finite and ultimately not enough, the new power has in fact sucked you into another *cul-de-sac*. And so it goes for most people until they truly see each new power as one more seductive enticement of *maya*.

Some people when they become aware of having gained a new power justify their use of the power in terms of social good, i.e., the welfare of their fellow man. However, to the extent

50

that they are attached to doing good, their desires affect their perception and they, in fact, cannot truly see what is best for the welfare of their fellow man. Often, in their zeal to do good, they only increase man's illusion and make perception of the truth more difficult.

These days most people put their faith in man's intellect and his power of reason. Consequently, those few who have powers which transcend the rational mind are in an unusual and extraordinary position. It becomes tempting for them to want to experiment. There are many stories in India of *yogis* who in the course of very intense *sadhana* have developed certain powers which they use either for fame or wealth or more subtle forms of ego enhancement. They read minds, change their physiological processes such as heart beat, body heat, reaction to cold, etc. As an example of a misuse of power, one *sadhu* lifts a 100 pound bag of sand with his penis.

The simple rule of the game, repeated in the most profound mystical texts, reminds us that it is not my but THY will, O Lord . . . not my trip but THY Trip. Quite simply, if **you** are wondering whether to use a power . . . don't! If, on the other hand, in the unfolding of your *karma,* some power is required, it will appear and serve. The only thing that will hold back your evolvement is the use of power in the service of the ego.

With each new level of surrender and purification, and of faith to give up your present control and power, you achieve new powers. Finally, when you have given up all of your position and power, you end up having all powers. When Jesus said, "Had ye faith ye could move mountains," he was speaking literal truth. The cosmic humor is that if you desire to move mountains and you continue to purify yourself, ultimately you will arrive at the place where you are able to move mountains. But in order to arrive at this position of power you will have had to give up being he-who-wanted-to-move-mountains so that you can be he-who-put-the-mountain-there-in-the-first-place. The humor is that finally when you have the power to move the mountain, you are the person who placed it there—so there the mountain stays.

One can only stand in total awe of such a divine plan, and experience much compassion about the poignancy of one's petty concerns about power.

SATSANG

Ramakrishna points out that when a tree is very small we protect it by surrounding it with a fence so that animals do not step on it. Later when the tree is bigger it no longer needs the fence. Then it can give shelter to many.

So it is with the spiritual growth. At the outset, just after we have begun to awaken to the possibility of living in the Spirit, we are vulnerable, for our faith is shaky. At this stage in our development it is important that we surround ourselves with other beings who share our faith in the Spirit. This is called *satsang,* or *sangha*—the community of monks on the path. And it is for this reason that there are such things as monasteries or *ashrams*. During this stage it is well to be with people who wish to discuss only ways and means of realizing enlightenment.

The progression is quite inevitable. After some time on the path of awakening, the type of associates you share time with changes. Finally you realize that except for existing *karmic* commitments—such as familial or societal commitments—there is no reason to spend time with anyone except as an aid to one's *sadhana*. So all new relationships, be they friendships, roommates, marriages, business partnerships, take on implicitly, and finally explicitly, this contractual basis.

When your center is firm, when your faith is strong and unwavering, then it will not matter what company you keep. Then you will see that all beings are on the evolutionary journey of consciousness. They differ only to the degree that the veil of illusion clouds their vision. But for you . . . you will see behind the veil to the place where we are all ONE.

Potent Quotes

"Our friends found us becoming dull. Gurdjieff said, 'There is worse to come . . . he is an interesting man who lies well . . . you have already begun to die. It is a long way yet to complete death but still a certain amount of silliness is going out of you. You can no longer deceive yourselves as sincerely as you did before. You have now got the taste of truth.' "—Ouspensky

"Bad company is loss, and good company is gain; . . . In company with the wind the dust flies heavenwards; if it joins water, it becomes mud and sinks."—Tulsi Das

"When going through spiritual exercises (*sadhana*) do not associate with those who never concern themselves with matters spiritual. Such people scoff at those who worship God and meditate upon Him and they ridicule piety and the pious. Keep yourself far aloof from them."—Ramakrishna

"I must now whisper very unceasingly I was not born separate from you." / Gv

GETTING STRAIGHT

Your understanding of what the universe is all about changes as you proceed further along the path towards enlightenment. As your vantage point or perspective changes, you begin to understand more and more of "how it is." With this greater understanding comes greater compassion . . . an acceptance of "how it is" . . . an ability to see the divine plan in everything . . . even in your failings and the failings of others.

In the course of your journey it is most likely that your day-to-day companions or friends may change. Some may fall away as your interest in the Spirit pulls you from the worldly interest which brought or kept you together, but new friends who share your current interests will appear. Of course, some of your existing relationships will move easily into this new domain and the relationship will become deeper and calmer . . . coming to exist in the

54

eternal present.

This transition in travelling companions is a delicate and troubling matter. To find that someone whom you assumed shared all your values and interests over many years has no interest what-so-ever in enlightenment or in becoming more conscious or coming into the Spirit is a shock. You want to share this "trip" with him in the same way as you shared others in the past. That desire to proselytize, to turn him on, to show him, to bring him to the light . . . is a reflection of your lack of wisdom. For only some people can hear. Only some can awaken in this lifetime. It's a little like seeing a friend drowning and being unable to catch his hand. You want so badly to DO something. But in truth you can only BE . . . be as straight and as open and as HERE as you can be . . . and if your friend can hear, he will hear. And if he cannot hear, he will turn away from you. No blame.

What is important is that you get your house in order at each stage of the journey so that you can proceed.

"If some day it be given to you to pass into the inner temple, you must leave no enemies behind."—de Lubicz

For example, if you never got on well with one of your parents and you have left that parent behind on your journey in such a way that the thought of that parent arouses anger or frustration or self-pity or any emotion . . . you are still attached. You are still stuck. And you must get that relationship straight before you can finish your work. And what, specifically, does "getting it straight" mean? Well, it means re-perceiving that parent, or whoever it may be, with total compassion . . . seeing him as a being of the spirit, just like you, who happens to be your parent . . . and who happens to have this or that characteristic, and who happens to be at a certain stage of his evolutionary journey. You must see that all beings are just beings . . . and that all the wrappings of personality and role and body are the coverings. Your attachments are only to the coverings, and as long as you are attached to someone else's covering you are stuck, and you keep them stuck, in that attachment. Only when you can see the essence, can see God, in each human being do you free yourself and those about you. It's hard work when you have spent years building a fixed model of who someone else is to abandon it, but until that model is superceded by a compassionate model, you are still stuck.

In India they say that in order to proceed with one's work one needs one's parents' blessings. Even if the parent has died, you must in your heart and mind, re-perceive that relationship until it becomes, like every one of your current relationships, one of light. If the person is still alive you may, when you have proceeded far enough, revisit and bring the relationship into the present. For, if you can keep the visit totally in the present, you will be free and finished. The parent may or may not be . . . but that is his *karmic* predicament.

And if you have been truly in the present, and if you find a place in which you can share even a brief eternal moment . . . this is all it takes to get the blessing of your parent! It obviously doesn't demand that the parent say, "I bless you." Rather it means that he hears you as a fellow being, and honors the divine spark within you. And even a moment in the Here and Now . . . a single second shared in the eternal present . . . in love . . . is all that is required to free you both, if you are ready to be freed. From then on, it's your own individual *karma* that determines how long you can maintain that high moment.

This getting straight not only applies to people but to things as well, such as favorite music, disliked foods, special treats, avoided places, all your toys, etc. Everything must be rerun through your compassion machine. You must revisit, at least in meditation, all your old attachments and re-see them in the light of the Spirit. As you do, they fall away . . . unless, of course, the attachment to them is so strong that you are not able yet to re-see them with pure compassion. To stumble in that way on the path merely indicates the work yet to be done. Thus it gives direction to your *sadhana* . . . which is work on those desires that cause you to stumble, by bringing them into the light of *mantra* or the witness until they fall away of their own.

56

TRUTH

Truth gets you high. There is no doubt about it. Lies bring you down. To lie to another person you have to see them as "him" or "her" or "them", i.e., as an object. Such distance that the act of lying creates turns out in the long run to cost more than the lie gained for you in the first place. Once you understand the workings of *karma* you see that there is no escape from the effects, both short and long term, of your acts, i.e., acts done in the service of the ego.

Reflect upon each of the following quotes. Then reflect upon some lie or half truth you have attempted to perpetuate with regard to yourself or with others. Notice the corrosive side effects of the lie. Now consider how your life would be changed were the truth "known." It is useful here to remember that your **guru**, even though you may not have met him in his manifest form . . . KNOWS EVERYTHING ABOUT YOU . . . EVERYTHING . . . And he understands why you do what you do and he has compassion for your predicament. And you look him directly in the eye . . . and you suddenly know that it is all right to live in truth. For where it counts . . . in the matters of the spirit . . . you are not vulnerable at all. So how can truth hurt? This may take a great deal of reflection.

Potent Quotes

"Moreover, Son of Pandu! wert thou worst of all wrong-doers, this fair ship of Truth should bear thee safe and dry across the sea of thy transgressions."—*Bhagavad Gita*

"Indeed we are running away all the time to avoid coming face to face with our real selves, and we barter the truth for trifles."—*Way of a Pilgrim*

"Our sins are created in secrecy. The moment we realize that God witnesses even our thoughts we shall be free."—*Wisdom of the Ages,* from Sat Sandesh

"What makes a man unworthy of the Temple is the cowardice which prompts him to avoid the experience of shame, for this avoidance breeds oblivion. For shame accepted is the greatest treasure. The Door will open before your eyes when you have understood this: the only thing that is humiliating is helplessness. The cause of such helplessness lies in ignorance of your errors; awareness thereof, on the contrary, attracts you to the power of your God.

If you deny the existence of your fault or error, it will strengthen its hold over you. If you recognize it, your awareness will destroy it. He who rejects this will never know the entrance to the Temple."—de Lubicz

"Illusions are like mistresses. We can have many of them without tying ourselves down to responsibility. But truth insists on marriage. Once a person embraces truth, he is in its

57

ruthless, but gentle, grasp."—Rabazar Tarzs

". . . When she caught me stealing jelly beans in the kitchen one day, she grabbed my closed fist in her palm and held it up to the light.

'Open up your hand, child,' she said, 'and don't be so prideful. It ain't nothing but stuff you got hiding there.' "—a novel

DROP OUT/COP OUT

Can you undertake *sadhana* without defaulting in your social responsibilities?

If you could stand back for but a moment you could see that if man were more conscious from moment to moment he could transcend most of the difficulties he now faces: poverty, war, pollution, neurosis, disease.

Where does such consciousness come from? From you!

"Can he rectify false weight whose own scales are uncertain? Can you enlighten your neighbor while you yourself have no light?"—Ramakrishna

Man is presently caught in a plane of consciousness which is nourished by the workings of his rational mind. That is, the plane of polarities . . . of good and evil . . . and left and right . . . of old and young . . . of us and them . . . and of man and woman.

To be "not caught" means to be unattached. To be unattached does not mean to be uninvolved, it means to be involved "without attachment."

A conscious being is capable of making as many discriminations among components of the Universe as anyone else (perhaps even more). However, he is not caught in them. Just because you are seeing divine light, experiencing waves of bliss, or conversing with Gods and Goddesses is no reason to not know your zip code. Keeping it together means keeping conscious at all levels—all planes—with no attachment to any of them.

Let us consider an example of the relation of a group called "hippies" and a group called "police." If a "confrontation" occurs during a protest, what is the result? . . . If the hippies see the police only as "them" and the police see the hippies only as "them" . . . then the result is an increase in polarization and distance between the two groups. Each returns to its headquarters and plans an increase in its own strength to overcome "them."

Why does the distance increase? Because nobody wants to be "them." Everyone wants to be "us." And if you meet someone who sees you as "him" or "one of them," that meeting arouses in you all your paranoia and you, in turn, see the other person as "him" or "one of them."

Such cycles get worse and worse until there is violent confrontation. What is the conscious alternative? It is not to avoid protest or confrontation. Rather it is for the participants to become more "conscious." And what does that mean? It means that though you may be protesting against someone or some group, you realize that behind the ways in which you differ, you are the same. That is, you understand protest as a form of social communication among US . . . and that "where it counts" there is only US. US includes: black and white, young and old, man and woman, American and Russian, rich and poor, saint and rogue.

So the simple rule of conscious participation is:

YOU MAY PROTEST IF YOU CAN LOVE THE PERSON YOU ARE PROTESTING AGAINST AS MUCH AS YOU LOVE YOURSELF.

You may disagree with all his values, but behind all of them . . . HERE WE ARE . . . all manifestations of the Spirit.

The effect of "conscious" protest is that it reduces the polarization and the paranoia and thus allows each side to hear the other's concern more clearly because there is less fear and anxiety. It's all so simple (and so difficult). There can be conscious revolution.

Thus, the rule of the game that everyone work on himself in order to find the center where "we all are"—within himself—in order that he can meet with other human beings in that place . . . is the *sine qua non* (without which nothing) of social responsibility.

What about helping suffering people—starving Biafrans and such? Sure. Do it. It's *karma yoga*. But do it without attachment. To be attached means that you identify with your role as the GIVER of help. This in turn casts the other person in the role of the RECEIVER of help. Such identification with roles may fill bellies, but it increases human distance. A conscious being knows that there is neither giver nor receiver . . . there are only empty bellies, storehouses of wheat . . . and effort required to move the wheat from the storehouses to the belly. It is OUR wheat, OUR belly, OUR effort. And when all this energy has been transferred, a conscious being realizes that nothing has happened. Thanks are absurd . . .

does your left hand thank your right hand?

To think that working on oneself requires "dropping-out" of society is to miss the point. Certainly you must drop out . . . but the drop-out is internal, not external. One drops out of one's attachments; one drops out of one's identification with the illusion of separateness.

Those who think the drop-out from one or another social institution is truly dropping out are naive. It is merely more of the illusion, for we can see that the dropouts almost immediately form new social institutions . . . new religions and priesthoods . . . new traps for keeping themselves in the illusion.

Buddha says:

"As long as you think there is a 'do-er' you are still caught in the wheel of birth and death."

Does that mean that you should sit in bed and not do anything? Well, that's doing something. In fact, as long as you are in your body you must do things. So that couldn't be what Buddha meant. No, he meant something much "farther out." He meant that you do what you do, but you do not identify with the doing of it. All "doing" is happening as part of the dance of nature . . . and though your body and mind speed about their business, you remain in your calm center . . . HERE . . . "where we all are."

Potent Quotes

"A man bound hand and foot in the endless chain of cause and effect cannot free another."—Ramakrishna

"Judge not, that ye be not judged.
For with what judgement ye judge, ye shall be judged:
and with what measure ye mete, it shall be measured to you again.
And why beholdest thou the mote that is in thy brother's eye,
but considerest not the beam that is in thine own eye?
Or wilt thou say to thy brother,
Let me pull out the mote out of thine eye;
and behold, a beam is in thine own eye?
Thou hypocrite, first cast out the beam out of thine own eye;
then shalt thou see clearly to cast out the mote out of thy
brother's eye."—Jesus

"He who has so little knowledge of human nature as to seek happiness by changing anything but his own disposition will waste his life in fruitless efforts."—Samuel Johnson

"The higher one climbs on the spiritual ladder, the more will he grant others their own freedom and give less interference to another's state of consciousness."—Twitchell

"Though I speak with the tongues of men and angels, and have not charity, I am become as sounding brass, or a tinkling symbol. And though I have the gift of prophecy, and understand all mysteries, and all knowledge; and though I have all faith, so that I could remove mountains, and have not charity, I am nothing.

And though I bestow all my goods to feed the poor, and though I give my body to be burned, and have not charity, it profiteth me nothing. Charity suffereth long, and is kind; charity envieth not; charity vaunteth not itself, is not puffed up.

Doth not behave itself unseemly, seeketh not her own, is not easily provoked, thinketh no evil;

Rejoiceth not in iniquity, but rejoiceth in truth;
Beareth all things, believeth all things, hopeth all things, endureth all things.
Charity never faileth: but whither there be prophecies, they shall fail; whither there be tongues, they shall cease; whither there be knowledge it shall vanish away.
For we know in part, and we prophecy in part.
But when that which is perfect is come, then that which is in part shall be done away.
When I was a child, I spake as a child, I understood as a child, I thought as a child: but when I became a man, I put away childish things. For now we see through a glass, darkly; but then, face to face: now I know in part: but then shall I know even as also I am known.
And now abideth faith, hope, charity, these three; but the greatest of these is charity."—Paul of Tarsus

(Brunton to Ramana Maharshi): "Will Maharaj-ji express an opinion about the future of the world, as we are living in critical times? M: Why should you trouble yourself about the future? You do not even properly know about the present. Take care of the present, the future will take care of itself."—Osborne
"Since the world points up beauty as such
There is ugliness too.
If goodness is taken as goodness,
Wickedness enters as well."—*Tao Te Ching*
"By passion for the 'pairs of opposites.'
By those twin snares of Like and Dislike, Prince,
All creatures live bewildered, save some few
Who, quit of sins, holy in act, informed,
Freed from the 'opposites' and fixed in faith
Cleave unto Me."—*Bhagavad Gita*

"If you call it a stick, you affirm. If you call it not a stick, you negate. Beyond affirmation and negation, what would you call it?"—Tai-hui

"Thus saith He who formulateth in darkness:
I am Lord, not of light alone,
But of darkness also,
For I the One am all-pervading."—*Book of Tokens*

"I, the Lord, destroy with darkness.
But with darkness do I also create.
The wise discern this.
Fools, deluded by outward appearance,
Create a demon out of the web of their folly."—*Book of Tokens*

"Take this word: 'grok'. Its literal meaning, one which I suspect goes back to the origin of the Martian race as thinking creatures—and which throws light on their whole 'map'—is easy. 'Grok' means 'to drink' . . . But a Martian would use 'Grok' even if I had named a hundred other English words, words which we think of as different concepts, even antithetical concepts. 'Grok' means **all** of these. It means 'fear', it means 'love', it means 'hate'—proper hate, for by the Martian 'map' you cannot hate anything unless you grok it, understand it so thoroughly you merge with it and it merges with you—then can you hate. By hating yourself. But this implies that you love it, too, and cherish it and would not have it otherwise. Then you can **hate**—and (I think) Martian hate is an emotion so black that the nearest human equivalent could only be called mild distaste . . .

'Grok' means 'identically equal'. The human cliche 'This hurts me worse than it does you' has a Martian flavor. The Martians seem to know instinctively what we learned painfully from modern physics, that observer interacts with observed through the process of observation. 'Grok' means to understand so thoroughly that the observer becomes a part of the observed—to merge, blend, intermarry, lose identity in group experience. It means almost everything we mean by religion, philosophy and science—and it means as little to us as color means to a blind man . . . If I chopped you up and made a stew, you and the stew, whatever was in it, would 'grok'—and when I ate you, we would 'grok' together and nothing would be lost and it would not matter which one of us did the eating."—Heinlein

"In the presence of a man perfect in *ahimsa* (nonviolence), enmity (in any creature) does not arise."—Patanjali

MONEY AND RIGHT LIVELIHOOD

Money is "green energy." And any energy you work with brings with it its own vibrations. If you are sufficiently evolved to be able to transmute negative vibrations, then it makes little difference where the energy comes from. For most of us, however, we are affected for good or ill by the energies with which we interact. Also, the manner in which you obtain the energy from others affects them. Because we are all interrelated, what affects another person affects you.

The method of gaining your livelihood must not, by its very nature, increase the paranoia and separateness in the world. A dishonest or exploitive venture would be a case in point. Most means of gaining livelihood do not, in and of themselves, increase the illusion of separateness. However, the beings who do the work do it—because of their own level of involvement—in such a way as to increase the illusion. When you are involved in such vocations, then it is your work on yourself which makes the particular vocation a vehicle for bringing man out of illusion and into *yoga*.

Suitable right livelihood for any specific individual is determined by the totality of forces acting upon him. These forces (vectors) include social, cultural, economic, hereditary, and experiential factors. To hear the way in which the interplay of all these forces determines your right livelihood requires much calming of the mind. The quieter you become the more you can hear.

As you progress with your *sadhana* you may find it necessary to change your occupation. Or you may find that it is only necessary to change the way in which you perform your current occupation in order to bring it into line with your new understanding of how it all is. The more conscious that a being becomes, the more he can use any occupation as a vehicle for spreading light. The next true being of Buddha-nature that you meet may appear as a bus driver, a doctor, a weaver, an insurance salesman, a musician, a chef, a teacher, or any of the thousands of roles that are required in a complex society—the many parts of Christ's body. You will know him because the simple dance that may transpire between you—such as handing him change as you board the bus—will strengthen in you the faith in the divinity of man. It's as simple as that.

IN GOD WE TRUST

ONE

KARMA YOGA

If you were to follow the instruction of Krishna in the *Bhagavad Gita*, you would "do whatever you do, but consecrate the fruit of your actions to me." Every act you perform, all day every day, would be done as an offering to Krishna.

If we recall that Krishna is synonymous with Love, with Highest Consciousness, with the Eternal Witness, with the Spirit . . . and that He is actually our innermost Self, then we can understand that by consecrating an act, we are indeed offering our every action into the service of higher consciousness. Our every act becomes an act of waking up.

Using the stuff that makes up your daily life as the vehicle for coming to Union is called *karma yoga*. It is a most available *yoga* for all, and at the same time a most difficult one. It is difficult because it starts with an action which you are initially performing for an end of maintaining your individual ego, and it overrides or converts that motivation into one of service to the higher Self which transcends ego.

In order to perform *karma yoga*, there is a simple general principle to keep in mind: bring a third component into every action. If, for example, you are digging a ditch, there is you who is digging the ditch, and the ditch which is being dug. Now add a third focus: say, a disinterested person who is seeing you dig the ditch. Now run the entire action through his head while you are digging. It's as simple as that. Through this method you would ultimately free yourself from identifying with him who is digging the ditch. You would merely see a ditch being dug.

The difficulty with adding just **any** third party is that you might attribute to that other person certain motives or values. In order to avoid that, it is useful to pick the third focal point with an eye towards your goal of enlightenment. That is, pick someone who is already enlightened, such as Krishna or Ram or a Buddha or Christ. They see it all. They are beyond it all. They understand how it all is. As they watch you digging the ditch, they see the act in all its cosmic significance . . . it's the first and last digging of a ditch. They understand why you are doing it and all the thoughts in your head, all your history, and they even understand the future—how it is when the ditch is all dug. And from this vantage point they have total compassion, total appreciation for all that is involved. To run the act of you digging a ditch through one of their heads allows you to get free of the ego-centric predicament, "I am digging a ditch."

There are a variety of techniques for introducing this third focal point into your life in a systematic fashion. It can be done in a devotional form through, as Krishna suggests, offering the fruit of each action to Him. Thus you keep in mind some manifestation of God—some form of a *guru*—to whom you are offering in loving service your every act. He may be felt to reside in your heart or your head or atop your head or on your shoulder or "out there."

Or you can introduce as a third focal point the thought—in one form or another—that all forms and acts are part of the One. A continuing thought such as, "It's all the Divine Mother," or repeating *japa* such as saying over and over *OM OM OM* or *RAMA RAMA*

RAMA, or *TAT TWAM ASI* or *OM TAT SAT.* All of these *mantras* are designed to remind you over and over that it is all One and that it only appears, within the illusion, as if something were happening such as digging a ditch.

Another systematic technique for introducing an additional focal point is the technique called **self-remembering**, which utilizes a device called the **witness**. The following is a description of this method.

The Witness

George Gurdjieff, a Russian philosopher-mystic, noted that if you set an alarm clock at night in order to get up early to get some work done, who you are in the morning when the alarm goes off is quite different from who you were the night before. In the morning you might even say, "Who the %X**!! set that alarm clock?" A moment's reflection will show you that you play many roles in the course of a day . . . and that **who you are** from moment to moment changes. There is the angry you, and the kind you, the lazy you, the lustful you—hundreds of different you's. Gurdjieff points out that sometimes one "you" does something for which all the other "you's" must pay for years or possibly the rest of this life.

Each of these "you's" reflects an identification with a desire, or a feeling, or a thought. If, as we have seen, the **work** is to break these identifications, we can work effectively throughout each day by making each of these "you's" objects, i.e., by breaking the identification with each of them. This is not so easy.

There is one technique which is known as adopting the role of the witness . . . and holding on to that role . . . ultimately to the exclusion of all other roles.

Who is the Witness?

1. It is a part of the rational mind. As such it is only useful up to a point . . . the point at which you go through the "doorway." When you go through the doorway you merge with the One . . . the Eternal Witness . . . Buddha Consciousness . . . (we differentiate these two witnesses by referring to the small, rational mind, ego witness without the capital letter).

2. The witness could be thought of as an eye . . . or "I" which sees, though it does not look. That is, it is not an active thing. It just sees it all happening.

3. The witness is not evaluative. It does not judge your actions. It merely notes them. Thus, if you perform an act because of desire, such as eating something that is not *sattvic* (helpful to your *sadhana*), and then you put yourself down for having eaten it . . . the witness—when it finally appears—would merely note: (a) he is eating such-and-such, and (b)

he is putting himself down for eating such-and-such. Thus the witness has noted a "you" of desires and a super-ego you . . . two "you's."

This point is important. Most of the time the inner voices of most people are continually evaluative. "I'm good for doing this," or "I'm bad for doing that." You must make that evaluative role an object of contemplation as well. Keep in mind that the witness does not care whether you become enlightened or not. It merely notes how it all is.

Appearance of the Witness

At first the witness is adopted because of an intellectual understanding of the need to separate the Self from the Doer. You probably remember your witness only now and then, when you are in a calm dispassionate state of mind. The moment you get distracted you lose the witness. Later you "come to" and remember that you forgot.

For example, you are walking down a street witnessing yourself walking down a street. You feel happy and witness feeling happy . . . and so it goes. Then you meet someone or see something that irritates you. Immediately you get irritated and forget all about the witness. The adrenalin pumps through you and you think angry thoughts. At this point "angry me" is who you are. Only **much** later do you remember that you were attempting to witness.

At that point you promise yourself that you won't forget again. Ah, how little you know about the subtleties of the seductions of the other "you's." Again you are walking and again witnessing walking and so forth. This time you meet with another situation which irritates you. Again you lose your witness (or **center** as it is called sometimes) and again your endocrine glands secrete and you think angry thoughts. But this time right in the middle of the entire drama you "wake up" . . . that is, you realize your predicament. But at this point it is difficult to get free of the angry you because you are already getting much gratification. (It's like trying to stop in the midst of a sexual act.) And so you use some rationalization such as "I know I should be witnessing but after all he deserves to be punished" and with that you climb back into the "angry you" role with a certain amount of self-righteousness. And so it goes through thousands of such experiences.

After a time (however long is necessary) you notice that although you still lose the witness (fall asleep) as often as before, you are starting to "remember" sooner. That is, you are getting to the point where the actual falling asleep is starting to "wake" you. This is a big step forward.

Again, after some time, it all gets much more subtle. Now you are walking down the street and again you are witnessing it all . . . and again an "irritant" presents itself. This time—as you are about to get angry—the witness says "Ah, about to get angry, I see." This often short-circuits the energy the "angry you" was fueling up with, and it falls away. So now the lapse between being awake and being asleep is getting much smaller. Simultaneously, you begin to note that you don't fall asleep (i.e., fall out of the witness) nearly as often. Throughout the day you are remaining centered in the witness watching the drama of life unfold.

On the surface, this method looks like what psychologists call the "defense mechanism of dissociation." A girl goes to a dance and no one asks her to dance . . . and she adopts a superior separateness . . . watching it all with the thought: "I couldn't be less interested in dancing." This response of separating herself from her desire arises because she so badly wants to dance. It must be differentiated from the adoption of a witness when you have **finished with dancing**, so to speak. The witness we are considering here is hardly an unconscious defense mechanism. Though they look alike on the surface, they are quite different. But only you know which is which.

There is a side effect which occurs while you are developing the witness which, though unpleasant, will soon disappear. It is the feeling that life has lost its zest as a result of keeping the witness going. It is difficult to fully get lost in the subtle sensual gratifications of eating when you are witnessing yourself eat. "He is chewing . . . tasting . . . savoring, etc." It all seems so dispassionate. And truly it is. Here it is well to remember the oft-quoted stipulation that you must "die to be reborn" or "give it all up to have it all ." Keep in mind that the loss of full sensory gratification is but a stage (and one of the more difficult ones at that) of your *sadhana*. And it will only be when you are living quietly and calmly in the dispassionate witness that you will be ready to "permanently" pass through the next doorway.

You will also note that as you break identification with more and more of your roles and begin to live more calmly in the witness, that you begin to be aware of much more. You begin to see how the laws of the universe are manifesting in all aspects of nature, outstandingly those which you have so recently been involved with, such as your own body and personality. Now you are beginning to live on the causal plane. This experience of seeing how it is . . . is a very heady feeling. It must be witnessed, too, or else you will get caught in a new ego game of playing "the eye of God"—while still being you. This is a sticking point for many intellectuals. They enjoy intellectual power so much that they cannot forego it by witnessing it . . . in order to go the final step in which they give up their separateness as an individual "knower" to dissolve in the sea of knowledge.

4. The witness is always in the Here and Now. It lives in each instant of living. It is well to keep in mind that whatever device you choose as a third focal point, it is a temporary crutch. It is dualistic in nature. Once you have successfully broken identification with the Doer, and are solely the witness or a servant of Krishna, or whatever, then you must go the

final step in which servant and master, witness and that which is witnessed, become One. The goal is non-dualistic. The means is dualistic. Such a means is a sturdy vessel to get you across the ocean of *samsara* (illusion). Once you reach the far shore, you leave the boat behind.

Potent Quotes

"Whatever you do, or eat, or give, or offer in adoration, let it be an offering to me; and whatever you suffer, suffer it for me. Thus you shall be free from the bonds of Karma which yield fruits that are evil and good; and with your soul one in renunciation you shall be free and come to me."—*Bhagavad Gita*

"In regard to every action one must know the result that is expected to follow, the means thereto, and the capacity for it. He, who being thus equipped, is without desire for the result, and is yet wholly engrossed in the due fulfillment of the task before him, is said to have renounced the fruits of his action."—Gandhi

"He who sees the inaction that is in action, and the action that is in inaction, is wise indeed. Even when he is engaged in action he remains poised in the tranquility of the Atman."—*Bhagavad Gita*

"But that state of Supreme Love and Immortality is made possible only by giving up the objective reality of the world as it appears to the ego-centric intellect and senses, and the consequent renunciation of attachment, by uninterrupted loving service."—*Narada Bhakti Sutras*

"To study Buddhism is to study ourselves. To study ourselves is to go beyond ourselves. To go beyond ourselves is to be enlightened by all things. To be enlightened by all things is to free our body and mind, and to free the bodies and minds of others. No trace of enlightenment remains, and this no-trace continues endlessly."—Dogen Zenji

"If you observe well, your own heart will answer."—de Lubicz

"An art of living which will enable one to utilize each activity (of body, speech and mind) as an aid on the path is indispensable."—*Tibetan Yoga and Secret Doctrine*

"How does the emancipated soul live in the world? He lives in the world like a diver bird. It dives into water, but the water does not wet its plumage; the few drops of water which may possibly stick to its body are easily jerked off when it once flaps its wing."—Ramakrishna

"At first whenever I fell back into sin I used to weep and rage against myself and against God for having suffered it. Afterwards it was as much as I could dare ask, 'Why has thou rolled me again in the mud, O my playfellow?' Then even that came to my mind to seem too bold and presumptuous; I could only get up in silence, look at him out of the corner of my eye and clean myself."—Aurobindo

"All the urges of the passions express vital natural impulses, and it is the animal in us which gives rise to them. The wise man is conscious of them, he knows how to give them their true name and to make use of them as you direct your donkey. But the wise man is rare, and egoism finds a thousand reasons for giving those impulses legitimate motives and flattering names. The human passions are life impulses which have been perverted . . . and so skillfully perverted that it is very difficult to discover, beneath their complications, the almost divine power which is their source—de Lubicz

"What you receive depends upon what you give. The workman gives the toil of his arm, his energy, his movement; for this the craft gives him a notion of the resistance of the material and its manner of reaction. The artisan gives the craft his love; and to him the craft responds by making him one with his work. But the craftsman gives the craft his passionate research into the laws of Nature which govern it; and the craft teaches him Wisdom."—de Lubicz

"But he learned more from the river than Vasudeva could teach him. He learned from it continually. Above all, he learned from it how to listen with a still heart, with a waiting, open soul, without passion, without desire, without judgement, without opinions."—Hesse

"As long as one feels that he is the doer,
he cannot escape from the wheel of births."—Buddha

"If you can serve a cup of tea right, you can do anything."—Gurdjieff

"Ch'ing, the chief carpenter, was carving wood into a stand for musical instruments. When finished, the work appeared to those who saw it as though of supernatural execution; and the Prince of Lu asked him, saying, 'What mystery is there in your art?'

'No mystery, Your Highness,' replied Ch'ing. 'And yet there is something. When I am about to make such a stand, I guard against any diminution of my vital power. I first reduce my mind to absolute quiescence. Three days in this condition, and I become oblivious of any reward to be gained. Five days, and I become oblivious of any fame to be acquired. Seven days, and I become unconscious of my four limbs and my physical frame. Then, with no thought of the Court present in my mind, my skill becomes concentrated, and all disturbing elements from without are gone. I enter some mountain forest, I search for a suitable tree. It contains the form required, which is afterwards elaborated. I see the stand in my mind's eye, and then set to work. Beyond that there is nothing. I bring my own native capacity into relation with that of the wood. What was suspected to be of supernatural execution in my work was due solely to this."—Chuang Tzu

BHAKTI YOGA

The *yoga* which is most available to all people at all times in all situations is *bhakti yoga*, the yoga of love and devotion. It is the method of merging in ultimate union through the heart.

The method of *bhakti yoga* is dualistic in the sense that one experiences love at first in relation to something separate from oneself. The goal and natural outcome of *bhakti yoga*, however, is non-dualistic in the sense that the ultimate state is one in which the lover and beloved merge in One.

It is a delicate *yoga* to work with properly because it is only too easy to get so much reward (bliss) from the dualistic stages that one cannot leave the separateness to proceed to the unitive stage. An excellent example is presented in the life story of Ramakrishna, the

Indian saint who was so in love with Kali, a manifestation of the Divine Mother, that he resisted breaking through into the Oneness. Only after his *guru* forced him, did he do so.

This *yoga* is difficult for us in the West to understand because we have used the term "love" in such a profance sense . . . that is, to reflect attachment to worldly objects or people. We speak of "loving" that food or drink or automobile or person . . . often in the same sense. We are so "action-oriented" that we think of love as "something to do." But most people have sadly found that you can't "make love" if love does not already exist. Meher Baba, a recent Indian saint who advocated love as the supreme vehicle said:

"Love has to spring spontaneously from within: and it is in no way amenable to any form of inner or outer force. Love and coercion can never go together: but though love cannot be forced on anyone, it can be awakened in him through love itself. Love is essentially self-communicative: Those who do not have it catch it from those who have it. True love is unconquerable and irresistable; and it goes on gathering power and spreading itself, until eventually it transforms everyone whom it touches."

The specific object of love which concerns the *bhakti yogi* is the Spirit or the manifestation of the Divine . . . in anything and everything. It is the love for light or for love itself or for the Life Force or for truth or beauty. It is love for the purest manifestations of these abstractions. The roles through which this love may be expressed are many: the relation of worship or piety; the pure relationship of servant to master; the relation of friend to friend; the relation of wife to husband; parent to child; child to parent; the lover to the beloved; etc. Though the "vehicles" differ from role to role, the essence—the love—is the same stuff. In each instance what one is loving in the object of one's love is love itself . . . the inner light in everyone and everything.

When we speak of falling in love, we might find that a slight restatement of the experience would help clarify our direction. For when you say "I fell in love" with him or her you are saying that he or she was the key that unlocked your heart—the place within yourself where you are love. When the experience is mutual, you can see that the psychic chemistry of the situation allows both partners to "fall in love" or to "awake into love" or to "come into the Spirit." Since love is a state of being—and the Divine state at that—the state to which we all yearn to return, we wish to possess love. At best we can try to possess the key to our hearts—our beloved—but sooner or later we find that even that is impossible. To possess the key is to lose it.

Just as with every other method of coming to the Light, if it works we get attached to the method, failing to realize that it is the goals and not the method which we crave. A relationship starting out as one that awakens love can only remain a living vehicle for love to the extent that it is continually made new or reconsecrated. That is, each partner in love must

73

always strain to see through the veils of personality and body to see the Divine Essence within—within himself and his partner. And he must come to see the veils as veils . . . as *maya*, the Divine Illusion, the Divine Mother . . . and worship even the veils without getting trapped into thinking them real. Such ideas are reflected in the highest marriages, or for that matter in the highest form of any relationship. Play your role in the Divine Dance, but know it to be such and worship its divinity.

Song, dance, chanting and prayer have been throughout the ages traditional forms of *bhakti yoga*. There are many levels at which you can participate in these rituals. At first such rituals are matters of curiosity, and you are the observer. Then you arrive at the stage of peripheral participation—a "sing along." Then in time you become familiar with the routines and you start to identify with the process. As your identification deepens, other thoughts and evaluations fall away until finally you and the ritual become one. At that point the ritual has become the living process and can take you through the door into perfect unity. To know that these stages exist does not mean that you can jump ahead of where you are. Whatever stage you are in, accept it. When you have fully accepted your present degree of participation, only then will you start to experience the next level.

Singing and music: Most familiar to us is the use of song to open the heart. Hymns such as "Holy, Holy, Holy" or "We Gather Together To Ask The Lord's Blessing" or "Mine Eyes Have Seen the Glory of the Coming of the Lord," "Stand Up, Stand Up for Jesus," "Amazing Grace"—have touched the hearts of millions with the Spirit. In India, *bhajan* (the singing of holy songs) has been until recent times practically the only social function in the villages. Evenings the men gather, squatting or sitting on the ground in a circle with their *chillums* (pipes) and a harmonium, a set of *tabla* (drums), perhaps a *serangi* or violin (stringed instruments) and cymbals . . . and they take turns singing the stories of the holy beings such as Krishna and Ram. Night after night they participate in this simple pastime, keeping themselves close to the Spirit.

It is often startling to a Westerner to realize that it is not the beauty of the voice but the purity of the spirit of the singer that is revered by these people. It was only when music was profaned that it became a vehicle for gratification of the senses. Prior to that it was a method of communion with the Spirit.

A special form of *bhajan* is called *kirtan* . . . which is the repetition in song of the Holy Names of God. Perhaps the most familiar of these in the West at present is:

HARI KRISHNA, HARI KRISHNA, KRISHNA KRISHNA,
HARI HARI. . .HARI RAMA, HARI RAMA, RAMA, RAMA
HARI HARI.

Hari can be translated as "Lord" and Ram and Krishna are names of incarnations of

74

God.

The melody of *kirtan* is usually basically simple and it is only after many repetitions that the process of coming into the spirit starts to happen. Singing the same phrases over for two to five hours is not unusual for the true seeker. And you will find as you let yourself into the repetitive rhythm and melody that you experience level after level of opening.

Exercises

On the record that is included in the box *From Bindu to Ojas,* there are a number of examples of *kirtan*. Take any one of them and tape one single repetition of it onto a tape loop which you can run over and over through your tape machine. Then turn up the volume and join US.

There are many records and tapes of *kirtan* available (and more appearing all the time). Work with a variety of these until they have worked deeply into your heart.

When you have an opportunity to join with others in the singing of *kirtan* . . . even a group of amateurs . . . do it. Remember it is inner singing . . . it is the spirit that you bring to it that counts.

Potent Quotes

"God respects me when I work
But he loves me when I sing."—Tagore

"Love me, my brothers, for I am infinitely superfluous, and your love shall be like His, born neither of your need nor of my deserving, but a plain bounty. Blessed be He."—C.S. Lewis

"Bhakti, love of God, is the essence of all spiritual discipline . . . Through love one acquires renunciation and discrimination naturally."—Ramakrishna

"Oh thou who art trying to learn the marvel of love from the copybook of reason, I am very much afraid that you will never really see the point."—Hafiz

"To savour in our hearts in a certain manner and to endeavor to experience in our souls the power of the Divine Presence and the sweetness of heavenly glory, and this, not only after death but even in this mortal existence. This is most truly to drink of the gushing fount of the Joy of God."—*Institution of the First Monks*

"Love without attachment is light."—N.O. Brown

"God alone is Real and the goal of life is to become united with Him through Love."—Meher Baba

"If you have love you will do all things well."—T. Merton

75

"Love suffereth long, and is kind; love envieth not; love vaunteth not itself, is not puffed up, does not behave itself unseemly, seeketh not its own, is not provoked, taketh not account of evil; rejoiceth not in unrighteousness, but rejoiceth with truth; beareth all things, hopeth all things, endureth all things. Love never faileth."—Paul of Tarsus

LOVE in the World's Great Religions:

Christianity: "Beloved, let us love one another, for love is of God; and everyone that loveth is born of God, and knoweth God. He that loveth not, knoweth not God, for God is Love."

Confucianism: "To love all men is the greatest benevolence."

Buddhism: "Let a man cultivate towards the whole world a heart of Love."

Hinduism: "One can best worship the Lord through Love."

Islam: "Love is this, that thou shouldst account thyself very little and God very great."

Taoism: "Heaven arms with Love those it would not see destroyed."

Sikhism: "God will regenerate those in whose hearts there is Love."

Judaism: "Thou shalt Love the Lord thy God with all thy heart and thy neighbor as thyself."

Jainism: "The days are of most profit to him who acts in Love."

Zoroastrianism: "Man is the beloved of the Lord and should Love him in return."

Baha'i: "Love Me that I may love thee. If thou lovest Me not, My love can no wise reach thee."

Shinto: "Love is the representative of the Lord."

I LOVE YOU

DANCE

TOWARD THE ONE

THE PERFECTION OF LOVE, HARMONY AND BEAUTY
THE ONLY BEING
UNITED WITH ALL THE ILLUMINATED SOULS WHO FORM
THE EMBODIMENT OF THE MASTER
THE SPIRIT OF GUIDANCE

Sufi Ahmed Murad, of the Chisti Order teaches in San Francisco, where most of his disciples and centers are located. Dance, movements and invoking the names of God are the main vehicles for the Murshid's teachings. They are of many forms, round, linear, counterclockwise, sunwise, with and without partners, with and without a specific leader, and with and without sound.

We in New Hampshire and in New Mexico have taken part in these dances, movements and invocations both directly under Murshid's direction and also using the patterns as he has instructed and found that they allow us to attain to ecstatic states and unitary experiences.

They are in Murshid's words "practical proof of higher states which are available."

We hope either to publish or to help see published both the patterns and words of the dances and the Murshid's commentaries on their meaning and significance.

Following are paragraphs excerpted from some of the Murshid's papers on "Spiritual Dancing" which give some impression of his style and method. Those interested in this material or in working/practicing under the Murshid should contact him thru his secretary Wali Ali, 410 Precita Ave., San Francisco, Calif. 94110.

"Spiritual Dancing" is that which elevates the consciousness. Dancing may be said to be the movement of the body or any of its parts to rhythm, and spiritual is that which helps to make man realise that this body is really the Divine Temple. Therefore the use of sacred phrases and words, or the practice of deep meditation before starting, are necessary. For no dance is a Spiritual Dance because it is called that; it does not mean a certain form or technique, nor a ritual, nor something so esoteric that there is no understanding by performers and no communication to audience.

"The principle of PATH appears in several religions. It is not only in their mystical aspects but in many ceremonies and rituals. Circumambulation of an altar or shrine is also important, even regarded as an important act of devotion. The very word 'path' signifies that which comes from the feet treading—it almost means 'what is footed'. It is now important to study the Walk both as a physical exercise and as a super-physical endeavor, making both movement and rest the most fundamental things in life.

"One thing almost obvious in the consideration of Walk is that the feet themselves are connected with Shrines. When one does the Lotus and other postures the human body is the shrine and the feet are accordingly tucked either under or over the legs. When one uses an external shrine, then there is Walking. But if one agrees with Kabir that God is everywhere, one can learn to walk that the body is the real temple and that every place is a holy shrine.

"It should be recognized that before we can run we must be able to walk, and by the same token even before we walk we should be able to breathe, to breathe is life . . . Breath-currents have energy-values as well as chemical and mechanical ones. These are studied in Sufi mysticism and also in the works of Rama Prasad. If one stops breathing, functions also stop and some Indians identify 'prana', the breath, with life itself . . . It cannot be emphasized too much that life depends on breath. Our willing has nothing to do with it. If one ambles, if one slouches, one does not manifest magnetism. From the very beginning of discipleships talibs in Sufism are given the instructions in breathing which aid in increasing both magnetism and the capacity for vitality.

"If one has a goal, physical or mental, while walking, it brings all the magnetisms together. It is a living concentration. For instance a loving person going to meet his or her

78

beloved, is endowed and imbued with a living spirit which makes action easier and fatigue disappears. If we practice a 'TOWARD THE ONE,' whatever be the goal or purpose, walking becomes much easier. And therefore also sacred phrases may be thought or repeated, consciously or unconsciously.

". . . one should breathe concentrating on 'TOWARD THE ONE' with both inhalation and exhalation, the same phrase. This can be done best by leaning on the breath, but also one can take so many steps to each breath. This is somewhat more complicated. In between comes in listening to music wherein the rhythm is most important . . . As one breathes in and out with this concentration all the essence of the universe can enter with the breath, and also all poisons can go out of the system. If this is not sufficient, one can be taught sacred phrases but for a group 'TOWARD THE ONE' is very good. Besides a group so joining builds up magnetism and as the group progresses from walk to ceremonial or ritual and from ritual to dance the dynamism and magnetism of both person and group increase; and also the capacity for the divine *baraka* manifesting on the earthsphere increases.

". . . no mechanical means, no rules, no rituals, nothing controlled by man alone can liberate man.

"The Japanese, concentrating on the abdomen, rid their minds of useless luggage. The Sufi dervishes, using their feet, also rid their minds of useless luggage. The ridding of luggage is more important than the method. What is needed is a method that works, not a philosophy about method which can be very confusing."

S.A.M.
BELOVED SAMUEL L. LEWIS
MURSHID: SUFI AHMED MURAD: CHISTI
1896-1971

THE WORK WILL CONTINUE
OM SRI RAM JAI RAM JAI JAI RAM

MEDITATION

The term **meditation** is used in such a variety of ways that it may mean anything from daydreaming or musing, to deliberating about a topic, to a specific discipline of working with the mind that can be so exact that every act of body and thought is prescribed. The way in which the term **meditation** is used in *yoga* is in the more formal and disciplined sense. As such it is distinguished from reflection or contemplation. It includes two processes: making the mind concentrated or one-pointed, and bringing to total cessation the turning of the mind.

Vivekananda says:

"The human mind is like that monkey, incessantly active by its own nature, then it becomes drunk with the wine of desire, thus increasing its turbulence. After desire takes

80

possession comes the sting of the scorpion of jealousy at the success of others, and last of all the demon of pride enters the mind, making it think itself of all importance."

As long as the mind is caught in the senses and you are caught in your mind, you remain in the illusion . . . since in the last analysis, your thoughts create your universe. Only when your mind has become completely calm will you reach **Buddhahood** or enlightenment.

"The soul has the means. Thinking is the means. It is inanimate. When thinking has completed its task of release, it has done what it had to do, and ceases."—Vishnu Parana

Exercises

1. The simplest instructions for meditation are given by Tilopa in the *Song of Mahamudra:*
> "Do nought with the body but relax
> Shut firm the mouth and silent remain
> Empty your mind and think of nought
> Like a hollow bamboo
> Rest at ease your body
> Giving not nor taking
> Put your mind at rest
> The great way is a mind that clings to nought
> Thus practicing, in time you will reach Buddhahood."

2. The southern Buddhists (Therevadin) practice a form of meditation called *Satipatthana Vipassana* (Application of Mindfulness). It starts with the simple exercise of **Bare Attention**. All that you do is register thoughts, states, etc. in the present. This process slows down the transition from the receptive to the active phase of the cognitive process. You don't think about your thoughts. You merely note them. This produces "peaceful penetration." You transcend conceptual thought.

Instructions:

(a) Find a quiet and peaceful place where you will not be disturbed. If you wish to purify the spot first before you meditate in it, stir a glass of water with the fourth finger of your right hand while repeating the following *mantra* three times:
> *OM APWITRAH PAVITRORWA*
> *SARVA WASTANG GATOPIWA*
> *YEH SMARET PUNDARI*
> *KAKSHAM SABAHYA*
> *BHUANTARAH SUCHIH*

81

Then sprinkle the water around the spot you plan to sit in (moving in a clockwise fashion). This *mantra* is used by jungle *sadhus* in India to purify the ground.

(b) Get into a comfortable seat. It should be a position you can remain in for at least thirty minutes without moving or discomfort. It is desirable that the head, neck and chest be in a straight line.

(c) At first let your mind wander and just watch it. Just note how your mind works. Don't think about the thoughts. Just note them. Do this for about thirty minutes a day for a week.

(d) Then find a muscle in your abdomen, just below your rib cage, which moves when you breathe such that it (the muscle) rises and falls. Attend to it. Every time the muscle rises, think "Rising," and every time it falls, think "Falling" . . . rising . . . falling . . . rising . . . falling. Let all other thoughts drift by and keep your attention focused on this muscle. Don't lose heart. At first the mind will wander frequently. Each time it does, follow it immediately upon becoming conscious of its wandering. Note where it wandered to, and then immediately return to rising . . . falling . . . rising . . . falling . . .

Or if you prefer, you can substitute counting for rising and falling. *Om* (in-breath) . . . 1 (out-breath), *Om* . . . 2 . . . *Om* . . . 3 . . . etc. Two or more syllable numbers can be divided into in and out breath, e.g., four . . . teen . . . etc. If you wish, you can set goals for yourself during the initial stages. Start with 250 and increase by 50 each day. Remember . . . your only task is to count that muscle going up and down. All other thoughts don't belong here. Don't try to suppress them (for that is just another thought). Rather, note the intruding thought, give it a label, and return to the task at hand. After about a month you will note a great calm and sense of peace from this exercise.

(e) After you get in the habit of merely noting each stimuli in the Here and Now without thinking about it, then add additional steps designed to further free you from illusion. Specifically, you add **Clear Comprehension**. This advanced practice involves describing the noted thought or state in terms of its purpose, its suitability, the way in which it relates to spiritual practice, and finally in terms of its total impersonality. These descriptions (which are described in detail in a number of books on Buddhist meditation) are ritualistic in nature and help you to see the impermanence of thought, the way in which it perpetuates suffering, and the fact that it does not in any way imply the presence of an ego or "I" who thinks it.

Great gains in meditative practice may be made without these advanced stages. The simple technique of bare attention is very powerful. With the advanced techniques available in the Buddhist texts you develop in time a totally dispassionate view of the thoughts which fill your consciousness.

3. *Tratak*

Set a candle at a distance of about twenty inches in front of you. The height of the flame should be at a level with a point between your eyebrows when you are sitting up straight. Sit comfortably, but with head, neck and chest in a straight line.

If you are able to do so, close your *muhlbandh*. That is, pull up at a point halfway between your genitals and your anus. This closes the sphincters and pulls energy up towards the upper part of the body. Don't strain to do this. With practice it comes naturally.

Starting with five minutes and increasing by about five minutes a day up to one hour . . . just sit with the candle.

Don't try to do anything. Just hang out with the candleflame. Let any thoughts that enter your mind pass by like clouds in the sky. See all thoughts and sensations as tiny insects hovering around the flame. Don't try to make the flame change or to focus or to see . . . just BE with the flame. If your eyes water it is all right. If your eyes hurt, then stop.

After a period of time there will be just you and the candle flame . . .

Note: You may do *Japa* (*mantra* on name of God) simultaneously if you wish.

4. *Nad Yoga*

This is a *yoga* of attending to the inner sounds. It is extremely effective and powerful.

Find a comfortable position where your head, neck and chest are in a straight line. You may lie down if reclining doesn't lead to sleep. You may wish to use earplugs if there is much erratic external noise. They are not necessary, especially if you can find a quiet place or time of night in which to do this exercise. Keep your eyes and mouth closed.

Now tune in on any inner sound in your head that you can find. Narrow in on that sound until it is the dominant sound you are attending to. Let all other sounds and thoughts pass by.

As you allow that sound to more and more fill your consciousness, you will ultimately merge with that sound so that you do not hear it any longer. At that point you will start to hear another sound. Now tune in on the new sound and repeat the process. There are seven or ten sounds (depending upon the number of discriminations you make).

The seven are described by Madame Blavatsky as follows:

"The first is like the nightingale's sweet voice, chanting a parting song to its mate. The next resembles the sound of silver cymbals of the Dhyanis, awakening the twinkling stars. It is followed by the plain melodies of the ocean's spirit imprisoned in a conch shell, which in turn gives place to the chant of Vina. The melodious flute-like symphony is then heard. It changes into a trumpet blast, vibrating like the dull rumbling of a thunder cloud. The seventh swallows all other sounds. They die and then are heard no more."

Other descriptions include: the buzzing of bees, the sounds of crowds in a large gathering place such as a railway station, drums, etc. You need not initially concern yourself with the order, for until the final stages there are some individual differences.

You can think of these sounds as the vibrations of various nerves. Or you can think of these various nerves as tiny receivers for various planes of vibration. Later in your work you will find that each of the sounds is associated with specific visual and kinesthetic experiences . . . each is a specific astral plane.

This is a technique of climbing the ladder of sound.

Notes: Some of these sounds, such as that of the flutes, are very attractive and may trap you in bliss. After a few days of such enjoyment it is well to get on with it.

Following the highest sound, you may have a fever for twenty-four hours. This will only occur when you arrive at a very high level of purification.

In meditation, perseverence furthers.

> "At first a yogi feels his mind
> Is tumbling like a waterfall,
> In mid course like the Ganges
> It flows on slow and gentle,
> In the end it is a great vast ocean
> Where the lights of Son and Mother merge in One."—Tilopa

Potent Quotes

"Right mindfulness snatches the pearl of Freedom from the Dragon Time."—*Heart of Buddhist Meditation*

"We are not trying to check the thought-waves by smashing the organs which record them. We have to do something much more difficult—to unlearn the false identification of the thought-waves with the ego-sense. This process of unlearning involves a complete transformation of character, a 'renewal of the mind' as St. Paul put it."—Isherwood

"A system of meditation which will produce the power of concentrating the mind on anything whatsoever is indispensable."—*Tibetan Yoga and Secret Doctrine*

"There are no impediments to meditation. The very thought of such obstacles is the greatest impediment."—Ramana Maharshi

THE RATIONAL MIND

Man's rational mind, the instrument with which he can think **about** things, has given him great power. This power he has used primarily to increase his potential for survival, to increase his pleasure or sensual gratification, and to enhance his ego through mastery or control of his environment. To visit one of the great cities of the world, to see a television image in your own home of the first man to set foot on the moon, to study the complexities of existing civilizations, cannot but fill one with awe as to the manifestations of the rational mind. And yet at the same time, to see the horror of urban living with its pollution and tensions, to see war and killing, to see the runaway imbalances in ecology, to study the statistics about neurosis and tranquilizers and crime and highway fatalities, cannot but lead one to wonder whether man's rational mind is enough.

The answer is that it is not. In an evolutionary perspective, the rational mind takes us a certain distance and no further, and we must be able to transcend it, to go on to other ways, other vehicles, if we are to cross the great ocean.

"A new type of thinking is essential if mankind is to survive and move towards higher levels."—A. Einstein

If you sense the limitations of a specific tool you do not necessarily throw the tool away. You first explore whether there is a way of using this very powerful tool in such a way as to develop a better tool or vehicle. That is, can you use the rational mind to transcend itself? The answer is yes. And the technique is known as *jnana yoga*, or the path of knowledge arrived at through reasoning and discrimination.

As with the use of sexual energies in *sadhana*, using the rational mind is making use of great powers which can lead to freedom or to greater enslavement. To understand the risk involved in *jnana yoga* you need to reflect upon the precise limit of the rational mind. The rational mind functions by separating subject from object, that is, the knower from the known. It works with data derived from the senses and the associative processes of the intellect (the memory). It works by analysis, a systematic processing technique that is based on the laws of logic.

Its limitations are that it cannot handle paradoxical or illogical information (e.g., that points at the opposite ends of a continuum are the same point, or that something can be "a" and "not a" at the same time) and that it cannot know that which can only be experienced subjectively.

It is interesting that in the autobiographical accounts of the great breakthroughs in man's understanding of the universe, the role of intuition, or some mysterious comprehension, led to the breakthrough rather than any systematic analytic process.

"I didn't arrive at my understanding of the fundamental laws of the universe through my rational mind."—A. Einstein

William James, the philosopher, pointed to other types of consciousness, or ways of knowing which are: (a) discontinuous with our rational mind, and (b) screened from us by the veil of our attachment to our rational mind. And he cautioned man against prematurely closing his accounts with reality before he had incorporated these other ways of knowing.

Now if you very dispassionately understand all the above, as well as understanding the truth of *yoga,* or union, and if you understand the essence of the fundamental truth that it is attachment that keeps man caught in the illusion of separateness, you begin to understand more and more of the way in which the universe functions. And with such study comes further discrimination, a further understanding and transcending of your own desires and thus a deeper and broader understanding of "how it all is." This is known as the work of the "causal plane" and is connected with the sixth *chakra* (the energy focal center located behind point between the eyebrows).

Finally you come to a point where you almost know it all. You are very wise. You are very pure . . . except for the fact that you may well have gotten caught in the last trap . . . the desire to know it all and still be you, "the knower." This is an impossibility. For all of the finite knowledge does not add up to the infinite. In order to take the final step, the knower must go. That is, you can only BE it all, but you can't know it all. The goal is non-dualistic—as long as there is a "knower" and "known" you are in dualism.

"There is only ONE GOD, and none else besides."—*Old Testament*

Many of the greatest minds in history have gotten caught in this trap of wanting to be God and at the same time to retain their separate identity. They are caught because they still have energy attached to the third *chakra*, the desire for ego power. And to be God is obviously the ultimate power trip.

In order to avoid this pitfall associated with *jnana yoga*, tremendous discipline is necessary. In Zen Buddhism, the relationship of the *koan* (the exercises in thought which confound the rational mind) to *zazen* (formal meditation) is an example of such discipline.

Exercises

One of the techniques used extensively in India was expounded by Ramana Maharshi and is called *Vichara Atma* (Who Am I?). It is a method for turning the mind in upon itself to first know its true nature and then to be its true nature. The method is technically simple, though extremely difficult to execute.

(1) You ask yourself, "Who am I?" Then step by step, in a systematic fashion, you

86

proceed to dissociate yourself from all the elements you previously identified as "I."

(2) You answer, "I am not my torso or body." Then you attempt to experience yourself as separate from your body. It is helpful to some people at the outset to place the "I" in the middle of the head and then see it as separate from the other parts to be set forth.

(3) Then you say, "I am not the five organs of motion: the arms, the legs, the tongue, the sphincter, the genitals." As you say each of these, experience your "I" as separate from that part of the body.

(4) Then you say, "I am not the five organs of sense: the eyes, the ears, the nose, the mouth, the skin." Again, stop with each and experience it as separate from "I".

(5) Then say, "I am not the five internal organs: the organs of respiration, digestion, excretion, circulation, perspiration." Again you stop with each of these sets of organs, attempt to experience the organ or to imagine its functioning, and then proceed to experience "I" as separate from that organ.

(6) If you have carried out the above instructions exactly, the only thing that is left are your thoughts. And, thus, the final step is to say "I am not these thoughts." Now the exquisite difficulty at this point is that the thought of "I" which you originally placed in the middle of your head is also (and specifically) a thought which you are not. So even the thought of "I" must go . . . It's a little like climbing out on the farthest branch of a tree and then cutting off the branch.

"The inert body does not say 'I.' Reality-Consciousness does not emerge. Between the two, and limited to the measure of the body, something emerges as 'I.' It is that that is known as Chit-jada-granthi (the knot between the conscious and the inert), and also as bondage, soul, subtle body, ego *samsara,* mind, and so forth."—Ramana Maharshi

If you have sufficient discipline of mind to carry this exercise through to completion, you have entered into the realm of *SAT CHIT ANANDA* (Reality-Consciousness) . . . your True Self . . . where there is only ONE.

Potent Quotes

"What can't be said can't be said, and it can't be whistled either."—Ram Tirtha

"All that the imagination can imagine and the reason conceive and understand in this life is not, and cannot be, a proximate means of union with God."—St. John of the Cross

". . . because the mind of the flesh is enmity against God."—Paul of Tarsus

"All that is made seems planless to the darkened mind, because there are more plans than it looked for. So with the Great Dance. Set your eyes on one movement and it will lead you through all patterns and it will seem to you the master movement. But the seeming will be true. Let no mouth open to gainsay it. There seems no plan because it is all plan: there seems no center because it is all center. Blessed be He . . ."—C.S. Lewis, *Perelandra*

"Kill therefore with the sword of wisdom the doubt born of ignorance that lies in thy heart. Be one in self-harmony, in Yoga, and arise, great warrior, arise."—*Bhagavad Gita*

"Have patience, Candidate, as one who fears no failure, courts no success. Fix thy soul's gaze upon the star whose ray thou art, the flaming star that shines within the lightless depths of ever-being."—Blavatsky

"Allegiance to the void implies denial of its Voidness
The more you talk about it, the more you think about it,
the further from it you go.
Stop talking, stop thinking, and there is nothing you will not
understand.
Return to the root and you will find the meaning
Pursue the light, and you lose its source.
Look inward and in a flash you will conquer the apparent and
the void.
All come from mistaken views
There is no need to seek truth, only stop having views."—Seng T'san

"A student once asked Joshu:
'If I haven't anything in my mind, what shall I do?'
Joshu replied: 'Throw it out.'
'But if I haven't anything how can I throw it out?' the student continued.
Said Joshu, 'Well, then, carry it out'."—Reps

"Our existence as embodied beings is purely momentary; what are a hundred years in eternity? But if we shatter the chains of egotism, and melt into the ocean of humanity, we share its dignity. To feel that we are something is to set up a barrier between God and ourselves; to cease feeling that we are something is to become one with God."—Gandhi

"Cease to seek after God as without thee
And the universe and things similar to these.
Seek him from out of thyself and learn who it is
Who once and for all appropriateth all in thee
Unto Himself.

And say, My God, My Mind, My Reason, My Soul, My Body, and learn whence is Sorrow and Joy and Love and Hate, and waking though one would not, and sleeping though one would not, and falling in love though one would not. And if thou shouldst closely investigate these things, thou wilt find Him in thyself, one and many, just as the atom. Thus finding, from thyself, a way out of thyself."—Manoimus the Heretic

"Make your will one! Don't listen with your ears, listen with your mind. No, don't listen with your mind, but listen with your spirit. Listening stops with the ears, the mind stops with recognition, but the spirit is empty and waits on all things. The Way gathers in emptiness alone. **Emptiness is the fasting of the mind.** It is easy to keep from walking; the hard thing is to walk without touching the ground."—Chuang Tzu

"If therefore thine eye be single, the whole body shall be full of light."—Jesus

"That which sees through the eye but whom the eye sees not; that is the Atman."—*Mundaka Upanishad*

"The Self is the witness, all-pervading, perfect, free, one, consciousness, actionless, not attached to any object, desireless, ever-tranquil. It appears through illusion as the world."—*Ashtavakra Gita*

"If it is said that Liberation is of three kinds, with form or without form, then let me tell you that the extinction of the three forms of Liberation is the only true Liberation."—Ramana Maharshi

"Who realizes what? That is realization."—Hari Dass Baba

"May all beings realize the ecstatic transparency of their own minds."—Karma LoTsu

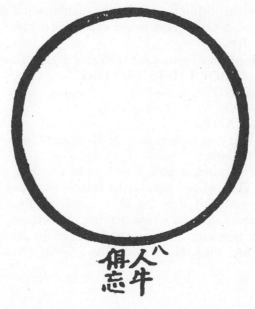

TIME AND SPACE

Exercises

1. Ask yourself: Where am I?
   Answer: Here.
   Ask yourself: What time is it?
   Answer: Now.
   Say it until you can hear it.

2. Set alarm clocks or design your day or put up notes on the wall so that a number of times during the day when you are in the midst of various occupations you confront yourself with the questions:

   (a) Where Am I?   and then answer (see answer below)
   (b) What time is it?   and then answer (see answer below)

Each time you do this, try to feel the immediacy of the Here and Now. Begin to notice that wherever you go or whatever time it is by the clock . . . it is ALWAYS HERE AND NOW. In fact you will begin to see that you can't get away from the HERE and NOW. Let the clock and the earth do their "thing" . . . let the comings and goings of life continue . . . But YOU stay HERE and NOW. This is an exercise to bring you to the ETERNAL PRESENT . . . where it all is.

3. For specific periods of time focus your thoughts in the present.
   DON'T THINK ABOUT THE FUTURE.
   JUST BE **HERE NOW.**
   DON'T THINK ABOUT THE PAST.
   JUST BE **HERE NOW.**

4. Reflect on the thought that if you are truly Here and Now—
   (a) it is ENOUGH, and
   (b) you will have optimum power and understanding to do the best thing at the given moment. Thus when "then" (the future) becomes Now—if you have learned this discipline—you will then be in a ideal position to do the best thing. So you need not spend your time now worrying about then.

5. Reflect on the fact that you can plan the future in the Here and Now as long as when then is Now . . . you are fully Here and Now. Seem paradoxical? Of course! Keep reflecting!

6. "Think that you are not yet begotten, think that you are in the womb, that you are young, that you are old, that you are dead, that you are in the world beyond the grace, grasp all that in your thought at once, all times and places . . ."— Hermetica

Answers: (a) HERE   (b) NOW

Potent Quotes

"The Oversoul is before Time, and Time, Father of all else, is one of His children."—Emerson

"Thought is time, and time creates fear."

"How are we to know that the mind has become concentrated? Because the idea of time will vanish. The more time passes un-noticed the more concentrated we are . . . All time will have the tendency to come and stand in the one present. So the definition is given, when the past and present come and stand in one, the mind is said to be concentrated."—Vivekananda

"A Zen student must learn to waste time conscientiously."—Suzuki Roshi

"If we could feel the **idea** of time itself, of all our life lying in Time, the momentary I of passing time would not have the same hold over us."—Nicoll

PSYCHEDELICS AS AN UPAYA (Method)

There are many paths that lead towards enlightenment. Some of these paths lead all the way, while others take a pilgrim only a little way. Some paths are steep and dangerous; others slow and gentle. You will notice that as you come to meet more and more pilgrims you will find that they are attached to the particular method they are pursuing at the moment. That attachment is because the method is giving them a return of some greater light or bliss or knowledge or sense of being than that to which they are accustomed.

In India, the trap of becoming attached or addicted to any particular method, be it *pranayam* or devotion, or whatever, is well known. As a safeguard against this there is a time schedule in a *sadhana*. The first twenty years of life are for study. The second twenty years are for worldly participation and family; the third twenty years are for religious study and the pursuit of various intense methods of *sadhana*. In the last twenty years, however, the *sadhak* forgoes all methods. He becomes a *sanyasi* and wanders without ties to family or temple or method . . . having given up all attachment.

Psychedelics as an *upaya* at first seem to hold infinite promise. But as one works with them further, one comes to realize the possible finiteness of the method. At this point, however, the individual may have become so attached to the experience of "getting high" that he doesn't want to continue on his way by finding other methods. At this point he is being dishonest with himself, conning himself. Such a tactic is a short-term strategy at best and usually produces negative emotions.

"A man who has attained certain powers through medicines, or through words, or through mortification, still has desires, but that man who has attained to *Samadhi* through concentration is alone free from all desires."—Vivekananda

"But when the King came in to look at the guests, he saw there a man who had no wedding garment; and he said to him, 'Friend how did you get in here without a wedding garment?' And he was speechless. Then the King said to the attendants, 'Bind him hand and foot, and cast him into the outer darkness; there men will weep and gnash their teeth'. For many are called, but few are chosen."—Jesus

What are psychedelics?

They are a group of chemicals which can expand consciousness. Included are such chemicals as LSD, marijuana, peyote, mescaline, psylocybin, DMT, DET, hashish . . . These vary in the degree to which they contain other than psychedelic components. Some have side effects of euphoria or agitation or nausea or lethargy.

Is speed (amphetamines, methamphetamines, etc.) psychedelic? It can be. However, it has very strong side effects which ultimately are seriously detrimental to one's work. They tend to facilitate thought loops or spinning out of old associations somewhat endlessly. In addition, speed is strongly habit forming and demands increasing dosage over time. Furthermore, speed slowly does your body in. And if you destroy the temple in which you must do the work before the work is finished . . . you lose.

How are the opium derivatives (heroin, morphine, etc.) different from psychedelics? The opiates are truly "drugs" in the exact sense of the term. That is, they allow an individual to escape from an unpleasant environment, be it physical or psychological. They make everything seem irrelevant. Their effect is sought by those deeply entrapped in the subtle sphere of sense enjoyment. They are not only habit forming but appear to be physiologically addicting. For someone who realizes that, as Buddha points out, attachment is the cause of suffering, heroin and other opiates which are a sure trip into new attachments hardly seem the path to enlightenment.

What use are psychedelics in this work?

The "pros" of psychedelics are as follows:

1. For a person deeply attached to any finite reality which he takes to be absolute, the psychedelics can, under proper conditions, help him to break out of the imprisoning model created by his own mind. Of course, there is a paradox here: if he wants to take a psychedelic in order to break out, he already knows of another possibility . . . and thus could proceed without psychedelics. If, on the other hand, he takes psychedelics for kicks or for other reasons without seeking to know another reality, the experience may help his spiritual work (the shock may be quite dramatic).

"LSD is like Christ in America which is awakening the young folk in Kali Yuga. America is most materialistic country therefore God has shown His Avatar in a form of LSD (a material). They wanted a material for approaching God and they got it in the form of LSD. A man who has not tasted things thinking as true, how he will get the feeling of those things?"—Hari Dass Baba

"To a few sincere seekers such as yourself, LSD may have served as a means to arouse that spiritual longing which has brought you into contact with Baba, but once that purpose is served further ingestion would not only be harmful but have no point or purpose." — An Indian Correspondent

2. The use of psychedelics can provide experiences which in the short term strengthen your faith in the possibility of enlightenment sufficiently to pursue systematic purification

(which ultimately will, of course, include giving up psychedelics). They often serve this function even though the glimpse they give may only be of a low astral plane.

3. Carefully programmed psychedelic sessions can have significant therapeutic value in providing new perspectives for areas of strong attachment. That is, for a person who is caught, for example, in strongly learned oral or sexual habits, a psychedelic session can provide a moment of transcending these habits, and thus experiencing the possibility of alternative reactions. This experience will be temporary, for you are merely overriding the desires which feed the habits in the first place. However, the experience may give leverage to your work with these strong drive areas.

4. The deepest psychedelic experiences allow one to transcend polarities and thus get beyond fears of death, or entrapments in the guilt created by attachment to the polarity of good and evil.

5. The milder psychedelics are used by many *sadhus* in *bhakti yoga*. They smoke in order to release emotion and allow them to commune with God with open hearts. This is true of many wandering *sadhus* in India. Smoking is looked down upon by most temple and *ashram* residents in India.

The "cons" of psychedelics are as follows:

1. You still come down. The experience is not permanent. Coming down brings despair.

2. Because the psychedelic agent is external to yourself, its use tends to subtly reinforce in you a feeling that you are not enough. Ultimately, of course, at the end of the path you come to realize that you have been Enough all the way along.

3. The intensity with which the psychedelics show you "more" makes you greedy to be done before you are ready. This attaches you to the experience of "getting high" which, after a period of time, becomes a *cul-de-sac*. The goal of the path is to BE high, not GET high.

4. Many people who use psychedelics primarily experience astral planes where their ego is present. Thus they often attempt to use the powers that are available in such an astral plane in the service of their own ego. This creates additional *karma* for them—for it is action which comes out of attachment. Many messianic trips are of this nature. Sometimes such individuals get stuck at one or another astral plane and lose contact with the gross physical plane. In the West such beings are usually hospitalized until they find their way back to the physical plane. Of course, what in fact has happened is that they have not gone far enough. For the psychiatrist is attached to the physical plane (denying the reality of other planes) in the same way that the patient is attached to the astral plane (denying the reality of other planes including the physical). The only true reality includes all these planes and is beyond them all at the same time. This is known as the paradox of *Mahamudra*—the paradox of two-in-one.

94

5. Using violent methods as one's *upaya,* such as strong psychedelics or *kundalini yoga**, severe fasts, etc., lead to an unevenness in the individual's vibrations. This creates waves in the environment because the person is not quite able to keep it all together. You should be able to remember your zip code even as you drift in intergalactic ecstasy. Keeping it all together is hard.

6. Psychedelics are, for the most part, illegal. This means that in order to use them you must break the law. Breaking the law involves risks which create anxiety and paranoia. Anxiety and paranoia are not good states of mind in which to pursue one's *sadhana.* Furthermore, breaking the law means that you must function within the polarity of "we" and "them." Only a very advanced being can do this without attachment.

7. There is at present no conclusive evidence that psychedelics are damaging to the physiological organism. The research on chromosome damage has been largely political in nature. There may be energy depletions and subtle physiological effects not yet measured. Most of the physiological reactions are psychological in origin and usually are the result of fear or anxiety.

*Kundalini yoga is a powerful method, and should be undertaken only under the guidance of a competent teacher.

THE COURSE OF SADHANA

Doing *sadhana* can be as much of a trap as any other melodrama. It is useful to have some perspective about the path in order to keep yourself from getting too caught up in the stage in which you are working. These pointers may help:

1. Each stage that one can label must pass away. Even the labelling will ultimately pass. A person who says, "I'm enlightened" probably isn't.

2. The initial euphoria that comes through the first awakening into even a little consciousness, except in a very few cases, will pass away . . . leaving a sense of loss, or a feeling of falling out of grace, or despair. *The Dark Night of the Soul* by St. John of the Cross deals with that state.

3. *Sadhana* is a bit like a roller coaster. Each new height is usually followed by a new low. Understanding this makes it a bit easier to ride with both phases.

4. As you further purify yourself, your impurities will seem grosser and larger. Understand that it's not that you are getting more caught in the illusion, it's just that you are seeing it more clearly. The lions guarding the gates of the temples get fiercer as you proceed towards each inner temple. But of course the light is brighter also. It all becomes more intense because of the additional energy involved at each stage of *sadhana*.

5. At first you will think of your *sadhana* as a limited part of your life. In time you will come to realize that everything you do is part of your *sadhana*.

6. One of the traps along the way is the *sattvic* trap—the trap of purity. You will be doing everything just as you should—and get caught in how pure you are. In India it's called the "golden chain." It's not a chain of iron, but it's still a chain. You'll have to finally give up even your idea of purity if you expect to do it all in this life-time.

7. Early in the journey you wonder how long the journey will take and whether you will make it in this lifetime. Later you will see that where you are going is HERE and you will arrive NOW . . . so you stop asking.

8. At first you **try**. Later you just do your *sadhana* because, "What else is there to do?"

9. At certain stages you will take your *sadhana* very seriously. Later you will see the wisdom of the statement of Jesus that to seek the Lord, men need not disfigure their faces. Cosmic humor, especially about your own predicament, is an important part of your journey.

10. At some stages you will experience a plateau—as if everything has stopped. This is a hard point in the journey. Know that once the process has started it doesn't stop; it only appears to stop from where you are looking. Just keep going. It doesn't really matter

whether you think "it's happening" or not. In fact, the thought "it's happening" is just another obstacle.

11. You may have expected that enlightenment would come ZAP! instantaneous and permanent. This is unlikely. After the first "Ah Ha" experience, the unfolding is gradual and almost indiscernible. It can be thought of as the thinning of a layer of clouds . . . until only the most transparent veil remains.

12. There is, in addition to the "up and down" cycles, an "in and out" cycle. That is, there are stages at which you feel pulled in to inner work and all you seek is a quiet place to meditate and to get on with it. Then there are times when you turn outward and seek to be involved in the market place. Both of these parts of the cycle are a part of one's *sadhana*. For what happens to you in the market place helps in your meditation and what happens to you in meditation helps you to participate in the market place without attachment.

13. What is happening to you is nothing less than death and rebirth. What is dying is the entire way in which you understood "who you are" and "how it all is." What is being reborn is the child of the Spirit for whom things all are new. This process of attending an ego that is dying at the same time as you are going through a birth process is awesome. Be gentle and honor him (self) who is dying as well as him (Self) who is being born.

Potent Quotes

"On the way of true development, something old must die and something new must be born in him . . ."—Collins

"How to get rid of the lower self: The blossom vanishes of itself as the fruit grows, so will your lower self vanish as the divine grows in you."—Ramakrishna

"Lakes in the Dry Season: drop by drop their depths are diminished, like as the enlightened gradually lose all notions of self."—Ramakrishna

"The Soul flees just at the very moment when we seem to hold its gleaming splendour in our hands and all we are left with is one more dead butterfly to add to our mouldering collection."—Krishna Prem

"All of a sudden the progress will stop one day, and you will find yourself, as it were, stranded. Persevere. All progress proceeds by such rise and fall."—Vivekananda

". . . every individual existence is brought into rhythm by a pendulum to which the heart gives type and name. There is a time for expanding and a time for contraction; one provokes the other and the other calls for the return of the first . . . Never are we nearer the Light than when the darkness is deepest . . ."—Vivekananda

"But first the disciple must pass through the complexity in order to exhaust the various possibilities until the awakening of the consciousness which leads towards simplicity: would he be able to bear the intermediate phase between his dream and reality."—de Lubicz

"Wipe out the delusions of the will, undo the snares of the heart, rid yourself of the entanglements to virtue; open up the roadblocks in the Way. Eminence and wealth, recognition and authority, fame and profit—these six are the delusions of the will. Appearance and carriage, complexion and features, temperament and attitude—these six are the snares of the heart. Loathing and desire, joy and anger, grief and happiness—these six are entanglements of virtue. Rejecting and accepting, taking and giving, knowledge and ability—these six are the roadblocks of the way. When these four sixes not longer seethe within the breast, then you will achieve uprightness; being upright, you will be still; being still you will be enlightened; being enlightened you will be empty; and being empty you will do nothing, and yet there will be nothing that is not done."—Chuang Tzu

"When crystallization is achieved, renunciations, privations, and sacrifices are no longer necessary. Then a man may have everything he wants. There are no longer any laws for him, he is a law unto himself."—Ouspensky

"Having, therefore, ascended all these degrees of humility, the monk will presently arrive at that love of God which, being perfect, casteth out fear; whereby he shall begin to keep, without labour, and as it were naturally and by custom all those precepts which he had hitherto observed through fear.

No longer through dread of hell, but for the love of Christ, and of a good habit and a delight in virtue: which God will vouchsafe to manifest by the Holy Spirit in his labourer, now cleansed from vice and sin."—*Rule of St. Benedict*

I know
that I know
and that I don't know.
But I forget.

I see that I am blind
and I see the blinding light
in everything,
but I forget.

I see what I know
I think
I know what I see.
But sometimes
I forget.

And This is the Way
It should be.
At the end of every forget
I remember.—Lonny Brown

SETTING

As you begin to calm your mind through meditation or *mantra*, you become increasingly aware of the forces acting upon you—forces within as well as outside your body. Previously you sought continuous stimulation but now you gravitate towards situations in which there is less and less stimulation. For some well advanced upon the path, the cave—the traditional haunt of *yogis*—is sought, for here the rock is insulation against many of the subtle vibrations which are distracting for those who have become sensitive.

"Where there is fire, or in water or on ground which is strewn with dry leaves, where there are many ant-hills, where there are wild animals, or danger, where four streets meet, where there is too much noise, where there are many wicked persons, Yoga must not be practiced."—Vivekananda

For most Westerners embarking upon their *sadhana*, a cave is neither a desirable or even a possible alternative. Not desirable in the sense that their *karma* still requires commerce with worldly stimulation. Under such conditions the seeking out of a cave and attempting to pursue a *sadhana* such as that of the Tibetan renunciate, Milarepa, can start out and remain a subtle ego trip. It would seem wiser to start your *sadhana* from exactly where you are, and then let any changes occur in your style of life and environment in a slow and natural fashion. For it is true that at the early stages, any waves you make in carrying out your *sadhana* merely created more *karma*. Let your inner pull towards enlightenment lead you, so to speak. Let the Light pull you towards itself (like a moth to a flame). You will finally seek more and more pure environments because you "have to"—because it's the only thing you **can** do, not because you think you **ought** to.

Where you are at this moment is the first thing to assess. Married or single? Children? Parents? Existing contracts with other beings (social, vocational, economic, religious, national, familial, etc.)? Available opportunities?

Perhaps the most appropriate initial step in view of your present predicament is to continue with your daily life in the customary manner with the simple addition of a *mantra*. Such a *mantra* can initially be used for 15 minutes in the morning and evening as suggested by Maharishi Mahesh in his program for Transcendental Meditation. You can set up a corner of your room for this purpose.

Create a quiet corner in your home . . . an *Om* Home . . . a launching pad to the infinite . . . a meditation seat . . . a shrine. Bring to it that which is simple and pure: a mat, perhaps a candle, maybe a picture of a realized being whose life has turned you on—Buddha, or Christ, or Ramakrishna, or Ramana Maharshi, possibly some incense. Create a seat in which you can sit comfortably with spine straight out and turn off your body. Those who have developed the triangular seat of *padmasa* (full lotus), *siddhasa* (half lotus), or even *sukhasa* (the easy pose) . . . remember, no suffering.

In this corner establish a regular ritual for purification, for reflection, for calming the mind. Just as water wears away stone, so daily *sadhana* will thin the veil of *avidya* (ignorance).

At quite the opposite end of the continuum is the total moment-to-moment discipline of each thought and act required in a monastery or *ashram*. Here is but one example, presently functioning in the United States. It is Tassajara, a Zen Buddhist center in California.

The Zen Center

Bell ringing at 4 a.m. You get up immediately.

Han (block of hard ash wood struck with wooden mallet) starts at 4:05. 15 minute *han*, 3 rounds. You should be in the *zendo* by end of second round.

Zazen (sitting meditation) starts at 4:20. 40 minute period. *Roshi* makes a round of the *zendo* in the beginning. People bowing as he approaches (actually, *gassho*-ing—hands together and bow).

Bell sounds after 40 minutes. *Kinhin* (walking meditation) begins. *Kinhin* for 15 minutes. (Hands on chest, walking very slowly in a line, about a half step with each breath).

Second period of *zazen* (40 minutes).

Service at 5:50. Consists of bowing to the floor 9 times, reciting the *Heart Sutra* 3 times, bowing to floor 3 times; lasts about 20 minutes. With bells and large wooden drum.

Study period. One hour. In large room with fire if it's cold. Kerosene lamps. Tea is served. Warmth often makes you drowsy. You read various texts. Short chant at beginning and end of period.

Han for breakfast starts at 7:10.

Breakfast is served in the *zendo*. You sit on cushions in meditation posture. Each student has: an *oryoki* (set of 3 bowls, spoon and chopsticks, a scraper, *setsu* (stick with cloth end), and 3 cloths (for napkin, bowl-wiping, and cloth in which entire *oryoki* is wrapped—folded and tied in prescribed manner). Ritual way for untying and removing bowls. Bowls are placed on an eating board in front of each student. Complicated *oryoki* ritual helps to focus attention. Meals are a sort of meditation, in silence, with as little noise as possible.

Chanting precedes meal (in English at breakfast, Japanese at lunch). After short chant, students set up their *oryokis*. Chanting resumes and servers enter. As server stops before student, they bow to each other, server kneels and dishes food into bowl, they bow again and server goes on to next student. There is chanting while food is served (reciting names of Buddha and Bodhisattvas). When servers leave there is more chanting (we should be mindful of where this food comes from and whether our practice deserved it). Meal is eaten. When meal is finished server enters with hot water and there is a short chant. Hot water is poured in large bowl. Bowl is cleaned and water poured in second bowl, bowl wiped with cloth, and so on until the bowls are cleaned. Water is drunk, with a little bit saved and collected at the end (it's taken out and poured on a plant). *Oryokis* are tied up and put away (placed by the side of each student). Clackers and bow at the end of meal, *roshi* and priests leave, then students leave. As students file out of *zendo* they exchange bows with the cook.

Short period (about 20 minutes) in which you change into work clothes, take care of toilet, etc.

Work drum sounds at 8:40. Students assemble for work meeting. Short informal meeting to make sure each student knows what he's doing, has some task assigned to him, and jobs are co-ordinated.

Work period until *han* 11:10. Gardening, carpentry, masonry, roofing, garbage collecting, cleaning, sewing, etc.

Han at 11:10. 20 minutes to clean up, change into robes and get to *zendo*.

(There is a 15 minute *han* for this, so one can gauge his time.)

Zazen (40 minutes).

Service (bowing and reciting *Heart Sutra).*

Lunch (same procedure as breakfast). Usually soup, bread, and vegetable.

After lunch there is a rest period, about 30-40 minutes. (This is the chance to get some sun.)

Work drum sounds at 2 (or 2:05). After short work meeting you return to your job.

At 3:30 a bell signals tea. Everyone gathers on steps in front of *zendo* (where there is still some sun), a short chant and tea is served. Sometimes there is a treat (crackers, cookies). A short chant at the end and people return to work. At 5 p.m. drum signals end of work. Clean up, put away tools, tidy work area.

Bath time. Everyone heads for the hot sulphur baths. Before entering bath student bows before altar and recites *gatha* (verse). Silence in bath. (It is already dark in the winter, and quite cold. Kerosene lamp, cement grotto, steam rising from water, shadowy forms. Bath, at about 110° is the one chance for the body—feeling all day like a piece of cold iron—to get really warm. Blood returns to body.) Students bow and recite *gatha* before leaving.

Bell begins at 5:35. 15 minutes to service.

Evening service (as before).

Supper. No chanting, simply clackers before and after meal.

Brown rice, miso soup, and vegetable.

After supper there is free time. You return to your cabin or go to the large room where there is a fire.

Han starts at 7:30.

Study period (at 7:45) when there is no lecture.

Lecture—by *roshi*, priest, or student—is in *zendo*, at 8.

Zazen (at 8:35, lecture may extend into this period). Ends with slow deep chanting of *Heart Sutra*.

Students return to cabins.

Lights out at 9:30.

There is a day off on 4 and 9 days (for example, the 4th, 9th, 14th . . .). This begins after breakfast. On 4 days (officially only 1/2 day off) there is a general discussion in the morning attended by all; completely open—gripes, questions, views, personal problems; feedback for those directing Tassajara; very helpful for students to know where other students are, what sort of problems they're facing. On days off, students are expected to take care of personal needs—laundry, mending, shaving head, and so forth.

The Fall Practice period is 2 months; the Winter (or Spring) Practice period is 3 months. Each period ends with a 7 day *sesshin*—periods of intense meditation—17 hours a day of *zazen* and *kinhin*, including meals, lecture, bath, and short work period.

Besides joining a traditional *ashram* or monastery, you may prefer to participate in a spiritual community in the country or the city. Here are some descriptions and helpful suggestions based on our experiences at the Lama Foundation.

103

The Spiritual Community

There are hundreds of communities in the U.S. at present. Many spiritual seekers have joined or started communities in order to provide a suitable environment for their inner work. Often they have been disillusioned by these experiments because of disorder, economic instability, ego struggles, and mixed motives on the part of the participants. Out of these early community experiments have evolved more structured attempts to provide the optimum environment for spiritual growth. These communities are usually less disciplined than traditional Eastern *ashrams* but more firmly structured than contemporary communes.

The community has within it two levels or components: the base camp and the hermitages. Ideally these are physically separate from one another, although they may exist within the same house if necessary. The base camp handles all matters pertaining to economics, food, children, pets, relationships to the larger community, while the hermitage is set aside solely for spiritual development in a formal sense.

Things which make it work:

1. The nature of the contract must be explicit. That is, each person participating in the experiment must understand the form, schedule and objectives . . . and not only share the objectives but feel that this form is the optimum one for them to pursue at this moment. This

experiment cannot work properly if the group has many ideas of "how it should be done." In traditional *ashrams* there is usually a **guru** or teacher who leads the way . . . or a traditional structure which is known to every one who seeks to participate.

2. All members of the community (with the exception of small children) have consciously and freely chosen to participate in the experiment. Any exceptions to this rule reduce the effectiveness of the experiment. In the most rigid selection procedures, if one partner of a couple does not wish to fully participate in the experiment, then neither would participate and they would leave the community, at least for the period of the experiment. It takes very few people who do not share the desire to work on themselves in this way to destroy the effectiveness of a spiritual community.

3. All participants in the community (with the exception of the smaller children) spend time in the hermitage as well as the base camp and share base camp activities and responsibilities.

If you are living with others who are sharing the journey even minimally, it is important that a group meditation room be set aside. In fact, it is wise when moving into a new home to create the center — the meditation room or alcove — **first,** before you get the kitchen and bedrooms in order.

1. Collaboratively pick the place for the meditation area.

2. Clean it up and bring the most beautiful things to it. Keep it simple.

3. Then light a candle and perhaps some incense . . . everyone sit together silently . . . and reflect on why you are here . . . the goal of your work together . . . and then perhaps read from some holy books. Perhaps take a reading of the *I-Ching* for your work together . . . and only after all that is done do you set up housekeeping.

4. Keep that area very special. No social conversations, no other books, no other uses, no sleeping there.

5. Try to build a natural ritual into your lives so that you use that space to share a daily moment when you transcend your ego games. Perhaps early morning silent meditations, or evening chanting, or reading from holy books aloud . . .

The Base Camp

The base camp includes all the living facilities with the exception of the hermitage rooms or buildings. Participants in the base camp follow a schedule as follows:

5:30	Rise
5:45- 6:30	Group silent meditation.
6:30- 7:00	Chanting, reading aloud, singing.

7:00- 9:00	Dancing, *asanas, pranayam,* breakfast, getting the children to school, clean up, etc.
9:00-12:00	*Karma yoga* (work) period — assignments for an entire week are usually made once a week on Saturday morning.
12:00- 2:00	Bringing food and supplies to hermit and preparing and having *prasad* (consecrated food), taken in silence. Then rest or relaxation and clean-up.
2:00- 4:00	*Karma yoga* period.
4:00- 5:30	Group study, and exercises in consciousness.
5:30- 6:30	*Pranayam, asanas,* preparing evening food, etc.
6:30- 8:00	Evening *prasad* (silently) plus clean-up and relaxation, reading, etc.
8:00- 9:00	Group meditation and chanting and singing.

By assigning the *karma yoga* tasks over a period of a week you can use the *karma yoga* periods in a fluid fashion. One person's *karma yoga,* for example, might include milking goats, making cheese, weaving, picking the kids up at school, getting the car fixed, etc. Also a person may design his schedule to use a few of the morning *karma yoga* periods for personal study or meditation. The use of these periods is largely dependent upon the number of participants, and the amount of man-hours required for right livelihood and community maintenance. Time not spent in fulfilling assignments should be used on inner work (study, meditation, *asanas,* singing *kirtan).*

Most activities can be carried on in silence. Groups working together on a shared project such as gardening, building, etc. can either do these tasks in silence or do *mantra* during the work. Silence is an important part of the work. Formal discussions at the base camp of the hermitage experiences of the participants can be useful. Gossip, small talk, and hanging out . . . have a limited value in breaking through the illusion.

It is well to realize that the relationships in this community are not the dominant concern. Ideally, personality falls away in the common endeavor. If you want at all costs to hold onto your personality, don't join a spiritual community . . . because no one is going to be interested. Interpersonal matters are dealt with only to the extent that they are disruptive (i.e., capture the consciousness of the group or some participants). Such matters can be dealt with at a group meeting if necessary . . . but the moment the group gets bogged down in heavy melodrama . . . it is well to call a meditation interlude until everyone can find a center again. Melodrama sucks us in again and again, but diminishes in power if actively thwarted.

The Hermitage

Each participant in the community spends a portion of his or her time in solitude in a hermitage. The amount of time spent by each individual is a function of the number of participants and the number of spaces. The minimum time for a hermitage visit is twenty-four hours. (The maximum we have worked with is three weeks.) Usually an initial period of three to five days is a good "shake-down cruise."

You bring into the hermitage the minimum requirements. A sleeping bag, toothbrush, blanket or cushion, candles, incense, etc. Beyond the requirements for survival the stay in a hermitage should be designed to include items useful to your specific *sadhana*. The fiercest confrontation is to merely walk into an empty room with your basic survival gear and close the door. The most gentle trip is to include knitting, books, notebook, drawing pad, walks in the woods, photo albums, etc. Only books written by very advanced beings should be brought in, only pictures of holy beings or religious subjects or nature should be around you.

Each day food is brought at noon. One large meal a day is usually enough. The tray may include enough fruit for the evening. Survival apparatus may include facilities for making tea. (Those who are ready for the fierce *tapasya* may choose to fast while in the hermitage.) The food and supplies are left outside the door by one of the members of the base camp. No social contact is made. Any needs are communicated by a note left outside the door for the messenger to pick up.

The only reason to leave the hermitage room is for toileting and washing, both of which should be done without social interaction.

If the hermitage is in a noisy place, ear plugs may be used during your stay.

As a hermit, you usually spend a good deal of your time in meditation. It is good to have a little training or knowledge of meditation to help you calm your mind. A good deal of the time is spent initially watching your wild out-of-control mind do "its thing." It is only under these minimal stimulus conditions that you can really watch it do its thing.

The Abbot

Unless there is a teacher in the group, leadership is risky. However, it is possible to rotate the duties of an abbot in the event that no teacher is available. The abbot has the responsibility for making things run smoothly on the physical plane as well as for keeping the objectives of the community uppermost in everyone's mind. In order to fulfill such responsibilities, the abbot must spend much time meditating to keep his own spiritual center in order so that he does not become an agent of more confusion and illusion and power trips. Perhaps the abbot could be the person who has just come out of the hermitage if rotation is required.

One of the functions of the abbot can be to visit a hermit if the hermit sends a note requesting such a visit. During his visit the abbot must keep his concerns strictly on the spiritual unfolding of the hermit. Often merely a silent meditation between the hermit and the abbot will suffice to fulfill the needs of the hermit.

Mood or Tone

All of this structure sounds heavy . . . and it is . . . but it need not be carried out in a serious or heavy mood. A light joyful style is not in any way incompatible with spiritual work. The ability to retain a sense of cosmic humor is very crucial for the effectiveness of a spiritual community. Heavy religiosity (much evaluation) is a drag.

If you are living in a city and are involved in *karma yoga,* it may be possible to design a modified form of the community-*ashram*. A large house, shared by a number of people who have consciously come together solely for the purpose of working on themselves, is a useful setting. Perhaps one or two rooms can be set aside in the quietest part of the house as hermitage quarters. Another room can be set aside as the group meditation room. It should be possible for each participant to spend some time in the hermitage, being cared for by the other members of the group. The value of this procedure is that it creates a collaboration specifically for the spiritual evolution of each individual, based on the assumption that the group members each directly profit from the spiritual evolvement of each of the other members.

Still another possibility for city dwellers is to have *satsang* (or a gathering of monks on the path) at a different apartment each evening. The formats should be kept simple and non-competitive. Perhaps some reading, a meditation, a few songs and light *prasad* (consecrated food). There should be a real effort to reduce the amount of talk or stimulation that is not definitely involved in the journey. Even cosmic gossip can slow down the work. Silence before and after the formal aspects of the evening helps.

FAMILY SADHANA

The course of family sadhana in the West in the 1970's is a difficult one to practice. Whereas in the past in both East and West there have been precise models these have been built around a culture and tradition which was supportive of this practice. In Western culture the support system has been destroyed by the industrial revolution and the money economy which has caused the virtual destruction of the family as a spiritual and psychic union by compelling at least one and often both principal members to become money earners. This necessitates daily absence from the home and reliance on day-care centers, nursery schools or regular schools to provide a spiritual foundation which one cannot expect them to provide as they essentially are educating and directing children to become "good members" of the same society which is in essence profane and in extension looking only to continue its existence at the present level of consciousness. Consequently the family is dispersed, its members isolated from each other and effectively only together as an economic and sleeping unit. The family thus has no center to radiate from and no spiritual-psychic support system. It is dead. The outlook is bleak from this vantage point.

However, in the last decade there has been a resurgence of spiritual life brought about by lysergic acid, the bomb, rock 'n' roll, visiting teachers from the East and the incredible vacuum and death that is the rot at the core. And as life will not permit a vacuum, the times they are a-changing.

SO
HOW?
TO BEGIN?

To begin we must begin at the beginning. At the beginning is the spirit. Spirit is a Latin word meaning breath. It's like breathing out and breathing in, NO THING-yup, no thing. And this no thing is basic for our life. Breathe spirit, this spirit which sustains and maintains, without which we die to this form. This no thing is the foundation upon which all must be based. Life must be dedicated to the spirit alone for as it has been laid out . . . seek you first the kingdom of heaven and all else shall be added to you . . . so . . . with the family *sadhana* as with all *sadhana* this is where we begin. The family and all it is thru/by/in extension must be dedicated solely to the spirit.

Next:

An earth-real consideration of physical plane realities. Food, shelter, and clothing. An examination in truth of real needs. Not desires, not fantasies, but you know: how many pairs of pants? what kind of food? what type of shelter? how big? who for? where? and then?

109

Can you afford to take a cut? Can you afford not to? Can you and will you let go of all the things and values and trips that you have gotten caught in? If you can adapt your present means of livelihood to your spiritual work than you're cool. (See section on "Money and Right Livelihood.") If you can't then you'll probably have to make a radical change in your life. Try getting into subsistence economy. Just making it. Not too much not too little but just enough to make it. Buy an old farm (there're lots—cheap) or set up a craft scene. Use the system to teach yourself how to operate these well and efficiently. Keep it all together. Run a good ship. This is our second base. Apply consciousness clearly. Understand values. Don't be afraid to make mistakes but don't court disaster.

Why a farm, why a small craft scene? Just this. The family can "be" together. There are functions in these situations for all the members from the children to the adults. The work is clear and definite. Jesus was a carpenter. Ghandi spun. This daily concern with the vehicle of sustenance on the gross plane must be clear, straight and simple. As work/time/space is shared (based all ways on the spirit) a family grows together. Here exists mutuality, trust, openness, a psychic organism develops—this is what a family is. The possibilities on this level are endless: farm, crafts, natural food store, general store, restaurant, creamery, small paper, bookstore. Drop into realtiy.

Now we have an environment and a basis for practice.

First turn the environment into a shrine, a temple. If the family is primarily *bhakti*, plaster the walls with holy pictures, light incense, radiate love; if it's Christian make it a home for Christ; if it's more austere, moving toward Zen, reflect nothingness. Whatever your trip make the whole environment support it.

Next set up a clear movement thru time. Rise daily at the same time, meditate together, pray together, offer all actions to the spirit, offer all food to the spirit, cook in love for love, keep the home clean, calm and clear so if Lord Buddha walked in he'd feel right at home. Maintain the body as a temple, clean it, feed it, take good care of it, have compassion for it, love it. The discipline of a daily schedule is a drag at first, after a while you will feel the results. It all runs on automatic. Don't think. Fill your whole mind with the spirit. BE! And in being together in the spirit be in love together. It's all making love. Make love in beauty, in joy, in seeing each other in truth, choose your marriage model. The Sun and the Moon, Heaven and Earth, Yab-Yum, Shiva-Shakti, Siva and Parvati, the Eternal Companions, the Alchemical Marriage, Mohammed and his Wives, Adam and Eve, Christ and his Bride.

Let the man worship woman as God, the Holy Mother, the Divine Shakti, the Mana, the Food of Life, the Sustainer of Being, Isis, Astarte, the Good Earth, Terrible Kali, and Herself—All Of It. She is all of it.

Let the woman worship man as God, the Son, the Sun, the Father, the Lite of Her Life, the Creator, the Provider, as Jesus, as Ram, as Shiva, as Krishna, as all of them and Himself.

Surrender and die to one another. Become one. The glorious Mystic Rose in the garden of the Heavenly Father. Permeate the universe, fill it, become it for this is the union beyond duality.

O Holy Family

This is the seat of the practice.

And as the children who are the fruit of the union appear, see them as divine avatars, holy beings who have come recently from our true HOME to teach. Nourish and feed them as they feed you. Listen for their tone, see their ray so as to help them fulfill their spiritual destiny, provide a matrix for their consciousness. Great care must be taken to guide the entity on this plane. Choose carefully the initial impressions which they will be registering as you would the food they eat. They are the hope and destiny of the universe. Respect and honor them. Guide them clearly. Keep the home calm and free of chaotic inputs. Let love burn in all the lamps. Thru all of this face and cope out the difficulties. For the woman there will be the heavy pull of the earth element. The children will feel any psychic withdrawal on her part. She must find a place a little removed for deep meditation. When they wake up during meditation explain clearly what you are doing. Read them holy stories to acquaint them with spirit life so that they may remember. Keep your practice regular and the children will stay in tune. Don't trip too far too fast or psychic disequilibrium will upset months of work. Do not sacrifice relationships with the children for what you may think is spiritual necessity. The whole thing is *sadhana*. Chant *mantras* together. The first word of one infant here was Allah (God). Children really love *bhajan*. They go around singing Bhaja Shri Krishna Chaitanya or Om Sri Ram Jai Ram Jai Jai Ram. Bring them in. Sing together.

For men it's most often astral tripping. Far out trips in far out worlds that get so far out they become disconnected and then have to find someone to understand and then its Drama Drama Drama instead of Rama Rama Rama. Men struggle with death and rebirth and fear it's a tough trip alone and being together makes it both easier and harder. The key to it all is absolute and total surrender to the spirit. With this it is all possible.

The real difficulty in family *sadhana* seems to be in the maintenance over a long period of time of the discipline. In most other *sadhana* there is either overt or covert reliance on a *sangha*. In any given area there are just not that many people who will gravitate towards family *sadhana*. Most people are on their own spiritual paths. While it is true that these people constitute a *sangha* of sorts the uniqueness of family *sadhana* makes it difficult to tie all of this together. A very good alternative is to join together with others and form a

111

spiritual community. That is, a community constituted solely for spiritual purposes.

In the end this is the nut. It's all or nothing. Constantly revised schedules to squeeze the Spirit in for 10 or 20 minutes a day won't make it. This is not criticism but observation. The practice is fierce because it is so easy to forget and fall asleep. The families we have seen who are practicing in communal context (using a vehicle disciplines ranging from *Sufi* ecstatic practice thru Christian fellowship and Hindu *bhakti* to deep Soto Zen practice) seem to be getting on with it.

SADHANA IF YOU LIVE ALONE

You naturally have more flexibility and more **life time** to work on your *sadhana* when you live alone. You can get up very early in the morning, chant your *mantras* out loud, light candles, burn incense, ring a bell, or do whatever brings you into the Spirit without disturbing anybody else. If you are fasting, nobody feels disturbed about it, or if you want to eat some special diet which makes you feel light and in the Spirit (but which tastes like a horsehair mattress) you can feast on it whenever you feel hungry.

And then there is the silence. If you prefer to live in a quiet world, free of radio, TV, or records, you can spend a lot of time, if you live alone, in a warm cocoon of silence.

And then there is noise. If you are developing the witness and want to carry on a dramatic monologue to help you **remember**, you can play the star role aloud:

"He's heading toward the refrigerator now. He's thinking about eating some ice cream. He's decided to do some *pranayam* instead . . ." A running commentary like this helps to keep you in the witness but it doesn't help you fill the role of the ideal roommate.

Although you may have more chance to work on your sadhana when you live alone, you have less chance to practice that most difficult of all paths, *karma yoga*. In solitude you don't have many demands made upon you, nor do you develop the elasticity which comes with the give-and-take of living with others. If your work is also solitary, you may want to preserve a balance by seeking opportunities to interact with others. You may look for continuing situations where the interaction will be on a deep rather than a superficial, social level, such as teaching at a community center, taking on a group of scouts, etc. Situations which are totally engrossing are most apt to capture you and therefore provide the best practice in keeping your witness and your center. (Working with others will also enable you to see how losing and regaining your center affects those around you.)

However, if you live alone, you probably spend a large part of your time in solitude. Solitude does not mean that you are really living alone, even if you **seem** to be living alone. You know that when you shut the door and darken the room and look within that the door is open, the light is on, and, "Someone is in your room . . . darkness like a dark bird, flies away . . . flies away."

DYING

You must live before you can die. But you must die before you can live.

Live consciously! Die consciously!

Gandhi, the Indian Politician-Saint, was assassinated as he walked out of his home by an assassin who fired four bullets directly into his body. In the moment Gandhi fell, he was heard to utter the name, "RAM." The *rishis* (the men of India who know) say that to die uttering the name of God takes you immediately "beyond the beyond" with no further effort.

Practice Dying

1. Experience your own death:

Ritual death has been practiced throughout the world for centuries. Many Buddhist meditation exercises are designed to take you through your own death. Christian ascetics experience their death through contemplation for a vision of life *sub specie aeternitatis* (as Eternal Present). (See, for example, St. Ignatius Loyola's recommendations in his *Spiritual Exercises*.)

Laura Huxley has members of her seminars experience their own death psychologically. For example:

"Have the room comfortably dark or dimly lighted.

Lie down on your bed or sofa or on the floor.

Let your body go. Imagine that the life is out of it. Do not speak or move.

Imagine that you have died: Your body is passive, lifeless, useless. Your body is discarded. Your funeral is about to take place.

Let go of your body. Let it be there as something which is no longer yours. Follow to the limit this feeling of being completely alone, abandoned, not loved—not in life, not in death. Cry, scream, curse, if this is what you feel. Go to the limit of your feeling. And after you have cried and screamed and cursed, when you are empty and exhausted, stop and listen.

This is your last party. Speak to everyone there, tell them all about yourself, about your mistakes and your suffering, about your love and your longings. No longer do you need to protect yourself, no longer do you need to hide behind a wall or a suit of armor. It is your last party: you can explode, you can be miserable or pitiful, insignificant or despicable. At your funeral you can be yourself.

This is your chance: do what others have failed to do. Look at the unloved one, the miserable one. This is your chance to do an act of love toward one who has had no love. This is your chance to do justice where intentional or unintentional injustice has been committed.

114

This is your chance to give warmth and courage to one who feels only coldness, loneliness and death.

Let your tears flow from the very depth of you. Let your bitterness flow out with them. And when the bitterness is out, your tears will be gentle and sweet. Then take the hand of this lifeless body of yours, take it in your hands and with respect and love bring it to your lips and kiss it.

Now gently come back to your living body.

With this feeling of respect and love, come back to your living body, and let this feeling remain with you, inside of you. Let it spread to each nerve, to each muscle, along every vein and artery. Let this feeling of respect and love spread inside you, throughout your entire organism, and then let it spread out around you in everything, object or animal or human, that is part of your life. Feel this feeling of love and respect circulating inside you with the force of life itself; let it be in your blood, in the air you breathe. Feel it—accept it—give it." (A "recipe" from *You Are Not the Target*, Laura Huxley.)

The *Tibetan Book of the Dead* is a manual of practices for dying, and being re-born. There have been many ancient manuals for dying, e.g., the *Egyptian Book of the Dead*. Their purpose is to take a dying person through the various steps in this energy transformation dance called dying.

The psychedelics have been used with these manuals and exercises as sets or programs to experience death/rebirth. (See *The Psychedelic Experience*.)

Each time we can "let go"—of goals, of our ego-image compulsions, of controlling, of driving ourselves—and BE instead of DO, we die (as ego) and are reborn (as Self, as Buddha). Use a signal (the name Ram, a mantra word or phrase, a mandala image) to trigger that death whenever you are aware of your body being up-tight in the shape its desire-tension holds it in; then feel your breathing distribute itself throughout your body diffusing and lightening it as you die to desire, to ego, and then "not I but He lives in me."

Suicide, we might be reminded here, is a different type of death in which one *remains* attached to his ego. Rather than liberation it is a manifestation of bondage . . . which is why it has been condemned at all times by enlightened men.

2. Experience death with someone else:

To be with a person who is dying, to share consciousness with him, and to help him die consciously is one of the most exquisite manifestations of the Bodhisattva role. It should be sought out.

A few suggestions for practicing this yoga:

Meditate together or separately, whichever feels right. Meditation helps you remain in the Eternal Present where no-thing is happening . . . and it helps you serve lovingly with total involvement and with no attachment.

Don't teach by other than your *being*. If you remain centered, your calm presence helps to free all those about you who are ready.

Speak the truth as you see it . . . but only if asked! Speak nothing untrue.

See in the dying person only that which is eternal. You are merely seeing the Divine Mother doing it again. *All forms you see in another person are, after all, but the manifestations of your own desire*. A realized being wherever he looks sees no-thing or all things simultaneously, and knows them to be the same.

Read silently or aloud from the words of Those Who Know.

Perhaps one day we will have in this country Centers for dying and for being born . . . places located near mountains or the ocean where anyone who wishes might go to be in the presence of conscious beings during these crucial events. There would be healers and helpers as well as guides to assist along the way of any path—religious-metaphoric, yogic, or psychedelic—anyone might choose.

We all die in each moment . . . and we are all born in each moment . . . in truth, whether this death/rebirth is called physical or psychological. We can apply all of the above suggestions every day and in every interaction with people so as to be aware of this and conscious in it.

"Lightly, my darling, lightly. Even when it comes to dying. Nothing ponderous, or portentious, or emphatic. No rhetoric, no tremelos, no self-conscious persona putting on its celebrated imitation of Christ or Goethe or Little Nell. And, of course, no theology, no metaphysics. Just the fact of dying and the fact of the Clear Light. So throw away all your baggage and go forward. There are quicksands all about you, sucking at your feet, trying to suck you down into fear and self-pity and despair. That's why you must walk so lightly . . ."

"The Light," came the hoarse whisper, "the Clear Light. It's here—along with the pain, in spite of the pain."

"And where are you?"

"Over there, in the corner. I can see myself there. And she can see by body on the bed."

"Brighter," came the barely audible whisper, "brighter," And a smile of happiness intense almost to the point of elation transfigured her face.

Through his tears Dr. Robert smiled back at her. "So now you can let go, my darling." He stroked her gray hair. "Now you can let go. Let go," he insisted. "Let go of this poor old body. You don't need it anymore. Let it fall away from you. Leave it lying there like a pile of worn-out clothes . . . Go on, go on into the Light, into the peace, into the living peace of the Clear Light."—Aldous Huxley, *Island*

GLOSSARY

A

ajna—the point between the eyebrows; third eye; sixth of the seven chakras; actually located in the midbrain, related to the thalamus.

akasha—ether; subtlest, all-pervading material manifestation.

asana—comfortable posture; seat; third of the eight parts of yoga.

ashram—monastic retreat, usually directed by a guru.

Atman—Soul-Spirit; individualized Brahman.

avatar—(lit. to come from without) an incarnation of the Supreme Lord in human form, e.g., Christ, Krishna, Rama, Zoroastor, Buddha.

avidya—ignorance.

B

ban marg—the left-handed path.

bardo—the state between death and rebirth.

Bhakti Yoga—the yoga of devotion.

bhajan—singing of holy songs; devotional music.

bindu—a lower form of pran.

brahmacharya—(lit. to live in Brahma) sexual continence (a frequent meaning).

Brahman—the absolute one from which all else emanates; Ultimate Reality.

C

chakras—(lit. wheels) psychic energy vortices in the body, associated with the plexuses.

chela—disciple.

chillum—an earthen pipe cylinder used for smoking ganga or chars.

D

Dharma—Universal Law; the Way.

dhyana—meditation; identification with the Divine One.

G

gasho—a bow in reverence to another being with the understanding of the essential Buddha nature in all sentient beings.

gopis—the dancing milkmaids charmed by the cowboy flute player, Lord Krishna.

guru—spiritual guide or preceptor.

117

H

Hatha Yoga—(ha-sun; tha-moon) work with the body.

hridayam —spiritual heart.

I

ida—subtle nerve on the left side of the shushumna (the kundalini channel within the spine); the lunar nadi. See pingala.

Ista Devata—a personal God (Ishvara) who receives prayers and protects the chela on the Path.

J

japa—repetition of the Name of God, usually with a mala.

Jnana Yoga—the path of knowledge arrived at through reasoning and discrimination.

K

Kargyupa—an ascetic Tibetan Buddhist sect.

karma—(lit. action) the law of cause and effect; the apparent spread of energy through thoughts, words and deeds.

Karma Yoga—realization through action; selfless service (Sat Sewa).

kinhin—walking meditation practiced in Zen Buddhism.

kirtan—repetition in song of the Names of God.

koan—meditation exercise in question or paradox form used in Rinzai Zen practice.

kundalini—energy channeled from the base of the spine; aroused like a serpent by various yoga exercises to light the chakra lamps of consciousness.

L

Love—say the Word and you will be FREE; we do not HAVE love when we ARE love.

lama—teacher.

M

Mahamudra—the union of opposites; the Middle Path; the Great Gesture; the Great Symbol.

Mahayana—the Great Vehicle or High Way of northern Buddhism, Tibetan, Chinese and Japanese.

maithuna—the practice of yab-yum (sexual intercourse in which the woman sits astride the man facing him).

mala—a string of 108 beads and a guru (Meru) bead, used for japa; rosary.

mandala—(lit. a circle) a geometric and psychometric arrangement of lines, forms and colors, used as a vehicle for meditation.

mantra—words, syllables or phrases manifested to effect psychic states by sounding the chakras.

maya—the phenomenal world.

Meru—the mountain in the Center.

mouni—a sadhu who uses silence as an upaya.

moxa—liberation.

mudra—a gesture of the fingers or hands or limbs, used to affect prana.

muhlbandh—the closing of the anal sphincter.

N

Nad Yoga—the yoga of inner sound (from nadi, nerve channel).

nadi—nerve channel.

nirvakalpa samadhi—the highest superconscious, formless state, in which there is no distinction between subject and object.

nirvana—at-one-ment with the all and everything, the everything and no-thing; beyond karma.

Nyingmapa—a Tantric Tibetan Buddhist sect which does not require its members to be monks.

O

ojas—the highest form of pran.

OM(AUM)—the sum total of all energy; the first cause; all-pervading sound.

P

padmasan—the full lotus asana in which the legs are crossed and the feet rest on the thighs.

pandit—a learned man.

pingala—subtle nerve channel on the right side; solar nadi. See ida.

prajna—supreme intuitive wisdom.

pran(a)—life energy.

pranayama—control of prana through control of breathing.

prasad—consecrated food.

R

Ram(a)—solar avatar incarnated in Satya Yuga.

Rimpoche—(lit. Precious One) title accorded high lamas and tulkus.

roshi—a zen guide.

S

sadhak—a spiritual aspirant doing sadhana.

sadhana—a spiritual way, work, or exercise.

sadhu—a full-time worker; a holy man.

samadhi—oneness of mind; undistracted union of subject and object.

samsara—the repetitious cycle of birth-death-rebirth.

sanyasi—a renunciate; a mendicant monk in achre robe.

Sat Chit Ananda—complete Being-Knowledge-Bliss; our true nature; reality.

Satipatthana Vipassana—application of mindfulness.

Satsang (Sangha)—communion or community of Workers on the Way. (Sat Guru - Sat Sang - Sat Seva: pure guide - pure companion - pure service)

Sattvic—pure.

Satya Yuga—the Golden Age of Truth-Purity.

siddhi—occult (hidden) power.

Siva—the dancing destroyer (of ego); e.g., incarnated as Shankara, Bhagavan Ramana Maharishi.

T

Tao—the way and The Way.

Tantra Yoga—the yoga of using the senses to go beyond the senses; often called the Rapid Path.

tapasya—austerity; penance; purification by fire.

tratak—the discipline of gazing at and "grokking" a seed object such as a candle flame, a flower, the Sun.

U

udyanahandh—closing of the upper intestinal door.

upaya—method.

V

vairag—the falling away of worldly desires.

Vajrayana—the Adamantine Way.
Vichara Atma—"Who Am I?"
Vishnu—the Preserver; incarnated as Rama, Krishna, Buddha, Jesus.

Y

yoga—a yoke; union; making straight the Path through which God realizes Himself.

Z

zazen—being in the natural state; ceasing conceptual activity.
zendo—the place where zazen is practiced.

LAMA FOUNDATION: a current note (summer '72)

Honest experimentation in the evolution of economic, social, and spiritual forms for communities of seekers is exceedingly difficult, and the moments of love and trust and consciousness are interspersed by periods of paranoia and struggle. Through honesty we grow, and the beings who work, pray, and live together at Lama are no exception.

For the integrity of our inner journey and the ecology of the land, the Lama Foundation must at present limit the number and frequency of visitors. We realize the great need for spiritual nourishment at this time of awakening, and while Lama cannot fulfill this need for all those seeking to come physically to the land, we pray that more learning and growing centers will evolve* and that we may all open our hearts to the movement of the spirit.

*for information see:

Spiritual Community Guide, Box 1080, San Rafael, Cal., 94902

Alternative Newsmagazine, P.O. Drawer A, Diamond Hgts, San Francisco Cal., 94131

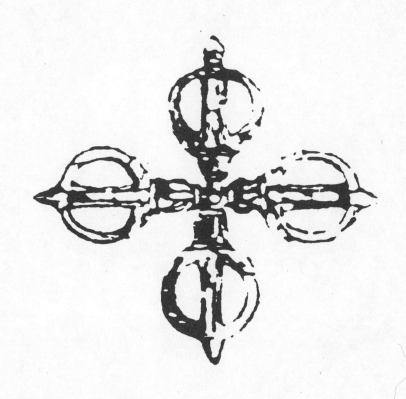

PAINTED CAKES DO NOT SATISFY

HUNGER

BOOKS TO HANG OUT WITH

BHAGAVAD GITA, Translations of:
    Arnold, Sir Edwin, THE SONG CELESTIAL. Dial.
    Besant, Annie. Theosophical Publ. House, India.
    Mascaro, Juan. Penguin Classic 1962 (pap).
    Prabhavananda & Isherwood. Mentor. (pap).
    Swami Sivananda. THE BHAGAVAD GITA.

THE HOLY BIBLE, King James version.

Blavatsky, Helen Petrovna. THE VOICE OF THE SILENCE. India: Theo-
    sophical Publishing House.

Blofeld, John (tr.) THE ZEN TEACHINGS OF HUANG PO. NY: Grove
    Press, 1959 (pap).

BUDDHA, THE LIFE AND SAYINGS OF
    Moore, J.H. (tr.) SAYINGS OF BUDDHA. AMS Press.
    Woodward, F. L. (tr.) SOME SAYINGS OF BUDDHA: ACCORD-
    ING TO THE PALI CANON. Oxford Press.
    Allen, G.F. (Ed.), WORDS OF WISDOM. Hillary, 1959.

Chang, Garma (tr.) THE HUNDRED THOUSAND SONGS OF MILA-
    REPA. University Books.
    TEACHINGS OF TIBETAN YOGA, NY: 1963.

Conze, Edward. SELECTED SAYINGS FROM THE PERFECTION OF
    WISDOM. London: Buddhist Society, 58 Eccleston Square.
    BUDDHIST MEDITATION, NY: Torch (pap).

DHAMMAPADA, Translations of:
    Babbitt, Irving, NY: New Directions, (pap).
    Lal, P. NY: Noonday.

Doresse, THE SECRET BOOKS OF THE EGYPTIAN GNOSTICS.
    Viking Press. (The Gospel of Saint Thomas is included. This is an
    important work.)

Evans-Wentz, W. Y. THE JEWEL OF LIBERATION.
    TIBET'S GREAT YOGI MILAREPA.
    TIBETAN YOGA & SECRET DOCTRINES.
    THE TIBETAN BOOK OF THE DEAD.
    THE TIBETAN BOOK OF THE GREAT LIBERATION.
    NY: Oxford University Press.

French, Reginald M. THE WAY OF A PILGRIM. NY: Seabury Press,
    (pap.).

Govinda, Lama. FOUNDATIONS OF TIBETAN MYSTICISM. London:
    Rider & Co.

Gunther, H. V. (tr.) THE JEWEL ORNAMENT OF LIBERATION.
    London: Rider.
Hafiz. FIFTY POEMS WITH TRANSLATION (Arberry, Ed.) Cambridge
    University Press. 1947.
Humphreys, Christmas. THE SUTRA OF WEI LANG. London: The
    Buddhist Society. (The Sutra of the Sixth Patriarch.)
Huxley, Aldous. THE PERENNIAL PHILOSOPHY. NY: Harper 1945,
    Meridian-World.
Kirpal Singh. THE JAP JI: THE MESSAGE OF GURU NANAK.
    THE CROWN OF LIFE (A Study in Yoga).
    MORNING TALKS.
    Delhi: Ruhani Satsang.
    (Available from Sant Bani Ahsram, Franklin, New Hampshire 03235).
Lao Tzu. TAO TE CHING (Blackney, tr.), NY: Mentor (pap.).
    Ch'u Ta-Kao (tr.) NY: Macmillan.
    Witter Bynner (tr.) Capricorn Press
    Many other translations available.
Lewis, Samuel, L.
    TOWARD SPIRITUAL BROTHERHOOD.
    INTRODUCTION TO SPIRITUAL DANCE.
    THE REJECTED AVATAR.
        All by Prophecy Pressworks.
M. (Swami Nikhilananda, tr.) THE GOSPEL OF SRI RAMAKRISHNA.
    NY: Ramakrishna Center, 1942. (Very high bhakti book.)
Meher Baba, DISCOURSES: VOLS. 1-4 (Adi K. Irani, Ed.) India: Meher
    Pub., Kings Road, Ahmednagar, Deccan, Bombay, 1954.
    Books on the works & life of Meher Baba include:
    GOD SPEAKS! THE THEME OF CREATION & ITS PURPOSE.
    NY: Dodd, Mead & Co.
Osborne, G. TEACHINGS OF RAMANA MAHARSHI. NY: Weiser.
PHILOKALIA — WORK OF THE EARLY CHURCH FATHERS.
Ramana Maharshi. TALKS WITH SRI RAMANA MAHARSHI.
    DAY BY DAY WITH BHAGAVAN.
    GURU RAMANA (S. S. Cohen).
    MAHARSHI'S GOSPEL.
    RAMANA MAHARSHI & HIS PHILOSOPHY OF EXISTENCE.
    REFLECTIONS ON "TALKS".
    SADDHU'S REMINISCENCES OF RAMANA MAHARSHI (Maj.
    S. W. Chadwick).

SELF-INQUIRY: WHO AM I?
(These books available at various bookstores, but can be ordered directly from: Arunachala Ashram, 342 E. 6th Street, NYC. "The Mountain Path," an excellent magazine, is also available.)

Shastri. ASHTAVAKRA GITA.

THE RAMAYANA OF VALMIKI. London: Shantisadam.

PRAKASHA BHRAMACHARI.

SATYA SAI BABA, BRINDAVAN, and other pamphlets. New Delhi. (C. Ramachandran, tr.).

THE SRIMAD BHAGAVATAM (THE WISDOM OF GOD). NY: Putnam (pap.).

Swami Prabhavananda (tr.) Capricorn, NY: (pap.).

St. John of the Cross. DARK NIGHT OF THE SOUL. NY: Doubleday, Image (pap.)

Tyagisananda, Swami. NARADA BHAKTI SUTRAS. India: Bharati. Vijayam Press. Triplicare, Madras.

UPANISHADS, THE. Mascara (tr.) Penguin Classic (pap.). Prabavananda & Manchester.

Vivekananda, Swami. RAJA YOGA. India: Advaita Ashram. (Patanjali's sutras with exposition.)

Watson, Burton (tr.) CHUANG TZU—BASIC WRITINGS. NY: Columbia University Press.

Wilhelm, Richard (tr.). I CHING—BOOK OF CHANGES. NY: Princeton University Press, Bollingen Series XIX. (Also Dutton (pap.), John Blofeld, tr.).

Willing, C. A. (publ.) THE IMPERSONAL LIFE. Sun Center Publication. New Canaan, Conn. (P. O. Box 54, San Gabriel, Calif.).

Yogananda, Paramahansa. AUTOBIOGRAPHY OF A YOGI. Los Angeles: Self-Realization Fellowship. 1959. (To get a great feeling for what it's really like in India. He tells it just like it is.)

BOOKS TO VISIT WITH NOW & THEN

Alexander, F. J. IN THE HOURS OF MEDITATION, Calcutta, India: Advaita Ashram.

Arberry, Arthur. DISCOURSES OF RUMI. University of Chicago Press. 1968.

Attar, Farid Ud-Din. THE CONFERENCE OF THE BIRDS. (Translation of Persian poem.) London: Routledge & Kegan.

Aurobindo, Sri. THOUGHTS & APHORISMS. Pondicherry, India.

Ayyangar. YOGA UPANISHADS. Adyar Library.

Avalon, Arthur (pseud. for Sir John Woodroffe). SERPENT POWER. INTRODUCTION TO TANTRA SASTRA.
SHAKTI POWER.
GARLAND OF LETTERS.
Ganesh: Vedanta Press.

Bailey, Alice A. THE LIGHT OF THE SOUL. (Paraphrase of Patanjali.) Lucis.

Blake, William. THE PENGUIN POETS. N Y: Penguin Books (pap.).

Blavatsky, Helena Petrovna. ISIS UNVEILED, 2 VOLS.
THE SECRET DOCTRINE. India: Theosophical Publishing House.

Bucke, Richard M. COSMIC CONSCIOUSNESS. University Books. 1961 Dutton (pap).

Bunyan, John. PILGRIM'S PROGRESS.

Byles, Maria. JOURNEY INTO BURMESE SILENCE. London: Allen & Unwin. (Day by day adventures at various Burmese Buddhist Meditation Centers).
PATHWAYS TO INNER CALM. London: Allen & Unwin.

Collin, Rodney. THEORY OF CELESTIAL INFLUENCE. London: Vincent Stuart.

Coomaraswamy, Ananda. BUDDHA & THE GOSPEL OF BUDDHISM. N Y: Torch (pap).

Danielou, Alain. YOGA: THE METHOD OF REINTEGRATION. London: C. Johnson. 1940.

Daumal, Rene. MOUNT ANALOGUE. N Y: Pantheon, 1962. Cal: City Lights, 1968. (The ascent of the soul symbolized by a mountain climbing expedition.)

David-Neel, Alexandra. INITIATIONS & INITIATES IN TIBET
SECRET ORAL TEACHINGS IN TIBETAN BUDDHIST SECTS.
Maha Bodhi Society, India.

de Chardin, Pierre Teilhard. THE PHENOMENON OF MAN.

THE FUTURE OF MAN.
THE DIVINE MILIEU.
HYMN OF THE UNIVERSE.
N Y: Harper

De Cusa, Nicholas. THE VISION OF GOD. N Y: Atlantic (pap).

de Lubicz, Isha Schwaller. HER-BAK: CHICK-PEA, EGYPTIAN INITI-
ATE, Vols. I & II. London: Hodder & Stoughten, 1967.

Duncan, Ronald. SELECTED WRITINGS OF MAHATMA GANDHI.
Boston, Beacon Press.

Dutt, R. C., the RAMAYANA and the MAHABHARATA, Everyman's
Library, Dutton, N Y.

Eliade, Mircea. YOGA, IMMORTALITY & FREEDOM. N Y: Pantheon,
1954.

Guillaumont, A. et.al. (tr.) THE GOSPEL ACCORDING TO THOMAS.
(Coptic Text). N Y: Harper Row, 1959

Gurdjieff, George. MEETINGS WITH REMARKABLE MEN. N Y: Dut-
ton (pap). 1963.
ALL AND EVERYTHING — BEELZEBUB's TALES TO HIS
GRANDSON. N Y: Dutton.

Herrigel, Eugen. ZEN IN THE ART OF ARCHERY. NY: McGraw Hill
(pap).

Hesse, Herman. JOURNEY TO THE EAST. N Y: Noonday (pap).
SIDDHARTHA. N Y: New Directions (pap).
STEPPENWOLF. N Y: Holt Rhinehart (pap).

MAGISTER LUDI (THE GLASS BEAD GAME). N Y: Unger, 1964

Hoffman. THE RELIGIONS OF TIBET. N Y: MacMillan, 1961.

Humphreys, Christmas. THE WISDOM OF BUDDHISM. N Y: Random
House.

Huxley, Aldous. ISLAND.

Huxley, Laura. THIS TIMELESS MOMENT.

Isherwood, Christopher. RAMAKRISHNA & HIS DISCIPLES. N Y: Simon
& Schuster.

Jack, Homer A. THE GANDHI READER. N Y: Evergreen, 1961 (pap).

Kapleau, Philip. THE THREE PILLARS OF ZEN. N Y: Harper & Row.
Beacon (pap).

Kirpal Singh. BABA JAIMAL SINGH: HIS LIFE AND TEACHINGS.

Delhi: Ruhani Satsang.

(Available from Sant Bani Ashram, Franklin, New Hampshire 03235)

Krishna Prem. THE YOGA OF BHAGAVAD GITA.

THE YOGA OF THE KATHUPANISHAD. London: J. W. Watkins.

Lefort, Rafael. THE TEACHERS OF GURDJIEFF. London: Victor Gollancz, 1960.

Legge, James C. (tr.) THE TEXTS OF TAOISM (in 2 parts). N Y: Dover.

Marsh, John. SAINT JOHN. NY: Pelican. Penguin (pap).

Meher Baba. LISTEN HUMANITY (Narr. & ed. by D. E. Stevens) N Y: Dodd, Mead, 1957

THE EVERYTHING AND THE NOTHING. (pap).

THE PERFECT MASTER. C. B. Purdom.

AVATAR. John Adriel. Calif: J. F. Rowny Press, Santa Barbara, 1947.

THE WAYFARERS. Dr. Wm. Donkin.

WHAT AM I DOING HERE? Ivy O. Duce (pap).

(May be purchased directly from Sufism Reoriented, 1290 Sutter Street, San Francisco, Calif.)

Merton, Thomas. THE WAY OF CHUANG TZU. NY: New Directions (pap).

THE SEVEN STORY MOUNTAIN. (Autobiography) NY: Signet.

SILENCE IN HEAVEN. (Book of the Monastic Life) Signet.

THE SIGN OF JONAS. (Day by day account of life in Trappist monastery) N Y: Image.

THOUGHTS IN SOLITUDE. N Y: Image.

NEW SEEDS OF CONTEMPLATION. New Directions.

Niehardt, J. G. BLACK ELK SPEAKS. N Y: Morrow & Co., 1932. University Nebraska (pap). 1961. (Life story of holy man of the Ogalala Sioux).

Nikhilananda, Swami. HOLY MOTHER (Life of Sri Sarada Devi—wife of Sri Ramakrishna). London: Allen & Unwin, 1962.

THE UPANISHADS. N Y: Harper Torchbooks (pap).

Orage, A. R., ON LOVE. London. The Janus Press.

Ouspensky, P. D. IN SEARCH OF THE MIRACULOUS. NY: Harcourt Brace. Bantam.

Percival, H.W. THINKING & DESTINY. Word Foundation, Inc.

Prabhavananda, Swami & Isherwood, HOW TO KNOW GOD. Hollywood: Vedanta Press. (Best introduction to Pantanjali Sutras).

VIVEKA-CHUDAMANI (CREST JEWEL OF DISCRIMINATION). Hollywood: Vedanta Press.

Price, A. F. (tr.) THE DIAMOND SUTRA OF THE JEWEL OF TRANS-CENDENTAL WISDOM. London: The Buddhist Society, 16 Gordon Square, 1947.

THE LIFE OF RAMAKRISHNA, Romain Rolland. Advaita Ashram. RAMAKRISHNA & THE VITALITY OF HINDUISM. (Solange Lamaitre) Funk & Wagnall's, 1969.

Ramdas, Swami. IN THE VISION OF GOD.

GITA SANDESH.
THE PATHLESS PATH.
WORLD IS GOD.
DIVINE LIFE.
By writer about Ramdas:
PASSAGE TO DIVINITY—A DEVOTEE'S DIARY.
SWAMI RAMDAS.
Order from: Anandashrama Kanhangad Rly. Stan Kerala, So. India. Plus many booklets.

Reps, P. ZEN FLESH ZEN BONES. A collection of Zen & Pre-Zen Writings. NY: Anchor Doubleday (pap).

Rilke, Rainier M. DUINO ELEGIES (MacIntyre, tr.) Cal: University of California (pap).

Saint Augustine. THE CONFESSIONS OF SAINT AUGUSTINE.
THE CITY OF GOD. Modern Library.
Westminster: Library of Christian Classics, Vol. 7, 1955.

Shah, Idries. THE WAY OF THE SUFI. London: Jonathan Cape. 1968.

Sivananda, Swami. CONCENTRATION & MEDITATION.
KUNDALINI YOGA.
THE PRACTICE OF YOGA.
SADHANA.
BHAGAVAD GITA.

Snellgrove (tr.) THE HERDJRA TANTRA, 2 Vols. London: Rider & Co.

Sobhana, Dhammasudhi. INSIGHT MEDITATION. London: Buddhapadipa Temple.

Shankaracharya. THE CREST JEWEL OF WISDOM. (Charles Johnston, tr. Watkins Press).

Szekely, Edmond Bordeaux (tr.) THE ESSENE GOSPEL OF JOHN—

FIRST CHRISTIAN (ESSENE) CHURCH. 1968. (Trans. from 1st century Aramaic & Slavonic texts).

Taimni, I. K. GAYATRI—DAILY RELIGIOUS PRACTICE OF THE HINDUS. India: Ananda Publishing House.
THE SCIENCE OF YOGA. Wheaton, Ill: Quest (pap). Theosophical Publishing House.

Thoreau. WALDEN.

Vishnudevananda, Swami. THE COMPLETE ILLUSTRATED BOOK OF YOGA. N Y: Julian Press, 1960. (Excellent help with Hatha Yoga theory & practice).

THE URANTIA BOOK. Chicago: Urantia Foundation, 1967.

Vithaldas, Yogi. THE YOGA SYSTEMS OF HEALTH & RELIEF FROM TENSIONS. N Y: Crown Publishers, 1957. (pap).

Waddell, Helen. THE DESERT FATHERS. N Y: Constable & Co. 1946

Waley, Arthur (tr.) MONKEY. N Y: Grove Press.

Whitman, Walt. THE LEAVES OF GRASS. N Y: Doubleday (pap).

Wilhelm, Richard. THE SECRET OF THE GOLDEN FLOWER. N Y: Harcourt, Brace.

BOOKS IT'S USEFUL TO HAVE MET

A Kempis, Thomas. THE IMITATION OF CHRIST. NY: Image (pap).

Asimov, Isaac. THE FOUNDATION TRILOGY. N Y: Doubleday.

Bailey, Alice. THE REAPPEARANCE OF THE CHRIST.
THE SOUL AND ITS MECHANISM.
FROM INTELLECT TO INTUITION.
INITIATION HUMAN & SOLAR.
LETTERS ON OCCULT MEDITATION.
A TREATISE ON WHITE MAGIC.
A TREATISE ON COSMIC FIRE.
TELEPATHY AND THE ETHERIC VEHICLE.
GLAMOUR: A WORLD PROBLEM.
A TREATISE ON THE SEVEN RAYS, 5 vols.
N Y: Lucis Publishing Co.

Beevers, John. STORM OF GLORY. (About St. Theresa of Lisieux) N Y: Image (pap).

Bernard, Theos. HATHA YOGA. NY: Columbia University Press, 1944.
     LAND OF A THOUSAND BUDDHAS. London: Rider.

Besant, Annie. KARMA.
     DEATH AND AFTER.
     DHARMA
     REINCARNATION.
     ESOTERIC CHRISTIANITY.
     India: Theosophical Publishing House. Adyar.

Blakney, Raymond B. MEISTER ECKHART, 14th CENTURY MYSTIC &
     SCHOLAR. Torch.

Boehme, Jacob. THE WAY TO CHRIST. (4 Treatises) London, 1961.

Borges, Jorge. LABYRINTHS, SELECTED STORIES & OTHER WRIT-
     INGS. N Y: New Directions (pap).

Bradbury, Ray. THE ILLUSTRATED MAN. N Y: Doubleday, 1958.

Brother Lawrence (tr. from French) THE PRACTICE OF THE PRESENCE
     OF GOD. Revell Inspirational Classics.

Buber, Martin. HASIDISM & MODERN MAN. (Friedman, M. tr.)
     N Y: Harper Row (pap).
     I AND THOU. (R. Gregor Smith, tr.) N Y: Scribner Lib. (pap).
     TALES OF THE HASIDIM.

Bucke, R. M. "Memorial Society Newsletter-Review" (An outstanding spir-
     itual newsletter. $1/copy). R. M. Bucke Memorial Society, 1266 Pine
     Ave. W. Montreal.

Campbell, Joseph. MASKS OF GOD. N Y: Viking (pap).

Castaneda, Carlos. THE TEACHINGS OF DON JUAN: A YAQUI WAY
     OF KNOWLEDGE. N Y: Ballantine (pap).

Dante, A. THE DIVINE COMEDY. (Tr. Carlyle) N Y: Modern Library.

de Lubicz, R. A. Schwaller. LE TEMPLE de L'HOMME. Blackwell's, Broad
     Street, Oxford, England.

De Ropp, Robert. THE MASTER GAME. N Y: Dell, 1969. (pap).

Descartes, Rene. MEDITATIONS (tr. Lafleur) N Y: Bobbs, 1951. (pap).

Dridedi, M. J. THE YOGA SUTRAS OF PATANJALI.

Fischer, Louis. THE LIFE OF MAHATMA GANDHI. NY: MacMillan,
     1962.

Fowles, John. THE MAGUS. N Y: Dell. (pap).

Giles, Herbert A. CHUANG TZU—TAOIST PHILOSOPHER & CHI-
     NESE MYSTIC. London: Allen & Unwin, 1961.

Govinda, Lama. THE WAY OF THE WHITE CLOUD. London: Hutchinson.

Heinlein, Robert A. STRANGER IN A STRANGE LAND. N Y: Putnam, 1961. Avon.

Hills, Christopher. NUCLEAR EVOLUTION.

Jha, Gangautha. THE YOGA DARSANA.

Johnston, Charles. THE YOGA SUTRAS OF PATANJALI. London: Stuart & Watkin.

Jonas, Hans. THE GNOSTIC RELIGION. Boston, Beacon Press.

Judge, William Q. YOGA APHORISMS OF PATANJALI.

Kazantzakis. THE LAST TEMPTATION OF CHRIST. N Y: Simon-Schuster (pap).

Kesey, K. ONE FLEW OVER THE CUCKOO'S NEST. N Y: Signet (pap).

Kierkegaard, Soren. FEAR & TREMBLING: SICKNESS UNTO DEATH. tr. Lowrie. N J: Princeton University Press (pap).
EITHER/OR. 2 Vols. N Y: Anchor-Doubleday.
AN ANTHOLOGY OF KIERKEGAARD. Modern Library, 1959.

King, C. Daly. THE STATES OF HUMAN CONSCIOUSNESS. Llevellyn Pub. (Pages 137-146 are excellent help in understanding pharaonic mentality.)

Kirpal Singh. PRAYER: ITS NATURE & TECHNIQUE.
THE WHEEL OF LIFE: THE LAW OF ACTION & REACTION.
NAAM OR WORD.
Delhi: Ruhani Satsang.
(Available from Sant Bani Ashram, Franklin, N. H. 03235).

KORAN. Everyman's Library.

Krishnamurti. EDUCATION & THE SIGNIFICANCE OF LIFE. N Y: Harper & Row.

Laing, R. D. THE POLITICS OF EXPERIENCE. N Y: Ballantine (pap).

Laski, Margharita. ECSTASY. London: Cresset Press, 1961
(A study of religious & secular experiences.)

Law. William. A SERIOUS CALL TO A DEVOUT & HOLY LIFE. Fontana Library.

Leadbeater, C. W. THE CHAKRAS. India: Theos. Publ. House, 1966.

Leary, T. THE POLITICS OF ECSTASY.

Lewis, C. S. PERELANDRA. N Y: Macmillan (pap).

Lu K'uan Yu (Charles Luk) THE SECRETS OF CHINESE MEDITA-
TION. N Y: S. Weiser.

Mahathera, P. W. BUDDHIST MEDITATION IN THEORY & PRAC-
TICE. 1962.

Maynard, Theodore. SAINTS FOR OUR TIMES. (18 saints) N Y: Image
(pap).

Mayrink. THE GOLEM. N Y: Ungar (pap).

Mead, G. R. S. (tr.) THRICE GREATEST HERMES, HERMES TRISME-
GISTUS. London.

Merton, Thomas. MYSTICS & ZEN MASTERS. N Y: Dell (pap). 1969.

Milton, John. PARADISE LOST: PARADISE REGAINED. N Y: Mac-
Millan, 1966. (pap).

Mishra, Rammurti. FUNDAMENTALS OF YOGA. N Y: Julian Press.
Lancer (pap).

Narayananda, Swami. THE SECRETS OF PRANA, PRANAYAM AND
YOGA ASANAS.

Nicholson. RUMI, POET & MYSTIC. London: Allen & Unwin.

Nicoll, Maurice. LIVING TIME—AND THE INTEGRATION OF LIFE.
London: Vincent Stuarts, 1964.
THE NEW MAN. London: Stuart & Richards, 1950.

Nin, Anais. SEDUCTION OF THE MINOTAUR & OTHER STORIES.
N Y: Swallow (pap).

Ouspensky, P. D. THE PSYCHOLOGY OF MAN'S POSSIBLE EVOLU-
TION.
A NEW MODEL OF THE UNIVERSE.
THE FOURTH WAY. N Y: Knopf.

Owens, Clifford P. A STORY OF JESUS. N Y: ARE, 34 W. 35th.

Pali Canon. JATAKA STORIES, Vols. 1-3. Pali Text Society.

Pascal, Blaise. PENSEES. N Y: Modern Library (pap).

Plotinus. ENNEADS (tr. MacKenna Stephen) NY: Pantheon, 1957.
ON THE IMPASSIVITY OF THE INCORPOREAL (tr. MacKenna)
Medici Society.

PLATO, THE WORKS OF. N Y: Modern Library.

Prasad, Ram. C. THE YOGA SUTRAS OF PATANJALI.

Rahula, Walpole. WHAT THE BUDDHA TAUGHT. N Y: Grove, 1962.

Ramanar K. Venkata. NAGARJUNA'S PHILOSOPHY. Tuttle.

Ram Tirtha. IN THE WOODS OF GOD-REALIZATION.

Reich, William. THE FUNCTION OF THE ORGASM. N Y: Noonday
Press.
    CHARACTER ANALYSIS.
    COSMIC SUPERIMPOSITION.
    THE SELECTED WRITINGS OF WILHELM REICH.
    REICH SPEAKS OF FREUD.
    (All Noonday Press)

Rice, Cyprian. THE PERSIAN SUFIS. London: Allen & Unwin. 1964.

ROSICRUCIAN. May be ordered from Rosicrucian Fellowship, Mt. Ec-
clesia, Oceanside, Calif.
    THE MESSAGE OF THE STARS. Max Heindel.
    ROSICRUCIAN COSMO-CONCEPTION OR MYSTIC CHRISTI-
ANITY. Max Heindel.
    ETHERIC VISION & WHAT IT REVEALS.

Runes, D. Dagobert. THE WISDOM OF THE KABBALAH. N Y: Citadel
(pap).

Saint Exupery, Antoine. (tr. Woods) THE LITTLE PRINCE. H. B. & W.
(pap).

Saint Francis de Sales. INTRODUCTION TO THE DEVOUT LIFE.
(Ed. Ryan) N Y: Image.

Salinger, J. D. NINE STORIES. N Y: Little, 1953.
    FRANNY & ZOOEY. Little.

Schopenhauer, Arthur. THE WORLD AS WILL & IDEA. (tr. Haldone)
N Y: Humanities.

Schrodinger, Erwin. MY VIEW OF THE WORLD. Cambridge University
Press.

Shabistari Mahmud. THE SECRET GARDEN. (tr. Johnson Pasha) London:
Octagon.

Shah, Idries. TALES OF THE DERVISHES. London: Octagon Press.

Shattock, E. H. (Rear Admiral) AN EXPERIMENT IN MINDFULNESS.
N Y: Dutton (Satipatthana Method).

Singh, Jogendra (tr.) THE PERSIAN MYSTICS. London: Paragon.
    THE INVOCATIONS OF SHEIKH ANSARI (Verses by 11th century
Sufi mystic) London: John Murray.

Snyder, Gary. THE BACK COUNTRY. NY: New Directions (pap).

Steiger, Brad. IN MY SOUL I AM FREE. NY: Lancer (pap), 1968.

Suzuki, D. T. ZEN DOCTRINE & NO MIND. London: Rider & Co. (pap).
THE TRAINING OF THE ZEN BUDDHIST MONK. N Y: University Books.

Swedenborg, Emmanuel. SWEDENBORG'S WORKS. NY: Houghton Mifflin.
AN INTRODUCTION TO SWEDENBORG'S RELIGIOUS THOUGHT. (J. H. Spalding) N Y: Swedenborg Publishing Assoc.

Tagore, Rabindranath. THE RELIGION OF MAN. Boston: Beacon Press, (pap).
POEMS OF KABIR.

Tennyson, H. INDIA'S WALKING SAINT.

Tolkien, J. R. R. THE HOBBIT, AND THE RING CYCLE. Boston: Houghton Mifflin. NY: Ballantine (pap). 1965.

Tookaran, Rajararm. YOGA PHILOSOPHY.

Trungpa, Chogyam. BORN IN TIBET. N Y: Harcourt Brace.
MEDITATION IN ACTION. London: Stuart Watkins. (pap).

Tucci, Guiseppe. THE THEORY & PRACTICE OF THE MANDALA. London: Rider (pap).

Underhill, Evelyn. THE ESSENTIALS OF MYSTICISM. N Y: Dutton (pap).
THE CLOUD OF UNKNOWING. London: Watkins.

Virajananda, Swami. PARAMARTHA PRASANGA—TOWARD THE GOAL SUPREME. Hollywood: Vedanta Press.

Waley, Arthur. THE NO PLAYS OF JAPAN. N Y: Grove Press.

Walker, Kenneth. THE CONSCIOUS MIND. N Y: Wehman, 1962

Warren, H. C. BUDDHISM. N Y: Atheneum Press, 1963 (pap).

Waters, Frank. BOOK OF THE HOPI. N Y: Viking Press, 1963.

Watts, Alan. PSYCHOTHERAPY EAST & WEST. N Y: Ballantine (pap). 1969.
BEYOND THEOLOGY: THE ART OF GODMANSHIP. N Y: Pantheon, 1964.

Whitehead, Alfred North. SCIENCE & THE MODERN WORLD. N Y: Free Press (pap).
PROCESS & REALITY. N Y: Free Press (pap).

Woods, J. H. YOGA SYSTEM OF PATANJALI. Harvard Oriental Series.

Workman, Herbert B. EVOLUTION OF THE MONASTIC IDEAL. N Y:

Beacon (pap).

Yesudian and Haich. YOGA AND HEALTH, NY: Harper & Bros., 1953.

Yukteswar, Swami Sri. KAWALYA DARSANAN or THE HOLY SCI-
ENCE. India: Yogoda Satsanga Society, Ranchi, Bihar, 1963.

Zehner. MYSTICISM SACRED AND PROFANE. Oxford Press (pap).

NEW ADDITIONS

Sat Prem, AUROBINDO OR ADVENTURES IN CONSCIOUSNESS
SRI AUROBINDO ASHRAM, Pondicherry, India.

Dane Rudhyar, PLANETARIZATION OF CONSCIOUSNESS (avail.
from Shamballa Pub., Berkeley, Cal.)

Nicholson, Reynold, THE MATHNAWI OF RUMI. Luzak & Co., 1968.

Khan, Hazrat Inayat, THE SUFI MESSAGE. (12 vols.) Barrie &
Rockliff, London, 1961.

Suzuki, Roshi, Shunryu, ZEN MIND BEGINNERS MIND, Walker/
Weatherhill, 1970.

SHRI SAI SATCHARITA of The Wonderful Life and Teachings
of SHRI SAI BABA of SHIRDI.

Where books may not be available at local bookstores, the following are
book specialists of the oriental and occult, etc.

SAMUEL WEISER, 734 Broadway, New York, NY 10003 (GR 7-8453)

ORIENTALIA, INC. 61 Fourth Ave., New York, NY 10003 (473-6730)

MASON'S BOOKSHOP, 789 Lexington Ave. New York, NY (832-8958)

SHAMBALLA BOOKSTORES, Telegraph Ave., Berkeley, Calif.

BROTHERHOOD OF LIFE, 110 Dartmouth St. S.E., Albuquerque, N.
Mex. 87106.

EAST-WEST BOOK SHOP, 1170 El Camino Real, Menlo Park, Calif.
94025.

THE PILGRIM'S WAY BOOKSTORE, P.O. Box 1044, Carmel, Calif.
93921.

PARAGON BOOK GALLERY, N.Y.C.

FIELDS, San Francisco, California

THE SPHINX, Cambridge, Mass.

THE BODHI TREE, 8585 Melrose Ave., L.A., Ca., 90069

THE RAINBOW BRIDGE DISTRIBUTING COMPANY, P.O. Box
40208, San Francisco, California 94140. FREE CATALOG.

OFFERINGS
from family and friends!

RAM DASS: Tapes, books, and teaching schedules—Ram Dass Tape Library,
524 San Anselmo Avenue, #203, San Anselmo, CA 94960
(www.RamDassTapes.org).

SWAHA: Bhagavan Dass and Amazing Grace, one cassette, $8—Ram Dass
Tape Library, 524 San Anselmo Avenue, #203, San Anselmo, CA 94960
(www.RamDassTapes.org).

AH!: Bhagavan Dass, one cassette, $8—Ram Dass Tape Library,
524 San Anselmo Avenue, #203, San Anselmo, CA 94960
(www.RamDassTapes.org).

BHAGAVAN DASS: For information about programs, write c/o Harbin Hot
Springs, P.O. Box 782, Middletown, CA 95461.

PIR VILAYAT KHAN: For information on the Sufi Order of North America,
write to P.O. Box 30065, Seattle, WA 98103.

HARI DAS BABA: For information about programs, write to Mount Madonna
Center, 445 Summit Road, Watsonville, CA 95076.

FLAG MOUNTAIN: For prayer flags, T-shirts, and rubber stamps, write to
Flag Mountain, Lama Foundation, Box 240, San Cristobal, NM 87564.